SCIENCE FICTION AFTER 1900

GENRES IN CONTEXT

Genres in Context is an essential series of critical introductions to major literary genres. Each book in the series includes:

- A historical overview of the genre
- In-depth analysis of key texts
- A list of works for further reading

- A chronology of authors, works, and historical events
- An annotated bibliography

Books in the *Genres in Context* series include:

BIOGRAPHY
Writing Lives
Catherine N. Parke

THE FAIRY TALE
The Magic Mirror of Imagination
Steven Swann Jones

FANTASY
The Liberation of Imagination
Richard Mathews

NATURE WRITING
The Pastoral Impulse in America
Don Scheese

SCIENCE FICTION AFTER 1900
From the Steam Man to the Stars
Brooks Landon

SCIENCE FICTION BEFORE 1900
Imagination Discovers Technology
Paul K. Alkorn

THE SEA VOYAGE NARRATIVE
Robert Foulke

THE SHORT STORY
The Reality of Artifice
Charles E. May

TRAVEL WRITING
The Self and the World
Casey Blanton

SCIENCE FICTION AFTER 1900

FROM THE STEAM MAN TO THE STARS

Brooks Landon

Routledge
Taylor & Francis Group

NEW YORK AND LONDON

Published in 2002 by
Routledge
29 West 35th Street
New York, NY 10001
www.routledge-ny.com

Published in Great Britain by
Routledge
11 New Fetter Lane
London EC4P 4EE
www.routledge.co.uk

Routledge is an imprint of the Taylor and Francis Group.
Printed in the United States of America on acid-free paper.

First Routledge paperback edition 2002.

Originally published in hardcover by Twayne Publishers, an imprint of The Gale Gr
This paperback edition published by arrangement with Twayne Publishers.

10 9 8 7 6 5 4 3 2 1

Library of Congress Cataloging-in-Publication Data

Landon, Brooks.
    Science fiction after 1900 : from the steam man to the stars / by Brooks Landon.
        p. cm. — (Genres in context)
    Originally published: New York : Twayne Publishers ; London : Prentice Hall
International, c1997, in series: Studies in literary themes and genres ; no. 12.
    Includes bibliographical references and index.
    ISBN 0-415-93888-0 (pbk. : alk. paper)
    1. Science fiction—History and criticism. 2. Fiction—20th century—History and
criticism. I. Title. II. Series.

PN3433.8 .L36 2002
809.3'8762—dc21   2002026724

For Larry McCaffery

Pomo's Pure Product, Cyberpunk's Critical Case Officer,
Avant-Pop's Main Man, and SF's Friend in the High Castle

Contents

Preface

Science fiction is the literature of change. More precisely, science fiction is the kind of literature that most explicitly and self-consciously takes change as its subject and its teleology. This essential presupposition holds as true for the earliest works to explore the new vantage point afforded fiction by scientific and technological developments, works such as Mary Shelley's *Frankenstein* and H. G. Wells's *The Time Machine*, as for the genre's most recent runs through cyberspace in novels by William Gibson, Pat Cadigan, and Rudy Rucker. This centrality of change was most firmly voiced by twentieth-century science fiction's most influential author, Robert Heinlein. "I think," claimed Heinlein in a 1941 Denver, Colorado, speech to the Fourth Annual Science fiction Convention, "that science fiction, even the corniest of it, even the most outlandish of it, no matter how badly it's written, has a distinct therapeutic value because *all* of it has as its primary postulate that the world does change."[1] Some 45 years later, the science fiction greats Jack Williamson, Frederik Pohl, and Brian Aldiss still invoked the concept of change to explain their common project. "I take seriously this notion that technology is changing the world and the future is going to be different," explained Williamson to the *Publishers Weekly* writer Rosemary Herbert.[2] Even more emphatically, Frederik Pohl specified: "The biggest reality in the world today is change, and that's what (science fiction) is about and other kinds of literature are not." And, suggesting the almost obsessive quality of this phenomenon,

Aldiss identified science fiction writers as "the ones who are pro-dromically moved to write of change."

What each of these writers left unspoken was science fiction's even stronger commitment to the postulate that the world can best be understood through change, whether rapid and radical or evolutionary over great periods of time. The extent of this commitment can perhaps best be seen in Octavia Butler's *Parable of the Sower* (1993), where her protagonist Lauren Olamina constructs "Earthseed," a secular religion, around the credo:

> All that you touch
> You Change.
> All that you Change
> Changes you.
> The only lasting truth
> Is Change.
> God
> Is Change.[3]

Butler's novel dramatizes the two key corollaries to a worldview built around the concept of change: (1) if you believe in change, you can prepare for it, and (2) if you believe in change, you damn well better prepare for it. In this sense, all science fiction is preparation.

There is an odd tension—almost a contradiction—in the notion of a genre devoted so strongly to the idea of change. Most popular genres depend on a view of the world frozen in time, a world whose features and rules remain fixed from book to book, but science fiction rises from change in the referential world, envisions change in fictional worlds, and paves the way for change in the worlds of its readers. Indeed, in exploring the kaleidoscopic human implications of science and technology, science fiction in the twentieth century has been not just the literature of change, but has become more: an epistemological force, an ideology having much more in common with the revolutionary project of modernism—and now, some would argue, with the cultural dominant of postmodernism—than with other popular literary genres.

The century that has seen science fiction first codified as a genre and—perhaps more important—as a publishing category has also seen that genre develop through distinct stages, mutate in innumerable and unpredictable directions, and finally over-flow the limits of genre to become a meta-genre so broad and so pervasive as to be a concept and force quite outside the bound-aries of fiction, and of art itself. As modes of science fiction have more and more become the new realism of technological society, the world itself has grown science fictional. The scientific, tech-nological, and industrial developments of the nineteenth century that made the rise of science fiction possible have inexorably led to twentieth-century conditions in which manifestations of sci-ence fiction have become inevitable and inescapable.

It is not too much to claim that, in the fifty years following Heinlein's frequently cited comments about change, something we might loosely call "science fiction thinking" has clearly over-flowed the formal bounds of literary genre to sustain both an identifiable science fiction subculture and a broad complex of science fiction–shaped cultural assumptions about science, tech-nology, and the future. Change—usually constructed as progress—has become the distinguishing mode of, as well as the subject of, science fiction in the twentieth century. Since 1900 we have seen the initial codification of futuristic stories into what Hugo Gernsback effectively first called "science fiction,"[4] have seen Gernsback's and John Campbell's prescriptions for this new genre fulfilled and then challenged and surpassed as writ-ers turned science fiction in a dizzying swirl of new directions. Moreover, in recent years we have seen the genre begin to shed its genre identity as it has (take your pick) more and more disap-peared into or significantly enveloped mainstream fiction. Many critics and science fiction writers alike explain this conflation by claiming that the felt experience of science and technology has so permeated contemporary life as to render our culture itself science fictional.

In the twentieth century the literature of change has itself never stopped changing, never stopped mutating, moving away from its European roots in satire and social criticism, moving closer and closer to the paradigms first of modernism and then of postmodernism. The audience of science fiction has repeatedly shifted as it has grown, ranging between intellectual and popular extremes. And the positivism and optimism of science fiction writing in the 1920s and 1930s has been tempered, if not sup-planted, by questioning and frequently apocalyptic pessimism in the years following World War II: science fiction is the only genre to truly feel the fallout from Hiroshima.

Some of the genre's most dramatic and most significant changes have seen the dime novel, boy-engineer appeal of pulp magazine "scientifiction" being wrestled into a useful and compelling vehicle for feminist expression, ecotopian protest, and wide-ranging explorations of difference and marginality of every imaginable kind. Both in popularity and in function the status of the genre has also changed, with science fiction texts and science fiction thinking becoming important influences in a self-replicating process—a feedback loop—involving science fiction cinema, TV, video games, music videos, computers, and comics, all sharing and developing science fiction assumptions, themes, and icons. This extraordinary feedback loop has made science fiction the first truly multimedia genre and, more important, the only popular genre to have a clear cultural impact. At the very least, science fiction is at the heart of a well-codified subculture; at its most influential, science fiction is what William Sims Bainbridge describes as "a popular cultural movement that develops and disseminates potentially influential ideologies."[5] Seeing in science fiction no less than the attempt to "create a modern conscience for the human race," Eric Rabkin and Robert Scholes have observed that science fiction has appeared in *every* medium of artistic creation, developing through dialectical stages "focusing on the popular medium of the moment," in great part simply because "science fiction is itself a major force in the continuing development of our culture."[6]

I mention all of this only to support my conviction that much is at stake in a study of science fiction since 1900, and that such a study must see the phenomenon of science fiction thinking as much more than a subject for genre analysis in only a formal sense and as much more than an exercise limited to literary history. Only the eclectic and expansive sense of literary genre advanced by this series can account for the many stages in the development of science fiction, and only an understanding of the importance of science fiction's unique extratextual dimension can account for its phenomenal growth in popularity and cultural influence in the twentieth century. Against the broad sweep of twentieth-century science fiction, my task in this necessarily brief study is a difficult one, sure to be incomplete, sure to be shaped by my personal reading preferences, sure to be weakened by the hundreds, if not thousands, of fine science fiction stories and novels that, even after a lifetime of enthusiastic reading, I do not know.

To give in a brief single work an accurate and systematic view of science fiction near the end of the twentieth century is, of course, impossible. In the first place, science fiction is no longer "just" fiction, but has become a universally recognized category of film, television, music, music videos, electronic games, theme parks, military thinking, and advertising, and its concepts and icons are now routinely appropriated for the development and marketing of products ranging from breakfast cereal to pickup trucks. Science fiction is not even only science fiction any longer, but "sci-fi" (a term hated by most science fiction writers) to those who consciously or unconsciously minimize its importance and SF to its well-informed fans and critics, some of whom see those initials standing for "speculative fiction," implicitly suggesting the contested status of "science" in twentieth-century SF, particularly that written since the 1960s. Some of the difficulty in describing science fiction is revealed in the sheer number of names that have been advanced for it: scientifiction, science fiction, SF, sf, stf, speculative fiction, speculative fabulation, structural fabulation, science fantasy (little wonder that one wag has suggested "sinus friction"). My personal preference is SF, and throughout this book I will use "SF" and "science fiction" interchangeably.

In the second place, the science in science fiction is no longer "just" science. Discoveries in quantum physics have more and more challenged science fiction's early identification of science with certainty and its positivistic optimism that everything could be known and all problems solved if only we thought long enough and well enough. The easily identifiable "big science" of rocket ships, robots, and atomic bombs has more and more in the twentieth century been augmented by what Bruce Sterling calls "science that sticks to the skin," the "little science" of a technological environment or technosphere that surrounds and involves everyone in the culture. Not only is SF not "fiction about science," but also it now rests more on debate than agreement about what it is that constitutes "science."

In the third place, even if we consider science fiction exclusively as a print phenomenon, its size and range of permutations demand encyclopedic rather than essentializing analysis. One of the most complicating variables in a study of twentieth-century SF is that while it has flourished since the 1940s in both short stories and novels, the genre's "golden age" had limited access to the novel format, and many of the genre's writers and critics argue that its strengths are most apparent in the short story rather than in the novel—another aspect that separates science fiction from other popular genres. Moreover, SF has more than any other popular genre been presented to its readers through the publishing hybrid of the fix-up, "novels" more or less smoothly cobbled together from short stories sharing the same "worlds"—themes, characters, settings, etc. As a result, even an exhaustive study of twentieth-century science fiction novels would give a very incomplete and misleading picture of the genre. A Borges might imagine a thoroughly satisfying overview of the genre on the shelves of the all-inclusive Library of Babel, but even such a heroic encyclopedic effort as John Clute and Peter Nicholls's magnificent 1,370-page *The Encyclopedia of Science Fiction* (1993) must acknowledge its many omissions and curtailed discussions.[7]

In the excellent volume that precedes this one Paul Alkon uses the title of Arthur C. Clarke's "The Nine Billion Names of God" to suggest the plenitude of science fiction works written before 1900; consider my task when the actual count of science fiction novels published in 1992 alone approached 300, and the sheer volume of SF novels and short stories made it virtually impossible for anyone to keep up with all developments in the field. A recent guide to science fiction that confined its attention to "the most significant English-language titles" and further limited itself to books that have largely remained in print during the past twenty years still found itself surveying over 3,000 titles. The Third Edition of Neil Barron's indispensable *Anatomy of Wonder: A Critical Guide to Science Fiction* (1987)[8] now contains annotated entries on over 550 critical works devoted to SF or SF authors, in addition to entries on some 2,000 works of SF, including 476 works of foreign-language SF. The recent fourth edition (1995) drops coverage of foreign-language and many older titles, and still contains over 1,000 entries on primary works. It also now annotates over 150 works of history and criticism of SF, not counting works devoted to individual authors. And finally, writers far more expert and experienced than I am in science fiction writing and scholarship have already tried their hands at such a single view of twentieth-century science fiction, with persuasive results almost uniformly at odds with each other in some significant respect. For the twentieth century has seen the dramatic proliferation of science fiction criticism just as surely as it has seen the flowering of science fiction writing, and even the attempt to survey this body of criticism would invoke, if not the number of Clarke's "Nine Billion Names of God," the number and frustration of R. A. Lafferty's equally classic "Nine Hundred Grandmothers."

Anyone who hazards generalizations about science fiction can ill afford to forget the laughter of the ultimate grandmother at the spaceman-anthropologist Ceran Swicegood's efforts to discover "how it all began."[9] Accordingly, my goal in this study is not to attempt a representative sampling, much less a comprehensive overview, of science fiction since 1900 but is instead to suggest some of the concerns that have allowed science fiction to become what J. G. Ballard claims is "the main literary tradition of the twentieth century" and what Istvan Csicsery-Ronay persuasively describes as an attitude toward life, a way of being in the world.[10] Following the wise example of Paul Alkon in *Science Fiction before 1900*, I will offer in this book "soundings rather than a survey," a mosaic rather than a manifesto. My soundings of science fiction works and criticism will be guided by my desire to avoid the descriptive extreme of exhaustive typologies (here are all the basic types of SF) and the normative extreme of essentializing theories (here is the way all "true" SF is or should be). While I will not advance either a systematic history or a theory of SF after 1900, my soundings will eclectically borrow from both. Inevitably, my soundings will strike many knowledgeable SF readers as idiosyncratic, since most have been chosen more for what I find representative in them than for their popularity or canonization as "SF classics." A number of the works I discuss will also be considered as potential metaphors for the protocols of reading SF, since I strongly share Alkon's "conviction that science fiction at its best is a distinctly self-conscious and self-referential genre that invites readers to appreciate the clever ways in which texts may allude to one another, to themselves, and to the act of reading."[11] Indeed, a major theme of this work will be that science fiction is perhaps the most recursive and most self-reflexive of all major literary movements.

One further problem concerns me—the question of audience for a brief book such as this. In some ways science fiction is like the joke that must be explained: after the explanation, you may get it, but the humor never works as well as it would have had you not needed its point spelled out. The experience gained from reading science fiction—the more the better—helps us to "get" each new SF work we come across, a process of creating and drawing upon a larger background of knowledge sometimes called a "megatext." Unlike other popular genres such as the hardboiled detective story, the western, or the romance, the megatext for science fiction holds concepts that have no close approximation in the referential world: there may be no detective like Philip Marlowe, but there are detectives in the referential world; there is no similar referential analogue for time travel, matter converters, or faster-than-light drives. In this respect, science fiction would seem to be similar to fantasy, which also has no referential analogues, but fantasy's concepts are anything but unfamiliar, drawing as they do on thousands of years of myth and superstition. In contrast, science fiction is in the process of creating myths grounded in science and technology—myths familiar to SF readers, but unfamiliar to those not informed by the SF megatext. Consequently, SF tends to make much more sense to and to appeal more to readers who have more extensive knowledge of the SF megatext, a kind of chicken-and-egg proposition that seems much more obvious and redundant than it really is, since the megatext for science fiction is arguably broader and more varied than for any other literary genre or mode. Science fiction, more than other literary genres, is itself intensely processual; in SF the dynamic interplay among writers, audiences, and conventions has operated at higher and higher rates of change.

My problem in writing this book lies in trying to decide how much familiarity with that megatext my reader is likely to have. Just as it's hard to imagine that a reader of this book will *never* have read a work of science fiction, it's hard to imagine that a reader will have exhaustive knowledge of the field. And the continuum between those two extremes is broad indeed. Accordingly, I've chosen to think of this work neither as an introduction to SF, nor as a comprehensive summary, but as a starting reference point for the reader with some familiarity with SF texts but with a desire to gain a better overview of the genre before reading the hundreds of works that constitute its vital core. Ideally then, my reader is someone who needs to make up ground in a hurry—perhaps a student preparing for a class or a project on SF, or a teacher who suddenly finds herself responsible for teaching a class or a unit on SF. In the megatext of SF criticism this work intends only to be a navigation beacon, not a star, but I write it in hope that some readers will find useful its arbitrary rationing of light.

My first chapter will discuss the culture of SF, including a brief analysis of three stories, one from each of the three main periods through which twentieth-century SF has evolved: the pre-pulp era dominated by the scientific romance, the genre SF era of Gernsback and Campbell, and the New-Wave-and-beyond era of reaction to and rebellion against the limitations of Campbellian SF. This chapter will also introduce some of the most common terms used in the ongoing critical discussions of SF. My primary concern, however, will be with suggesting the need for a conceptually expansive rather than a formally limited understanding of science fiction—a need to understand SF as a culture of readers rather than as a set of rules for writers.

The development of the genre's characteristic twentieth-century face as popular American SF moved from dime novels through the pulp era and into its "golden age" will be the focus of my second chapter, which will devote particular attention to the work and influence of John Campbell and Robert Heinlein. Chapter three will turn from the heavily Americanized face of twentieth-century SF to consider the quite different traditions of SF written on the continent and in the former Soviet Union. Stanislaw Lem's *His Master's Voice* and Arkady and Boris Strugatsky's *Roadside Picnic* will be the texts most closely examined in this chapter. My fourth chapter will return to the predominately American protocols of genre SF but will focus on two of the significant dialectical oppositions or "countertraditions" that have emerged within the genre's broad outlines. The first of these countertraditions I will examine stems largely from the work of one writer, Philip K. Dick, whose fiction insists on radically questioning the stability of reality itself, and thus the "knowability" of the universe. The second countertradition has been even more important for the maturation of SF as a genre and has had much to do with the genre's current cultural authority. This countertradition rises from a nexus of SF works by women, SF works that are explicitly feminist, and works that Marleen S. Barr calls "feminist fabulation."[12] I am particularly interested in feminist SF as a doubly oppositional literature that challenges the patriarchal mindset of the culture at large and the concentratedly patriarchal assumptions and traditions of the genre itself. The writing of Joanna Russ, Ursula K. Le Guin, and James Tiptree Jr. will suggest the range of concerns of this vital strain of SF.

My final chapter will follow the developments in SF, starting with its "New Wave" in the 1960s and 1970s and continuing through cyberpunk in the 1980s and through a number of as yet unnamed trends and movements in the 1990s, which have blurred, if not destroyed, distinctions between SF and "mainstream" fiction, a trajectory that can be seen both as SF's ultimate triumph and as its ultimate disaster. J. G. Ballard's *Crash*, the novel Jean Baudrillard claims shifted SF from an "elsewhere" to an "everywhere," suggests some aspects of this phenomenon, as does his *The Atrocity Exhibition*.[13] Finally, I will turn to Gardner Dozois's highly respected *The Year's Best Science Fiction: Twelfth Annual Collection* (covering SF published in 1994) to suggest some of the current trends in SF and possible directions in which the genre may continue to evolve.[14] Even though the combination of my bibliographic essay and my list of recommended titles will still not allow me to do justice to the wonderful range of SF written since 1900, it can at least point readers toward some of the works claimed as common heritage by the culture of science fiction.

Acknowledgments

Since this book does not attempt to offer a new theory or revisionist history of SF, but a synthesis and overview of the many histories and theories that have helped and continue to help shape the genre, it is particularly and heavily indebted to earlier studies and to other SF writers and scholars. My friends and colleagues in the Science Fiction Research Association (SFRA) and the International Association for the Fantastic in the Arts (IAFA) have taught me more about SF than I can ever adequately acknowledge, although I'll no doubt dismay them with what I've forgotten or gotten wrong. Ditto for George Slusser and Eric S. Rabkin and the fascinating blend of scholars who make the Eaton Conference such a yearly treat. Writing by and/or conversation with James Gunn, Brian Attebery, Gary K. Wolfe, H. Bruce Franklin, Brian Stableford, David Hartwell, Samuel R. Delany, Joanna Russ, Istvan Csicsery-Ronay, Gary Westfahl, Edward James, John Huntington, Rob Latham, Veronica Hollinger, Scott Bukatman, Marleen Barr, and Larry McCaffery have especially shaped my thinking about SF. And even this long list undoubtedly omits influences who deserve recognition. Shaping is not the same as sharpening, however, and the very number of major influences on my thinking suggests an embarrassment of riches: many of the above critics do not see eye to eye with each other about the nature of SF, and many will not see eye to eye with me.

James Gunn and Frederik Pohl have given me a strong sense of SF's formative ethos, while Lewis Shiner and Bruce Sterling have helped me see how that ethos can continue into the future. I've also been very lucky to have students who have patiently expanded my knowledge and understanding of SF—Joan Gordon, Aaron Barlow, Elyce Helford, Brooks Peck, Jim Connor, and Doug Hanke have all kept me moving. I've also been extremely fortunate to have had colleagues in the University of Iowa English Department who would listen to my rants and ramblings about a literature they did not necessarily know. I've consistently profited from Kate Hayles's knowledge not only of SF, but also of science. From Claire Sponsler I've borrowed the term "zones of possibility," and it was Claire who started me thinking about SF in terms of these zones. I'm eternally grateful to Paul Diehl and Ed Folsom for their willingness to listen to and comment on my work; good friends are an influence beyond measure.

But most important have been the hundreds of times from junior high through the army to the present when I've discovered that someone I was with also read SF and we started to share our favorite authors and reads. "What if" may be the operating heuristic for science fiction, but "Have you read the one where . . . ?" is surely its most rewarding refrain.

Chronology

1901   Wells, *The First Men in the Moon*. M. P. Shiel, *The Purple Cloud*.

1902   Georges Melies, *Le Voyage Dans la Lune* (film).

1903   Wells, "The Land Ironclads"; *The Food of the Gods*. Street and Smith's *Popular Magazine* founded.

1905   *All-Story Magazine* founded. H. Rider Haggard, *Ayesha*. Verne, *The Master of the World*.

1906   Wells, *In the Days of the Comet*. *The People's Magazine* published. *The Railroad Man's Magazine* becomes the first category pulp magazine.

1907   Jack London, *The Iron Heel*. *The Monthly Magazine* renamed *Blue Book Magazine*.

1908   Wells, *The War in the Air*. Hugo Gernsback founds *Modern Electrics*.

1909   E. M. Forster, "The Machine Stops."

1911   Gernsback, *Ralph 124C 41+* published in *Modern Electrics*. J. D. Beresford, *The Hampdenshire Wonder*.

1912   Edgar Rice Burroughs, *Under the Moons of Mars*; *Tarzan of the Apes*. Arthur Conan Doyle, *The Lost World*.

1914   Burroughs, *At the Earth's Core*.

1915   Charlotte Perkins Gillman, *Herland*. London, *The Scarlet Plague*.

1917   Burroughs, *A Princess of Mars*.

1918   A. Merritt. *The Moon Pool*. London, *The Red One*.

1919   Ray Cummings, "The Girl in the Golden Atom."

1920   David Lindsay, *A Voyage to Arcturus*.

1921   Karel Čapek, *R. U. R.*

1922   Alexei Tolstoy, *Aelita*.

1923   Gernsback devotes entire issue of *Electrical Experimenter* to "scientific fiction." *Weird Tales* founded. René Clair, *Paris qui dort* (film).

1924   Yevgeny Zamyatin, *We*. Burroughs, *The Land That Time Forgot*. *Aelita* (film).

1925 Gernsback, *Ralph 124C 41+*. *The Lost World* (film).

1926 Gernsback founds *Amazing Stories*. Lang, *Metropolis* (film).

1927 Wells, *The Short Stories of H. G. Wells*.

1928 E. E. "Doc" Smith, *The Skylark of Space*. Edmond Hamilton, *Crashing Suns*.

1929 Gernsback founds *Science Wonder Stories*.

1930 *Astounding Stories* founded. Olaf Stapledon, *Last and First Men*. John Taine, *The Iron Star*.

1931 James Whale, *Frankenstein* (film).

1932 Aldous Huxley, *Brave New World*.

1933 C. L. Moore, "Shambleau." *King Kong* (film). F. Orlin Tremaine becomes editor of *Astounding*. Edwin Balmer and Philip Wylie, *When Worlds Collide*.

1934 John W. Campbell, Jr., "Twilight." Stanley Weinbaum, "A Martian Odyssey." Jack Williamson, *The Legion of Space*.

1935 Stapledon, *Odd John*.

1936 Čapek, *War With the Newts*. Alexander Korda, *Things to Come* (film). *Flash Gordon* (serial).

1937 Campbell becomes editor of *Astounding*. Katherine P. Burdekin, *Swastika Night*. Stapledon, *Star Maker*.

1938 C. S. Lewis, *Out of the Silent Planet*. Smith, *Galactic Patrol*. Lester Del Rey, "Helen O' Loy." Campbell (Don A. Stuart), "Who Goes There?"

1939 *Buck Rogers* (serial). A. E. van Vogt, "Black Destroyer." Sprague De Camp, *Lest Darkness Fall*.

1940 Van Vogt, *Slan*. Robert A. Heinlein, "The Roads Must Roll." L. Ron Hubbard, *Final Blackout*.

1941 Theodore Sturgeon, "Microcosmic God." Isaac Asimov, "Nightfall."

1942 Del Rey, "Nerves."

1943 Lewis Padgett (Henry Kuttner and C. L. Moore), "Mimsy Were the Borogroves."

1944   Stapledon, *Sirius*. Moore, "No Woman Born."
       Donald A. Wollheim, *The Pocket Book of Science
       Fiction*. Fredric Brown, "Arena."

1945   Murray Leinster, "First Contact." Van Vogt, *The
       World of Null-A*.

1946   E. J. Carnell founds *New Worlds*. Moore, "Vintage
       Season." Groff Conklin (ed.), *The Best of Science
       Fiction*.

1947   Heinlein, *Rocket Ship Galileo*. Brown, *What Mad
       Universe?*

1948   Judith Merril, "That Only a Mother." Bradbury,
       "Mars Is Heaven." Smith, "Scanners Live in Vain."

1949   *The Magazine of Fantasy and Science Fiction* is
       founded. George Orwell, *1984*. George R. Stew-
       art, *Earth Abides*. Williamson, *The Humanoids*.
       Captain Video (TV).

1950   Horace L. Gold founds *Galaxy Science Fiction*. Asi-
       mov, *I Robot*. Ray Bradbury, *The Martian Chroni-
       cles*. Van Vogt, *The Voyage of the Space Beagle*. C. M.
       Kornbluth "The Little Black Bag." Fritz Leiber,
       "Coming Attraction." Katherine Maclean, "Con-
       tagion." *Destination Moon* (film). *Space Cadet* (TV).

1951   Asimov, *Foundation*. Heinlein, *The Puppet Masters*.
       John Wyndham, *The Day of the Triffids*. *The Day
       the Earth Stood Still* (film). *The Thing* (film).

1952   James Blish, "Surface Tension." Norton, *Star
       Man's Son*. Bernard Wolfe, *Limbo*.

1953   Alfred Bester, *The Demolished Man*. Bradbury,
       Fahrenheit 451. Arthur C. Clarke, *Childhood's End*.
       Frederik Pohl and C. M. Kornbluth, *The Space
       Merchants*. *It Came from Outer Space* (film). *Invaders
       from Mars* (film). *The Adventures of Superman* (TV).

1954   Asimov, *The Caves of Steel*. Hal Clement, *Mission of
       Gravity*. Tom Godwin, "The Cold Equations."
       20,000 Leagues under the Sea (film). *Space Patrol* (TV).

1955   Leigh Brackett, *The Long Tomorrow*. *This Island Earth* (film).

1956   Bester, *The Stars My Destination*. Clarke, *The City and the Stars*. Merril, *The Year's Greatest Science-Fiction and Fantasy*. *Forbidden Planet* (film). *The Quatermass Experiment* (film).

1957   Sputnik. Ivan Antonovich Yefremov, *Andromeda*.

1958   Brian Aldiss, *Starship*.

1959   Heinlein, *Starship Troopers*. Daniel Keyes, "Flowers for Algernon." Andre Norton, *The Beast Master*. Kobo Abe, *Inter Ice Age 4*. Rod Serling, *The Twilight Zone* (TV). Walter M. Miller, *A Canticle for Leibowitz*.

1960   Sturgeon, *Venus Plus X*. Norton, *Storm Over Warlock*.

1961   Stanislaw Lem, *Solaris*. Heinlein, *Stranger in a Strange Land*. Cordwainer Smith, "Alpha Ralpha Boulevard." Anne McCaffrey, "The Ship Who Sang."

1962   Philip K. Dick, *The Man in the High Castle*. Anthony Burgess, *A Clockwork Orange*.

1963   Roger Zelazny, "A Rose for Ecclesiastes." Walter Tevis, *The Man Who Fell to Earth*. Clifford D. Simak, *Way Station*. *La Jetée* (film). *The Outer Limits* (TV). *My Favorite Martian* (TV).

1964   Michael Moorcock becomes editor of *New Worlds*. Arkady and Boris Strugatsky, *Hard to Be a God*. J. G. Ballard, *The Terminal Beach*. Leiber, *The Wanderer*. Edgar Pangborn, *Davy*.

1965   Frank Herbert, *Dune*. Thomas M. Disch, *The Genocides*. Harry Harrison, *Bill the Galactic Hero*. Monique Wittig, *Les Guerillères*. Jean-Luc Godard, *Alphaville* (film). *Lost in Space* (TV).

1966   *Orbit* founded. R. A. Lafferty, *Nine Hundred Grandmothers*. Samuel R. Delany, *Babel-17*. Heinlein, *The Moon Is a Harsh Mistress*. Sonya Dorman Hess, "When I Was Miss Dow." Pohl, "Day Million." Strugatsky brothers, *The Snail on the Slope*. Gene Roddenberry, *Star Trek* (TV).

1967   Harlan Ellison (ed.), *Dangerous Visions*. Pamela Zoline, "The Heat Death of the Universe." Bob Shaw, *Night Walk*. Delany, *The Einstein Intersection*. Zelazny, *Lord of Light*.

1968   Disch, *Camp Concentration*. Dick, *Do Androids Dream of Electric Sheep?* Keith Roberts, *Pavane*. McCaffrey, *Dragonflight*. John Brunner, *Stand on Zanzibar*. Italo Calvino, *Cosmicomics*. Stanley Kubrick, *2001: A Space Odyssey* (film). *The Prisoner* (TV).

1969   Moorcock, *Behold the Man*. Dick, *Ubik*. Ursula K. Le Guin, *The Left Hand of Darkness*. Norman Spinrad, *Bug Jack Barron*. Angela Carter, *Heroes and Villains*. Moon landing.

1970   Ballard, *The Atrocity Exhibition*. Larry Niven, *Ringworld*. David R. Bunch, *Moderan*. Joanna Russ, *And Chaos Died*. Herbert, *Whipping Star*. Robert Silverberg (ed.), *The Science Fiction Hall of Fame*, Vol I.

1971   Delany, *Driftglass*. Spinrad, *The Iron Dream*. Kubrick, *A Clockwork Orange* (film).

1972   Gene Wolfe, *The Fifth Head of Cerberus*. Ellison (ed.), *Again, Dangerous Visions*. Silverberg, *Dying Inside*. James E. Gunn, *The Listeners*. Disch, *334*. Strugatsky brothers, *Roadside Picnic* (in English, 1977). Barry N. Malzberg, *Beyond Apollo*.

1973   James Tiptree Jr., "The Women Men Don't See." *Ten Thousand Light-Years from Home*. Ballard, *Crash*. Clarke, *Rendezvous with Rama*. Vonda N. McIntyre, "Of Mist, and Grass, and Sand." Ian Watson, *The Embedding*.

1974   Le Guin, *The Dispossessed*. Larry Niven and Jerry E. Pournelle, *The Mote in God's Eye*. Suzy McKee Charnas, *Walk to the End of the World*. Christopher Priest, *Inverted World*. Doris Lessing, *Memoirs of a Survivor*.

1975   Russ, *The Female Man*. Pamela Sargent (ed.), *Women of Wonder*. Joe Haldeman, *The Forever War*. Delany, *Dhalgren*. Shaw, *Orbitsville*. Brunner, *The Shockwave Rider*. *A Boy and His Dog* (film).

1976   Marge Piercy, *Woman on the Edge of Time*. Kate Wilhelm, *Where Late the Sweet Birds Sang*. Pohl, *Man Plus*. Delany, *Triton*. Gordon R. Dickson, *Dorsai!* Sargent (ed.), *More Women of Wonder*.

1977   Carter, *The Passion of New Eve*. Russ, *We Who Are About To . . . .* Pohl, *Gateway*. Dick, *A Scanner Darkly*. Moorcock, *The Cornelius Chronicles*. Gunn (ed.), *The Road to Science Fiction*. Steven Spielberg, *Close Encounters of the Third Kind* (film). George Lucas, *Star Wars* (film).

1978   John Varley, *The Persistence of Vision*. Tiptree, *Star Songs of an Old Primate; Up the Walls of the World*. McIntyre, *Dreamsnake*.

1979   John Crowley, *Engine Summer*. Douglas Adams, *The Hitchhiker's Guide to the Galaxy*. Ridley Scott, *Alien* (film). Strugatsky brothers, *The Ugly Swans* (1968). *Star Trek—The Motion Picture*.

1980   Gene Wolfe, *The Book of the New Sun* (published in four volumes from 1980–1983). Russell Hoban, *Riddley Walker*. Gregory Benford, *Timescape*. Octavia E. Butler, *Wild Seed*. Walter Tevis, *Mockingbird*.

1981   William Gibson, "The Gernsback Continuum." Carol Emshwiller, "The Start of the End of the World." C. J. Cherryh, *Downbelow Station*.

1982 Michael Bishop, *No Enemy but Time*. Rudy Rucker, *Software*. Spielberg, *E. T.: The Extra-Terrestrial* (film). Scott, *Blade Runner* (film). *TRON* (film).

1983 Lem, *His Master's Voice*. Spinrad, *The Void Captain's Tale*. David Brin, *Startide Rising*. Hubbard, *Battlefield Earth*. Benford, *Against Infinity*.

1984 Butler, "Bloodchild." Gibson, *Neuromancer*. Kim Stanley Robinson, *The Wild Shore*. Suzette Haden Elgin, *Native Tongue*. Russ, *Extra(ordinary) People*. Delany, *Stars in My Pocket Like Grains of Sand*. Gardner Dozois, *The Year's Best Science Fiction: First Annual Collection*.

1985 Margaret Atwood, *The Handmaid's Tale*. Connie Willis, *Firewatch*. Greg Bear, *Blood Music*. Bruce Sterling, *Schismatrix*. Brin, *The Postman*. Gibson, *Count Zero*. Orson Scott Card, *Ender's Game*. Le Guin, *Always Coming Home*.

1986 Karen Joy Fowler, *Artificial Things*. Gibson, *Burning Chrome*. Marc Laidlaw, *Dad's Nuke*. James Morrow, *This Is the Way the World Ends*. Sargent, *Venus of Dreams*. Joan Slonczewski, *A Door into Ocean*. Frank Miller, *The Dark Knight Returns* (graphic novel). *The Terminator* (film).

1987 Butler, *Dawn*. George Alec Effinger, *When Gravity Fails*. Pat Murphy, "Rachel in Love." Michael Blumlein, *The Movement of Mountains*. Vernor Vinge, *True Names . . . And Other Dangers*. Rebecca Ore, *Becoming Alien*. Lucius Shepard, *Life During Wartime*. Willis, "Schwarzschild Radius." Benford, *Great Sky River*. *Star Trek: The Next Generation* (TV). Alan Moore and Dave Gibbons, *Watchmen* (graphic novel).

1988 Cherryh, *Cyteen*. Lois McMaster Bujold, *Falling Free*. Gibson, *Mona Lisa Overdrive*. Robinson, *The Gold Coast*. Sterling, *Islands in the Net*. Sheri S. Tepper, *The Gate to Women's Country*. Brian M. Stableford, *The Empire of Fear*. Paul J. McAuley, *Four Hundred Billion Stars*. Ian McDonald, *Desolation Road*. Rucker, *Wetware*. Elizabeth Vonarburg, *The Silent City*.

1989 John Kessel, *Good News from Outer Space*. Katherine Dunn, *Geek Love*. Dan Simmons, *Hyperion*. Candas Jane Dorsey, "(Learning About) Machine Sex." Sterling, "We See Things Differently."

1990 Bujold, *The Vor Game*. Gibson and Sterling, *The Difference Engine*. Robinson, *Pacific Edge*. Simmons, *The Fall of Hyperion*. Kessel, "Invaders." Murphy, *Points of Departure*. Rucker, *The Hollow Earth*. Howard Waldrop, *Night of the Cooters*.

1991 Piercy, *He, She, and It*. Stephen Baxter, *Raft*. Emma Bull, *Bone Dance*. Pat Cadigan, *Synners*. Fowler, *Sarah Canary*. Haldeman, *The Hemingway Hoax*. Elizabeth Hand, *Winterlong*. Gwyneth Jones, *White Queen*.

1992 Maureen F. McHugh, *China Mountain Zhang*. Willis, *Doomsday Book*. Ben Bova, *Mars*. Robinson, *Red Mars*. Neal Stephenson, *Snow Crash*. Harry Turtledove, *The Guns of the South*. Varley, *Steel Beach*. Tom Shippey (ed.), *The Oxford Book of Science Fiction Stories*. Richard Calder, *Dead Girls*.

1993 Lewis Shiner, *Glimpses*. Nicola Griffith, *Ammonite*. Bear, *Moving Mars*. Robinson, *Green Mars*. Nancy Kress, *Beggars in Spain*. Terry Bisson, *Bears Discover Fire*. Ursula K. Le Guin and Brian Attebery (eds.), *The Norton Book of Science Fiction*. Gibson, *Virtual Light*. Butler, *Parable of the Sower*. Spielberg, *Jurassic Park* (film).

1994   Bear, *Moving Mars*. Cadigan, *Fools*. John Barnes,
        Mother of Storms. Sterling, *Heavy Weather*. Nancy
        Springer, *Larque on the Wing*. Arthur C. Clarke
        and Gentry Lee, *Rama Revealed*. Jones, *North
        Wind*. Charnas, *The Furies*. Bishop, *Brittle Innings*.
        Morrow, *Towing Jehovah*. David G. Hartwell and
        Kathryn Kramer (eds.), *The Ascent of Wonder*,
        Baxter, *Ring*. Greg Egan, *Permutation City*. Kress,
        Beggars and Choosers. Charnas, *The Furies*. Le
        Guin, *A Fisherman of the Inland Sea*. Willis, *Impos-
        sible Things*. Benford, *Matter's End; Furious Gulf*.
        Kit Reed, *Little Sisters of the Apocalypse*. Rachel
        Pollock, *Temporary Agency*. *Star Trek: Voyager*
        (TV). *The X-Files* (TV). *Earth 2* (TV).

1995   Griffith, *Slow River*. Robinson, *Blue Mars*. Ballard,
        Rushing to Paradise. Jeff Noon, *Vurt*. Richard
        Kadrey, *Kamikaze l'Amour*. Benford, *Sailing Bright
        Eternity*. Tepper, *Gibbons' Decline and Fall*. Ore,
        Gaia's Toys. Jonathan Lethem, *Amnesia Moon*.
        Stephenson, *The Diamond Age*. Linda Nagata, *The
        Bohr Maker*. Baxter, *The Time Ships*. Hand, *Waking
        the Moon*. Ron Howard, *Apollo 13* (film).

1996   Willis, *Bellwether*. Bisson, *Pirates of the Universe*.
        Haldeman, *None So Blind*. Sage Walker, *Whiteout*.
        Hartwell (ed.), *Year's Best SF*. Cherryh, *Inheritor*.
        Bishop, *At the City Limits of Fate*. *Independence Day*
        (film).

Chapter One

THE CULTURE OF SCIENCE FICTION— RATIONALIZING GENRE

To romance of the future may seem to be indulgence in ungoverned speculation for the sake of the marvelous. Yet controlled imagination in this sphere can be a very valuable exercise for minds bewildered about the present and its potentialities. Today we should welcome, and even study, every serious attempt to envisage the future of our race; not merely in order to grasp the very diverse and often tragic possibilities that confront us, but also that we may familiarize ourselves with the certainty that many of our most cherished ideals would seem puerile to more developed minds. To romance of the far future, then, is to attempt to see the human race in its cosmic setting, and to mould our hearts to entertain new values.

Olaf Stapledon

Criticism of science fiction cannot possibly look like the criticism we are used to. It will—perforce—employ an aesthetic in which the elegance, rigorousness, and systematic coherence of explicit ideas is of great importance. It will therefore appear to stray into all sorts of extra-literary fields, metaphysics, politics, philosophy, physics, biology, psychology, topology, mathematics, history, and so on.... Science-fiction criticism will discover themes and structures ... which may seem recondite, extra-literary, or plain ridiculous. Themes we

1

customarily regard as emotionally neutral will be charged with emotion. Traditionally "human" concerns will be absent; protagonists may be all but unrecognizable as such. What in other fiction would be marvelous will here be merely accurate or plain; what in other fiction would be ordinary or mundane will here be astonishing, complex, wonderful.

Joanna Russ

Everything considered, the world of science fiction is not a bad place to live.

Frederik Pohl

Science Fiction Thinking

In 1981 Jove Books published a series of "No-Frills" genre paperbacks, one for mystery, one for romance, one for the western, and one for science fiction. Its stark white cover with black print designed to look like generic grocery products, *Science Fiction* identified no author but promised to be "Complete with Everything: Aliens, Giant Ants, Space Cadets, Robots, One Plucky Girl." In short, the cover of this paperback promises that it will deliver *generic* genre literature, boiling SF down to its undifferentiated essence. An inner page explains that this No-Frills book contains "everything Science Fiction lovers look for," and suggests that this approach offers "the latest in economy and convenience to today's readers." "Why pay more?" the ad asks. "Why shop around? After you've read one, you won't mind the others."

Its 58 pages overflowing with the promised science fiction "stuff" (aliens, rockets, robots, scientists, and so on), *Science Fiction* puts its hero, space cadet Alex Harrison, through a fast-forward series of adventures—at the end of which he has saved his scientist father's reputation, saved Earth from some really nasty aliens, and won the heart of plucky girl Space Patrol Officer Dana Drew. Clearly meant to be a pastiche of SF formulas, *Science Fiction* offers instead a feeble parody only of the most unsophisticated examples of space opera circa the late 1920s. The only impressive part of this otherwise undistinguished effort is the book's plain white cover, since the often garish and always colorful covers of SF books provide a distinct reminder of the importance of packaging and marketing of science fiction. You may not be able to judge a book by its cover, but you certainly can identify most SF books by cover alone. Apart from its cover, however, this book joins a long line of uninformed dismissals of the genre based only on its crudest icons and actions, only on its weakest works. Like so many other criticisms of SF, the No-Frills book pointedly ignores Theodore Sturgeon's reminder, now immortalized as "Sturgeon's Law":

> Ninety percent of everything is crud.
> Corollary 1: The existence of immense quantities of trash in science fiction is admitted and it is regretted; but it is no more unnatural than the existence of trash anywhere.
> Corollary 2: The best science fiction is as good as the best fiction in any field.[1]

(While I'll not attempt in this book to argue for Sturgeon's second corollary, it is important, and only fair, that overviews of SF acknowledge corollary one.)

The No-Frills attempted parody starts from the assumption that science fiction is simply adventure built around SF props, that its contents are the same as content, that what SF "is about" is more important than what it does. It also assumes that science fiction is a static genre whose essential features remain unchanged through time, ignoring the fact that twentieth-century science fiction has mutated through at least three main periods and through more variations of plot and theme than could be counted. From the era of the scientific romance made famous by H. G. Wells, science fiction moved in 1926 into an era of pulp and magazine stories influenced by the vision of editors Hugo Gernsback and John Campbell. Then, starting in the 1960s with the experimental writing of the British New Wave, writing particularly associated with editor Michael Moorcock's *New Worlds* magazine, science fiction entered its contemporary phase, an era characterized by reaction against genre constraints, but in which almost all older forms of science fiction continue to enjoy success.

To the extent that it parodies anything recognizable, the No-Frills *Science Fiction* may capture some of the excesses of bad pulp SF from the 1920s, but even the least sophisticated of those early stories, such as Hugo Gernsback's *Ralph 14C41+: A Romance of the*

Year 2000 and E. E. "Doc" Smith's *The Skylark of Space*, possess a celebratory enthusiasm for the new, a kind of tall-tale exuberance that the No-Frills parody misses entirely. As a result, *Science Fiction* is not even funny to readers who know SF because it parodies images and ideas that have never been the heart of the genre, confusing props with essential processes, ignoring the fact that the genre has been characterized far more by flux than by stasis. Certainly, very effective, very funny parodies of SF do exist, but this No-Frills effort is not remotely in the league of parodies written by SF writers. Harry Harrison's *Bill, the Galactic Hero*, Bob Shaw's *Who Goes Here?*, Barry Malzberg's *Galaxies*, Douglas Adams's *The Hitchhiker's Guide to the Galaxy*, and Howard Waldrop's "Night of the Cooters" are just a few works readers might turn to in search of successful SF parodies. Most of all, however, *Science Fiction* reveals a complete lack of understanding of what might be called "science fiction thinking."

I use this purposefully fuzzy term in lieu of a definition of science fiction because it allows me to cover three different aspects of the culture of SF, as these aspects have developed through time. First, science fiction thinking encompasses the all-important fact that science fiction has moved in the twentieth century from being only a literary category to being a set of attitudes and expectations about the future. These attitudes reveal themselves in almost every medium and are prevalent throughout contemporary culture, more than justifying Paul Alkon's observation that "common habits of thinking have become science fictional" (8). Secondly, science fiction thinking refers both to the assumptions that guide the writing of SF and to the crucial assumptions and protocols that are central to its reading. And finally, science fiction thinking is a term that can reflect that during the twentieth century we have evolved a number of generally agreed upon ways of thinking and talking about science fiction as a body of literature. Terms such as "icon," "sense of wonder," "hard and soft SF," "cognitive estrangement," "subjunctivity," "genre SF," and "fandom" make the discussion of SF a fairly specialized activity, and at least a general introduction to these terms and the concepts they represent is crucial to the understanding of the critical enterprise that has grown around SF since 1900.

Science fiction thinking reflects the fact that science fiction in the twentieth century has moved from the fringes to the center of modern consciousness. In the twentieth century SF has become a multimedia genre with SF narratives prominent in movies, TV, comics, graphic novels, music videos, and video and computer games. SF icons and images have become prominent in commercial art and advertising, and SF ideas have been appropriated (or misappropriated) by government and the military who insisted on seeing in "Star Wars" more than just a movie. Responding to these changes, science fiction writers from James Gunn to Bruce Sterling have routinely noted the narrowing of whatever gaps exist between science fiction and "reality." "The world finally has caught up with science fiction," is how James Gunn begins his *Alternate Worlds: The Illustrated History of Science Fiction.* Gunn's contention in 1975 that "we live, indisputably, in a science fiction world" closely followed J. G. Ballard's introduction to the French edition of *Crash* in 1974, where he detailed the new responsibilities of the writer in a world where fiction and reality seem to have switched places.[2] Some dozen years later, when Bruce Sterling prefaced his *Mirrorshades* anthology with the suggestion that "Cyberpunks are perhaps the first SF generation to grow up not only within the literary tradition of science fiction, but in a truly science fictional world," he did not even need to explain his claim.[3] Brian Aldiss, however, did try to explain in *Trillion Year Spree* his sense that SF had "come to the crest of an ever-breaking wave":

> Films, TV series, computer games, toys, media advertising, music— the science fiction mode is more diverse in its forms than ever before. We live in an SF environment where our children's toys are robots and spacecraft, their cartoon adventures set in the 31st Century or on another planet. We see computer technology proliferating unchecked. We also see our oldest SF dreams being made into believable visual images on the wide screen.[4]

It has fallen to noted American literary and cultural critic H. Bruce Franklin, however, to remind us that it is not just children's toys and popular entertainment that have become science fictional, but all aspects of our culture: "Science fiction has moved inexorably toward the center of American culture, shaping our imagination (more than many of us would like to admit) through movies, novels, television, comic books, simulation games, language, economic plans and investment programs, scientific research and pseudo-scientific cults, spaceships real and imaginary."[5] Throughout his wide-ranging and provocative scholarship, Franklin has pursued the thesis that attitudes and beliefs derived from and promoted by science fiction have influenced even American military and foreign policy.[6]

While this book must necessarily concern itself only with print SF, it is imperative to keep in mind that SF has long since ceased being only—or even primarily—a literary phenomenon. Science fiction books and stories are now produced in a world where they are but one of many manifestations of science fiction thinking. When applied to the body of literature that is its textual dimension, science fiction thinking has to do with the rhetoric that manages the tension between what Gary Wolfe calls "the known and the unknown," between what is and what might be. Science fiction thinking generates the rhetoric that bridges the gap between the givens of science and the goals of the imaginary marvelous, the emphasis always on "explaining" the marvelous with rhetoric that makes it seem plausible, or at least not yet impossible. Joanna Russ provides a useful summary of this process:

> Science fiction is What If literature. All sorts of definitions have been proposed by people in the field, but they all contain both The What If and The Serious Explanation; that is, science fiction shows things not as they characteristically or habitually are but as they might be, and for this "might be" the author must offer a rational, serious, consistent explanation, one that does not (in Samuel Delany's phrase) offend against what is known to be known.[7]

"SF is the literature of change," says Frederik Pohl, "and writing it consists in looking at the world around us, dissecting it into its component parts, throwing some of those parts away and replacing them with invented new ones—and then reassembling that new world and describing what might happen in it."[8]

Perhaps most singularly, science fiction thinking refers to the process by which science fiction is read, for twentieth-century science fiction has become an extratextual phenomenon as well as a body of texts sharing similar characteristics. Whether in the form of organized "fandom" or in a more loosely held sense of participation among science fiction readers, science fiction has become something too important to leave to its writers alone, a subculture of values and expectations endlessly discussed and debated by its writers, readers, and critics across a range of media and forums. It is this subculture of readers and fans that has given science fiction, a literature in which many conflicting ideologies are advanced, an overarching sense of mission, a broad agenda of change that sets science fiction apart both from other popular genres and from the two broad forms of fantasy and mainstream writing.

John Kessel has said that all science fiction writers want to change the world, and much the same could be said for SF readers, many of whom would argue that the world *is* changed by the protocols at the heart of science fiction thinking. During the twentieth century, this way of seeing the world has evolved through distinct periods and along often contradictory ideological and aesthetic axes, leaving any formal attempt to define this attitude doomed to certain imprecision, if not outright failure. Most broadly, science fiction thinking is a sense of common enterprise that underlies the discussion of science fiction, a belief that better thinking is a desirable goal for humanity and that science fiction can somehow promote that improvement. "Science fiction is a tool to help you think," is the way Samuel Delany puts this broad proposition about what SF does or what readers expect it to do—what some call its "cultural instrumentality."[9]

Most SF writers, readers, and critics would agree that there is something different about the way we read science fiction, a difference divorced from standards of "literariness" that keeps some very sophisticated readers from making much sense at all of SF. This difference can be so pronounced that it may be useful to think of SF as a language that must be learned or as a mode of writing as distinctive as poetry, complete with its reading protocols quite different from those used for reading other kinds of fiction. In this sense, the stories of SF are not just "about" new ways of seeing, new perspectives, but actually demand new ways of seeing from its readers. Brian Stableford discusses the "perspective-shift of science fiction," as largely a function of reader expectation, as he argues that "there is an important difference between an act of reading in which a book is read *as science fiction* and an act of reading in which a book (whatever its content) is read *as a novel*."[10] A good example of the kind of reading Stableford refers to would be Karen Joy Fowler's delightful *Sarah Canary*, a novel seen by enthusiastic mainstream reviewers as the story of a band of politically powerless outcasts in the Pacific Northwest of the 1870s, but seen by SF writers and readers as an alien encounter story and promptly nominated for a Nebula Award in 1992.[11] The same perspective shift would of course also apply to science fiction in its shorter forms—the story and the novella.

In his frequently cited essay, "About Five Thousand One Hundred and Seventy Five Words," Samuel R. Delany suggests that part of this perspective shift occurs in the very way SF readers respond word-by-word to the sentences of SF stories.[12] What is different in SF, says Delany, is its level of "subjunctivity," the tension between the words of an SF story and their referents—what Brian Attebery calls their degree of "ifness." Illustrating his argument with sentences such as "The red sun is high, the blue low," "Her world exploded," and "He turned on his left side," Delany carefully makes the case for his essential claim: "On the most basic level of sentence meaning, we read words differently when we read them as science fiction" (Delany 1984, 165). More recently, Ursula K. Le Guin has added to Delany's examples sentences such as "I'm just not human till I've had my coffee," "He was absorbed in the landscape," and "The chairman kept putting out feelers."[13] She explains that one of the ways we read SF differently is to expect from it the literalization of metaphor ("He was walking on air"), a process that serves "to put reality into question, making us aware of our assumptions concerning what is real, as well as our perceptions or convictions of continuity and identity." Or, as Le Guin wryly restates her point: "The reader can't take much for granted in a fiction where the scenery can eat the characters" (NBSF, 31).

Other kinds of writing may lack any tie to the referential (or "real") world, but the concept of subjunctivity specifies the precise form of the relationship between SF and the referential world. The degree of subjunctivity accounts for part of this difference. Reportage, naturalistic fiction, fantasy, and science fiction depend on their readers' expecting different levels of subjunctivity: the reader of reportage assumes that its words refer to *what has happened*, the reader of naturalistic fiction to *what could have happened*, the reader of fantasy to *what could not have happened*, and the reader of SF to *what has not happened*. What has not happened, in turn, subsumes stories about events that will not happen and events that might happen. Although Delany has since stopped using the term *subjunctivity* for reasons of linguistic theory, this explanation for the way an SF reader approaches the words and world of an SF story remains very useful. It is the notion of subjunctivity that best accounts for the relationship in SF between known science and its necessary deformations, between the reader's world and the world of the SF semblance.

What further distinguishes SF from other prose modes, explains Delany, is that its imaginary worlds must be constructed by the reader with each word of the text, a process of addition and correction. This reverses the process of mundane fiction that allows readers to "subtract" the world of a naturalistic text from what the reader considers the known or given world. "To read an SF text," Delany observes, "we have to indulge a much more fluid and speculative kind of game. With each sentence we have to ask what in the world of the tale would have to be different from our world for such a sentence to be uttered—and thus, as the sentences build up, we build up a world in specific dialogue, in a specific tension, with our present concept of the real" (Delany 1984, 89). Of course, this sentence-by-sentence process of building and correction is aided when we read a new work of SF by what we know of previous works and by what we know, in a general way, about science. This all-important context in which the reading of SF unfolds has been called SF's "megatext" by Brian Attebery, and it is perhaps the degree of familiarity with this megatext that most determines the degree of satisfaction in a reader's response to SF.[14]

This focus on expectations echoes that of Mark Rose, who in *Alien Encounters* advises that we think of genre as "a social phenomenon, as a set of expectations rather than as something that resides within a text."[15] Comparing the perspective shift of SF to the "gestalt shift by which an ambiguous drawing can suddenly shift the mind of the observer from one of its appearances to the other," Stableford continues that in search of it the science fiction reader seeks it in stories that suggest "a vast universe of possibility beyond the everyday," and he calls attention to the fact that "several of the most popular science fiction stories ever written are stories *about* perspective shifts of this kind" (Stableford, 72–73).

I will return to this key idea of the perspective shift or conceptual breakthrough of science fiction thinking at the end of this chapter, but before doing so I want to look at three very different twentieth-century science fiction stories in order to suggest a number of other terms and concepts that have become prominent in the discussion of twentieth-century science fiction. While these stories, E. M. Forster's "The Machine Stops" (1909), John Campbell's "Twilight" (1934), and Pamela Zoline's "The Heat Death of the Universe" (1967), come from each of the three main eras of science fiction since 1900, they cannot reveal all the essential paragraphs of science fiction or lead to its rigorous definition, but they may allow us to survey some of the issues subsumed in science fiction thinking. Remember that these stories are soundings rather than any kind of representative sample. Even if we somehow identify an essential commonality between "The Machine Stops," "Twilight," and "The Heat Death of the Universe," they remain a descriptive index to where science fiction has been rather than a definitional prescription for where it is now or should go. What Forster's, Campbell's, and Zoline's stories *can* do is illustrate some of the behaviors we characteristically associate with SF, some of what John Huntington calls "the thought processes of the genre." A brief summary of these thought processes appears in Ursula K. Le Guin's introduction to *The Norton Book of Science Fiction*, where she notes:

> Materialistic cause and effect; the universe conceived as comprehensive object of exploration and exploitation; multiculturalism; multispeciesism; evolutionism; entropy; technology conceived as intensive industrial development, permanently developing in the direction of complexity, novelty, and importance; the idea of gender, race, behavior, belief as culturally constructed; the consideration of mind, person, personality, and body as objects of investigation and manipulation: such fundamental assumptions of various sciences or of the engineering mind underlie and inform the imagery and the discourse of science fiction. (NBSF, 23)

Le Guin's list is not exhaustive, nor can it stand without her further explanation of the ways in which SF can cast these assumptions both positively and negatively, but it does offer an effective index to the critical discourse that has sprung up around twentieth-century SF, starting with critical discussions in the letter columns of the pulps and proceeding through fan mags and fanzines to the now well-established classics of SF scholarship.

Two Cities and a House:
A Range of Fiction and Criticism

"Imagine, if you can," challenges the first line of E. M. Forster's "The Machine Stops," "a small room, hexagonal in shape, like the cell of a bee."[16] The underground room is easy to imagine because it contains only an armchair and a reading desk, with lighting and ventilation produced by unseen means. All the needs of Vashti, the woman who is the room's sole inhabitant, are met at the touch of a button: "There were buttons and switches everywhere—buttons to call for food, for music, for clothing. There was the hot-bath button, by pressure of which a basin of (imitation) marble rose out of the floor, filled to the brim with a warm deodorised liquid. There was the cold bath button. There was the button that produced literature" (MS, 39). That the room's inhabitant is only described as "a swaddled lump of flesh—a woman, about five feet high, with a face as white as a fungus" completes both the imaginary picture and Forster's heavily slanted setup for a story intended by its author as "a counterblast against one of the earlier heavens of H. G. Wells." As a protest against what Forster feared in a Wellsian enthusiasm for technological progress, "The Machine Stops" advances a dystopian view of technology that reappears in Yevgeny Zamyatin's *We* (1924), Aldous Huxley's *Brave New World* (1932), George Orwell's *1984* (1949).

Electric buttons so stud Vashti's automated room that while it may seem empty it can provide for her physical wants as well as putting her in electronic contact with thousands of people. The Machine provides all she cares for in the world. Which turns out to be not much, since Vashti so fears direct experience that she almost never leaves her room, almost never has direct contact with other people, and is even resentful of the time it takes to communicate with her son, Kuno, who lives "on the other side of the earth," by means of a device that seems to be a telephone with a visual screen, allowing callers to see as well as hear each other. Vashti resents using this device because it distracts her from giving a totally impersonal lecture over the Machine's communications net; Kuno wishes to see his mother in person because he resents having contact with her mediated by the Machine. In response to his mother's complete devotion to

11

Machine-mediated life, Kuno raises a cry that has been heard throughout the history of science fiction:

> Cannot you see . . . that it is we who are dying, and that down here the only thing that really lives is the Machine? We created the Machine, to do our will, but we cannot make it do our will now. It has robbed us of the sense of space and the sense of touch, it has blurred every human relation and narrowed down love to a carnal act, it has paralysed our bodies and our wills, and now it compels us to worship it. The Machine develops—but not on our lines. The Machine proceeds—but not to our goal. We only exist as the blood corpuscles that course through its arteries, and if it could work without us, it would let us die. (MS, 54)

First published in 1909 in *Oxford and Cambridge Review*, "The Machine Stops" presents a stridently dystopian view of a future society so completely run by ostensibly benevolent machinery that its inhabitants have forgotten not only how to run the machine but also how to be human. Forster's "Machine" is a totalizing environment, a technosphere whose hum penetrates the blood and the thoughts of the humanity it maintains. Here, the machine environment functions metonymically, standing for technology, science, progress, just as in science fiction most "gadgets" or technologized or technologically reached settings function to invoke the semblance of science and the scientific method. Claustrophobically oppressive when it functions efficiently, the Machine seems capricious as it begins to break down long after humans have forgotten how to repair its own "mending apparatus," and its ultimate failure is apocalyptic, leading to the deaths of mother and son and most other inhabitants of the machine environment.

The science fiction writer and scholar James Gunn sees Forster's story as part of a larger reaction of literary culture against the belief in progress and faith in science and suggests that "The Machine Stops" was written as something of a refutation of the Wellsian future city. Most Forster scholars find little of interest or merit in the story, probably because they see it as "science fiction," and, if they discuss it at all, concentrate not on its construction of technology, but on its construction of the conflict between mother and son. Agreeing with Gunn that the story is a reaction to Wells's *The Time Machine*, Wilfred Stone nevertheless claims that this "moral allegory warning men not to become the tools of their tools" is mainly interesting in personal rather than social terms as "another tale of the psychic escape of a boy hero."[17] Gunn's view of the story as science fiction rests precisely on its "social" rather than "personal" aspects, while both Gunn and Stone seem to share the assumption that science fiction has to do with the social rather than the personal. It's almost as if these two readers confronted two different stories, Gunn seeing a warning about progress, Stone seeing a castrating mother and her "maimed and impotent prophet" son. Stone cursorily acknowledges that "The Machine Stops" is science fiction, even "a small masterpiece in the genre," but reduces its conflict to that between mother and son and sees Kuno's death as possibly "the only atonement for the guilt of having opposed the mother-defender of the establishment." Immersed in the megatext of SF—its history, traditions, and stories—Gunn reads "The Machine Stops" *as science fiction*, in the manner previously described by Brian Stableford. Stone recognizes that the story may be labelled SF, but *does not read it as SF*, focusing instead on what the story has in common with other Forster works and with the body of realist or mainstream fiction. In the differing emphasis Gunn and Stone place on aspects of this story can be seen one of the distinguishing traits of science fiction, that, probably more so than is the case with any other popular genre, science fiction depends more on the eye of the beholder than on the intent of the creator and that different beholders read it for differing purposes.

Somewhat ironically, this "anti-" or at least "a-" science-fictional story is now widely anthologized as an example of early twentieth-century science fiction. For my purposes, Forster's story offers an instructive introduction to some of the difficulties of discussing science fiction after 1900, since it can be discussed at once as a publishing phenomenon; as an historical "artifact" in the body of science fiction texts written since 1900, as a "container" of science fiction iconography, themes, and behaviors (aspects of what I call science fiction thinking); and as purposive discourse informed by and advancing a belief system or ideology. In each of these three senses "The Machine Stops" can reasonably be called science fiction, but each sense offers a different understanding of that term as it has evolved during the twentieth century. Accordingly, I'll use this well-known story as a starting point for surveying some of the ways of talking about science fiction that have been advanced since 1900, a brief sampling of the main critical approaches that shape our recognition and understanding of the genre as it nears the end of the twentieth century.

Science fiction writer and editor Damon Knight is credited with defining science fiction as "that which we point to and call science fiction," and even a quick look at a contemporary chain bookstore suggests the inescapable construction of the genre as a publishing category yielding clearly marked products to which we can point. Science fiction is what is marketed in the science fiction section of the bookstore, published in lines of science fiction books (such as the famed ACE Doubles series of the 1950s and 1960s, or the DAW Books of the 1970s), published in science fiction magazines, or otherwise identified, advertised, and marketed as science fiction. "Science fiction," SF writer Norman Spinrad pragmatically insists, "is what is published as SF." Indeed, for the first 30 or so years after science fiction became a clearly identified category of literature it was almost literally the case, as famous SF writer and editor John W. Campbell claimed, "Science fiction is what science fiction editors publish." In this sense, science fiction as a publishing category began in 1926 when Hugo Gernsback published *Amazing Stories*, the first magazine devoted exclusively to science fiction. *Amazing* published what Gernsback termed "scientifiction," describing it as "the Jules Verne, H. G. Wells, and Edgar Allan Poe type of story—a charming romance intermingled with scientific fact and prophetic vision," and through it and its successors such as *Wonder Stories* Gernsback became the first and arguably most important of a long and distinguished line of editors who have exerted tremendous influence (for better and for worse) on the development of science fiction. One other aspect of science fiction publishing should be noted here—the publishing by science fiction fans of "fan mags" and "fanzines," an important but hard to quantify factor in the development of a steady audience for science fiction and the starting point for a number of the best known science fiction writers of the twentieth century.

Considered solely as a publishing phenomenon, "The Machine Stops" was *not* science fiction when it was first published in *Oxford and Cambridge Review*, nor when it was reprinted in Forster's *The Eternal Moment* in 1928. British readers of both early editions might well have seen it as a "scientific romance," a term codified by Wells and used to describe much of the future-oriented fiction written between 1850 and 1926.[18] However, Forster's story almost surely *is* science fiction when read in *The Science Fiction Hall of Fame, Volume IIB: The Greatest Science Fiction Novellas of All Time* (1973), or James Gunn's *The Road to Science Fiction #2: From Wells to Heinlein* (1979), or in *Science Fiction: The Science Fiction Research Association Anthology* (1988). Here, the line between the story considered in terms of publishing category or considered in terms of reader expectations blurs; what seems clear is that, in Delany's and Stableford's terms, "The Machine Stops" can be read as science fiction, even if retroactively, and that its inclusion in well-known SF anthologies strongly encourages such a reading. While vagaries of publishing and marketing do construct science fiction as a genre in one very arbitrary and often confusing sense, the useful corollary to this view is that science fiction is a category constructed by what readers expect.[19]

While Forster's story clearly is science fiction in terms of some publishing contexts, it was not, at least originally, an example of what John Clute and Peter Nicholls have usefully identified as the most distinct publishing context for the genre of science fiction—what they term "genre SF".[20] If science fiction after 1900 can be said to have a core body of texts that not only are science fiction but also cannot be mistaken for anything else, it would be genre SF, which Clute and Nicholls precisely define as "SF that is either labelled science fiction or is instantly recognized by its readership as belonging to that category—or (usually) both" (ESF, 483). Since their view of genre SF rests on the codification of science fiction publishing and readership, they also specify that genre SF "will be a story written after 1926, published (or theoretically publishable) in a US SF magazine or specialist press." In specifying 1926 as the starting point for genre SF they refer to the very widespread view that science fiction began to form a recognizable genre only when Hugo Gernsback published the first issue of *Amazing Stories*. What this understanding of genre SF (as opposed to the genre *of* SF) does is to suggest the inescapable hierarchies that inhere in even the least theoretical of attempts to identify science fiction.

Regardless of the context of its publication, however, Forster's story displays many features that are now widely associated with SF. Crude content analysis (picking out aspects of the story's referents) of "The Machine Stops" turns up many elements, icons, and "moves" that most readers would associate with science fiction. Set in "the future," the story brims with descriptions of futuristic science whose impact can be seen in everything from birth to transportation. Visual phones, a worldwide communications net, public nurseries that assume responsibility for all children at the moment of birth, automatic cars and airships, respirators, and automatic repair devices are all manifestations of the Machine and all would identify this story for most readers as science fiction, a literature that can often be inventoried. Considered in terms of its semblance, then, this story contains several of the semantically resonant ideas and images Gary Wolfe discusses as "icons" in his invaluable *The Known and the Unknown: the Iconography of Science Fiction* as central to science fiction.[21]

Even though the movement of the action in "The Machine Stops" seems inexorably toward apocalypse as its technology succumbs to entropy, Forster's story suggests for future generations a way out of the madness of machine-mediated life. In this way, the story displays a behavior Wolfe sees in much science fiction: "The transformation of Chaos into Cosmos, of the unknown into the known, is the central action of a great many works of science fiction" (Wolfe, 4). Kuno cannot save himself or his mother from the Machine's collapse, but he has ventured onto the unknown surface of Earth (believed to be Chaos) and found there the promise of "Cosmos," a life once more in tune with nature, "life as it was in Wessex, when Aelfrid overthrew the Danes" (MS, 66). More obviously, Forster's worldwide underground city shares with much SF the "icon of the city" as discussed by Wolfe and in keeping with Brian Aldiss's observation that "Science fiction is a literature of cities." Moreover, in finding a way out of the underground city through its deserted airshafts, Kuno both solves a puzzle (one of the characteristic metaphorical moves of science fiction thinking) and breaches a barrier, a literal move whose importance to SF is also persuasively detailed by Wolfe.

To consider Wolfe's discussion of barriers in slightly different terms, "The Machine Stops" posits two very different spaces or zones: the largely abandoned and Machine-proscribed surface of the Earth where rebels against the Machine hide "in the mists and the ferns" and the automated underground environment controlled by the Machine. While much of science fiction is not set in outer space, most science fiction rests on carefully articulated and demarcated spaces, or zones of possibility and impossibility. Kuno's brief movement from the underground zone of impossibility of "human" independence from the Machine to the surface zone of human possibility reminds us that science fiction often rests on narrative progression as simple as the move from "here" to "there," with the added understanding that "there" in science fiction is usually quite far removed in distance and/or time and/or in degree of difficulty of attainment. One of the most recent SF moves into a newly conceived "zone of possibility" has been the move into cyberspace in novels such as William Gibson's Neuromancer trilogy. Indeed, one of the underlying assumptions of this study is that science fiction itself can best be thought of as a zone of possibility, both in the sense that it is a literature where almost any formulaic deformations are possible and in the sense that it is a literature of the possible—or the not yet impossible, as opposed to fantasy, where the impossible holds sway.

"The Machine Stops" also seems to fit Carl Malmgren's understanding of science fiction primarily in terms of its "science fictional worlds" rather than story. Arguing in his *Worlds Apart: Narratology of Science Fiction* (1991) that far too much analysis of science fiction concerns itself with story—what SF most frequently has in common with other literatures, Malmgren identifies the world of an SF story as one whose characters and setting "contains at least one factor of estrangement from the basic narrative world of the author" and which attempts to naturalize this world "by rooting it in a scientific episteme."[22] In other words, following Darko Suvin's discussion of SF as "the literature of cognitive estrangement" (1979), Malmgren requires that SF present a world containing at least one novum, a novelty or innovation that presents some disjunction from the basic world of the writer and that attempts to explain this disjunction in terms that invoke the rhetoric of science to suggest the plausibility of the novum.[23] Certainly Forster's hexagonal room presents such a disjunction from the world of 1909, where there were no visual telephones and electric buttons did not provide all of the needs for existence. And, while Forster does not attempt to explain how this technological environment came into being in technical terms, he does explain it in evolutionary terms based on human psychology, making his radically estranged technological setting seem "natural" in terms of human nature.

Although it seems safe to assume that "The Machine Stops" displays more than enough symptoms to be called science fiction, it is important to note that what it *does* as science fiction is much less clear. Unmistakably polemical, the story shares what Joanna Russ identifies as SF's didactic nature, but her claim that science is the theology behind this didacticism does not seem to apply— until we add a qualifier by Ursula K. Le Guin that the content of SF "may be not scientific but scientistic" with science and technology portrayed as either deity or demon.[24] Forster thought of his story as a "counterblast" to Wells, and Kuno's criticism of machine dominated society seems to suggest that only a kind of primitivism can preserve "beautiful naked man" from the "invincible pressure" of progress. It is to the ninth-century world of Aelfrid that Kuno would return, not to the Edwardian world of 1909. In the human/machine conflict limned by Kuno can be seen one of the four significant forms of the human/inhuman conflict that Mark Rose identifies as the paradigm of science fiction, "the semantic space, the field of interest, within which science fiction as a genre characteristically operates" (Rose, 32). However, Rose points out that the machine often functions ambivalently in science fiction, that Wells's time machine loses some of its wonder when considered in the context of the underground machinery of the Morlocks. Likewise, it should be noted that Forster's determined attempt to demonize the machine has, at least for many readers of science fiction, the sense of wonder so often identified as one of the most important aspects of SF.

References to this "sense of wonder," a term appropriated and popularized by Damon Knight, appear over and over in twentieth-century discussions of SF and may at least in part reflect SF's debt to its Gothic and Romantic forerunners. From its modern birth in *Frankenstein*, notes Paul Alkon, science fiction "has been concerned as often to elicit strong emotional responses as to maintain a rational basis for its plots," and while the sense of wonder may be produced by "big ideas," it is essentially an emotional response (Alkon, 3). Roughly equating the sense of wonder with "awe at the vastness of space and time," influential SF editor and critic David Hartwell locates this response "at the root of excitement of science fiction."[25] Associating the term with mystery and the thrill of the unknown, Alexei and Cory Panshin rather imprecisely claim that the sense of wonder is crucial to the "transcendence" they reverentially describe as the true goal of science fiction.[26] John Clute and Cornel Robu acknowledge the importance of this valorizing invocation of the term, but add that it has also become enough of a cliche to be referred to by cynical SF fans as a "sensawunna" (ESF, 1083–85). Indeed, this least rigorous of all critical concepts brought to bear on the discussion of science fiction seems to have become the ultimate "fudge factor" in explaining the popularity of science fiction stories, since this shape-shifting extraliterary affective quality can be invoked to praise virtually any aspect of a narrative. The sense of wonder is not a quality that can be found in or pointed to in a work of science fiction, but is a response to which something in the experience of reading the work gives access. No matter how poor the writing, the SF reader or critic can claim that a sense of wonder springs from the novelty of a story, from a dramatically new perspective it presents, from its scale, from its setting, from its "scientific" ideas, etc. And, no matter how critical a story may seem to be of science and technology, the sense of wonder may arise from descriptions the writer intended to be entirely negative. In other words, once the sense of wonder has been invoked to praise an SF story there can be no real debate: *de gustibus non disputandam est.*

For all of its lack of critical rigor, however, the concept of the sense of wonder is probably indispensable for explaining why so many twentieth-century "classics" of SF seem so crudely written when subjected to contemporary standards of "literariness" (standards at best poorly suited, if not actually counterproductive, to the criticism of SF). Perhaps the only comparable literary phenomenon would be the Romantic concept of the sublime, but only if the sublime were invoked as the most important aspect of a Romantic text.[27] And, while the Romantic concept of the sublime was limited to amazing events and natural vistas (mountains, ice fields), the sense of wonder has been associated with technological, spatial, and temporal phenomena. Arthur C. Clarke's observation that a technology advanced far beyond our present knowledge would be indistinguishable from magic suggests one final dimension of the sense of wonder: the wonder is that a science fiction story can present an action or artifact that seems magical but that can be "explained" in rhetoric that makes the magic seem a plausible product of advanced science or technology. As David Hartwell concludes:

> Science fiction promises wonder outside the confines and limitations of the story. The wonder we perceive in the story could be real in a faraway place, or might be real someday. Science fiction delivers us from the written page into a universe of wonder infinitely renewed. It is the transcendence of the written page that is at the core of the appeal of science fiction. Science fiction makes *us* transcendent. (Hartwell, 55)

In a very important way, this concept of the sense of wonder points to one of the distinguishing features of science fiction— that its appeal is not only extraliterary, but extratextual. Many science fiction stories that do not hold up well when reread still provide ideas that reward rethinking and reworking into new stories. Surely SF is the genre that not only invites but also often demands paraphrasing, as the literary shortcomings of many of its best-known stories fade in the light of claims that these stories evoked the sense of wonder, science fiction's version of "the right stuff." While it may be fondly remembered, the affective impact of the sense of wonder often does not repeat on rereading. Noting that a typical 1940s SF magazine story may not hold up well when reread, Brian Attebery offers a crucial qualification: "If you try to go back to it there's nothing there but a burned-out firecracker, and yet readers can testify the explosion was real enough the first time through."[28] What's more, the sense of wonder seems to be a largely atemporal phenomenon: it may be that the sense of wonder rose from the historical innovation of the story (the first story set outside the galaxy or inside the atom), from the wonder that the story evoked from a juvenile reader, or from ideas or images in the story that remain so far beyond what is known as to achieve a kind of affective immortality—wonder that proves timeless.

I do not know of any reader or critic who has identified "The Machine Stops" as a site of wonder, but it seems very likely to me that its status as a staple in histories of SF rests in great part on the wonder of Forster's semblance. For, no matter how terrible a picture Forster hoped to paint of a technologized future, he implicitly posited that there would be a future, that it would be radically changed from the present, and that the primary agent of this radical change would be technology. To argue with Wells, Forster had to concede much of the Wellsian worldview. Accordingly, I suspect that many science fiction readers appropriate from this story not the inevitability of technology run amok, but the inevitability of a future transformed by technology. That Vashti doesn't want to look out the windows of a gigantic automated airship doesn't necessarily mean that Forster's readers would not be intrigued by the prospect of such a technological marvel, a marvel that technologically frames the Romantic sublime of sweeping natural vistas, making them accessible through the wondrous technology of the giant airship. Or, to put this another way, Forster's indictment of technology necessarily contains descriptions of many technological advances that seem desirable even if the dehumanized end to which they have led does not. "If nothing else," points out Gary Wolfe, "science fiction is a literature of alternatives" (Wolfe, 104), and it's not that difficult to imagine technologized futures that offer many of the wonders of Forster's Machine without leading to the totalized extreme of his warning. And, to support my case for the possibility of such a reading so at odds with Forster's apparent intent, I need turn no further than to John Campbell's famed story "Twilight."[29]

Forster's underground city in "The Machine Stops" is so totalizing as to be unseeable: one city spans the entire world. In "Twilight" Campbell lets his readers glimpse several wondrous cities of the far future, but these cities are so uniformly wondrous as to seem identical. We learn of this marvelous future from Jim Bendell, who somewhat agitatedly tells Campbell's narrator the story told by a mysterious hitchhiker he has recently picked up. The hitchhiker claimed to be a time traveller from 3059 who mistakenly went too far back in time—to 1932—on his return from a trip seven million years into the future. Campbell's time traveller, Ares Sen Kenlin, is a kind of scientific superman, magnificent in appearance and thoroughly impressive in manner. Kenlin is triply credentialled as a scientist: his middle name, Sen, literally is science in the classification system of his time, he is an experimenter who has discovered a source of power ("the release") so impressive that he finds signs of its continued use seven million years in the future, and perhaps best of all, he himself is an experiment, the first of a race of super beings created by his father's genetic engineering. It is important to note Sen Kenlin's heavily foregrounded ties to science because they offer one of several optimistic readings of the ostensibly pessimistic view he offers of the far future, and it is important to note his "brainpower," a sign of the fascination with intellectual power that John Huntington has so persuasively documented in his *Rationalizing Genius: Ideological Strategies in the Classic American Science Fiction Short Story*.[30]

Sen Kenlin tells Jim Bendell of a future in which most gleaming, fully automated cities have been deserted for three hundred thousand years, leaving the running and repair of the cities to tireless machines. The first technologically marvelous city Kenlin visits still provides perfect food, shelter, and transportation, but is "a city of the dead ashes of human hopes" because it continues where the human race has failed. Humanity is dying out and its few remaining members have not only forgotten how to run the machines but have also forgotten how to be curious—much like the inhabitants of Forster's Machine. Here Campbell tries to make a fine distinction, as Kenlin explains that these people of the future still possess super-evolved brains, "minds far greater than yours or mine," but have lost one crucial quality, the "instinct" of curiosity. After some five million years of steady intellectual progress, the human race "matured," and with maturity began the gradual dissipation that led to the bewildered and lost survivors encountered by Kenlin. In the world of "Twilight," entropy has ultimately overtaken upward evolution, and the heat death of the universe has been previewed by the intellectual death of the human race. Machines, however, the magnificent products of humanity at its height, are perfect enough to have held off entropy, and they remain as a kind of terrible tribute to the former greatness of humans. "When Earth is cold, and the Sun has died out," Kenlin muses, those machines will go on. When Earth begins to crack and break, those perfect, ceaseless machines will try to repair her—" (TWI, 45).

The future Campbell offers us in "Twilight" has been in some ways even more dominated by technology than is the future offered by Forster in "The Machine Stops." When Forster's Machine breaks down, it causes many deaths, but the "Homeless" survivors on Earth's largely deserted surface can look forward to "life, as it was in Wessex, when Aelfrid overthrew the Danes." Forster's survivors have learned not to trust the machine, that "man is the measure," that the senses can not be mediated by technology. When Forster's Machine stops, the problem is solved, but the fact that machines in Campbell's story "don't know how to stop" seems part of a problem that has no solution: the machines seem likely to go on forever, but the human race is on the inexorable path to extinction. Yet, while "Twilight" was written as a "mood piece," and Kenlin tries to set the mood by singing two songs from the far future, the "Song of Longings" and the "Song of Forgotten Longings," which we are told are really, *really* powerfully mournful, the mood of Campbell's story is more triumphant than melancholy—*precisely because the machines don't stop*.

Mankind may be finished, but those machines have a future! Before Kenlin made his return trip through time, he located not just one but five of the most advanced machines—"machines that could really think" but had been turned off so long ago that no one could remember how to restart them. Connecting these machines together "as the records directed," Kenlin directs them to solve "a great problem." They are to make a curious machine, a machine that will have the instinct lost by man, and there's no rush, since this proto-computer can grind away at the great problem for a million years if necessary. And, while Kenlin expresses some doubt about the success of his project early in his narrative to Jim Bendell, by the end he matter-of-factly claims that he had "brought another machine to life, and set it to a task which, in time to come, it will perform." The key phrase here is "brought to life," as Kenlin's rhetoric indicates Campbell's apparent satisfaction with the prospect of an evolutionary shift from man to machine as the only way of continuing the upward spiral of progress. In this view, the human race atrophied not so much because of machines, but despite them, failing to match their excellence and failing to anticipate the possibility of the evolution of machine intelligence—an oversight Kenlin corrects. "Can you appreciate the crushing loneliness it brought to me?" Kenlin asks Jim, exclaiming "I, who love science, who see in it, or have seen in it, the salvation, the raising of mankind—to see those wondrous machines of man's triumphant maturity, forgotten and misunderstood. The wondrous, perfect machines that tended, protected, and cared for those gentle, kindly people who had—forgotten" (TWI, 56). The implications of this valorizing rhetoric are clear. "Humans have no moral superiority to machines," concludes Huntington, who suggests that in this story "A curious machine is as good as a curious human, perhaps even better if it will not succumb to despair" (Huntington, 162).

Campbell wrote "Twilight" in 1932, but it was not published until 1934 in the November issue of *Astounding*—after having been rejected by all other SF pulps. It was published under the pseudonym Don A. Stuart and is one of a number of "Stuart" stories in which Campbell tried out a voice quite different from that of his earlier published fiction. His earlier stories had tended toward the action-packed superscience extravaganzas made popular by E. E. "Doc" Smith's *The Skylark of Space* (1928), and by 1934, when "Twilight" appeared, Campbell had become—along with Smith—one of the most popular writers in genre SF. Unlike "The Machine Stops," Forster's one try at science fiction, "Twilight" was written by a man claimed by many to have been primarily responsible for evolving the protocols at the very heart of twentieth-century SF, a man whose influence as writer and editor will be examined in chapter two. "Twilight" was at the very center of genre SF when first published and has been repeatedly anthologized (for example, in volume I of *The Science Fiction Hall of Fame* and in volume 2 of *The Road to Science Fiction*) as one of the key stories in the development of twentieth-century science fiction, a story that privileged idea over action, mood or atmosphere over space opera conflict.

When "Twilight" proved very popular with *Astounding*'s readers, Campbell's writing settled into the new "more poetic" style of the Don A. Stuart stories. "The Last Evolution," published in *Amazing* in August 1932 under Campbell's name, indicated the direction the "Stuart" stories would take. While "The Last Evolution" depicts Earth's victory over alien invaders, the victory is won by a machine-evolved entity of pure force and intelligence and it occurs only after the last humans have died. Before dying, however, one of Earth's last two scientists somewhat ponderously spells out the idea that Campbell seems to have reworked in "Twilight" and its sequel, "Night":

"The end of man.... But not the end of evolution. The children of man still live—the machines will go on. Not of man's flesh, but of a better flesh, a flesh that knows no sickness, and no decay . . ."[31]

"Night" features a time traveller who makes Sen Kenlin seem a piker as he travels 120 billion years into the future only to discover pretty much what Kenlin could have told him: the Sun is going out, the Earth is dead—including its machines, and the few machines that still run on Neptune are themselves ready for death. In all three of these stories (and somewhat more obliquely in "The Machine") Campbell seems determined to establish the immensity of evolutionary time and the inevitability of eventual entropic decline, while at the same time reminding us of the way marvelous technology can fight the good fight against the heat death of the universe. Even at its gloomiest, Campbell's version of the future offers us some five million years of human progress as a distinct zone of possibility in which most obstacles short of the second law of thermodynamics can be overcome.

The "mood" of "Twilight," for all its reminders that in only seven million more years humanity will be on its last legs, gets much of its power by offering a veritable catalogue of ideas and images that are calculated to evoke from readers the sense of wonder. While there may seem to be a conflict in this story between science fiction's characteristic optimism and faith in unlimited progress on the one hand, and the story's suggestion on the other hand of an evolutionary dead end for the human race, this latter possibility is framed in such a way as to make it an interesting but unthreatening part of the anything-but-pessimistic thrust of Campbell's message. "That's what happens to civilizations," was Campbell's matter-of-fact explanation of the story to an interviewer in 1971, and in this reply can be heard something of the exhilarated faith in science at the core of Campbell's worldview.[32] To this view the second law of thermodynamics was cause for celebration rather than despair because it proved the perfect immutability of science. "Science doesn't argue with the intransigent objector to the laws of Nature," was the way Campbell put this in a 1957 editorial. "It simply proceeds without him. If he shouts a defiant 'Over my dead body!' it proceeds with perfect equanimity, and without the slightest hesitancy, over his dead body."[33] And it is this "perfect equanimity," the "certainty" of human devolution after the peak of human progress, that is almost triumphantly proclaimed in "Twilight," much as it would be proclaimed in 1954 in Tom Godwin's "The Cold Equations," one of the most controversial stories in SF.[34] Godwin's "cold equations" have to do with the "irrevocable and immutable" laws of nature decreeing that a young girl must be ejected into space after she has stowed away on a supply rocket designed for a single occupant. Campbell is said to have insisted on the "surprise" ending of "The Cold Equations," in which no way could be found to save the innocent stowaway, and this patently contrived and misogynistic tale seems to have derived its popularity among "hard" SF readers by grimly celebrating the myth of scientific certainty that also drives "Twilight."

However, even that grim satisfaction is de-emphasized in "Twilight," first by Campbell's suggestion that Kenlin has already changed part of the future (and with the faint implication that a superscientist such as Kenlin might still find some other way to preclude man's devolution), and then by his much less theoretical celebration of concepts and gadgets. As John Huntington has pointed out in his fine discussion of this story, Campbell "remains deeply enthralled by technology" even as he echoes "pessimistic myths of decline," leaving untouched at the heart of "Twilight" "the source of pleasure that inspires the optimistic prophetic forecasters of this century" (Huntington, 161). The story initially borrows from Wells as Sen Kenlin conquers the barrier of time, and uses his time travelling to foreground a sense of temporal scale clearly designed by Campbell to appeal to the sense of wonder. Just in case readers failed to comprehend that seven million years is a *long* time, long enough for the very position of the stars to have changed, Campbell's unnamed narrator points out that Jim Bendell, a realtor, might miss the sweep of Sen Kenlin's story and use it as a forecast of land value, buying land where Kenlin told of future cities under the mistaken and short-sighted notion "that seven million years was something like seven hundred, and maybe his great-grandchildren would be able to sell it." And, in a kind of wonderful conceptual one-upsmanship, Campbell stresses how long seven million years is in human terms but notes that this time span is nothing in the life of the sun, whose "two thousand thousand thousand" risings between Kenlin's time and the future of the abandoned cities might have made some difference only if those two thousand thousand thousand days had been two thousand thousand thousand years. As Campbell well knew, one sure path to the sense of wonder was big numbers.

Moreover, while Kenlin may claim that the far future contained "the dead ashes of human hopes," his narrative regularly introduces marvels that make the future seem anything but used up. Almost gratuitously, Kenlin's narrative includes a catalogue of "big" ideas: gravity nullifiers, acceleration neutralizers, the death of all marine life, the achievement of super-evolved highly intelligent dogs, and even the possibility of man's developing intelligent and mobile plant life. In the midst of such wonders Kenlin still finds time to describe in some detail the operation of the small flying machine he uses to reach a city where some few humans still live, a description that at once shows Kenlin solving a puzzle and reveals what one critic accurately characterizes as "pleasure in sheer technology for its own sake" (Huntington, 161). In this writer-centered pleasure in sheer technology is the explicit exposition of the reader-centered pleasure I suggest can be found in "The Machine Stops," and in both Forster's and Campbell's visions of the future can be found the somewhat contradictory constructions of science and technology that can be found throughout science fiction's history.

Sometimes, however, science and technology enter SF through the back door, stripped of wonder, submerged in the details of mundane life, offering neither pleasure nor horror. This is the case with Pamela Zoline's celebrated story "The Heat Death of the Universe," a brilliant counterpoint to Campbell's macrocosmic consideration of entropy.[35] Consisting of 54 mostly short numbered paragraphs, some of which are titled and several of which are only one sentence long, Zoline's story interrogates ontology and entropy in a day in the life of Sarah Boyle, a California housewife, mother, and battler for order in a world where pet turtles die, the house is always dusty, and the children demand Sugar Frosted Flakes for breakfast. Combining technical inserts on entropy and the second law of thermodynamics with observations on love, despair, housework, and parenting, Zoline's story has one foot in the camp of "hard" SF with its traditional interest in physics, astronomy, and chemistry, and the other foot in the camp of "soft" SF with its traditional interest in psychology, sociology, and anthropology.

No cosmic vistas of time or space can be found in "The Heat Death of the Universe," but the story is in some respects a more rigorous consideration of entropy than is Campbell's "Twilight." After paragraphs detailing breakfast at the Boyle's house—with particular attention to the print on the Frosted Flakes box, Zoline's story presents in paragraph 13 the first of several "inserts," this one a definition of entropy. For Sarah Boyle, however, entropy has an emotional impact, is never abstract, and is never in the future, as paragraph 36 explains:

> Housework is never completed, the chaos always lurks ready to encroach on any area left unweeded, a jungle filled with dirty pans and the roaring of giant stuffed toy animals suddenly turned savage. Terrible glass eyes. (HD, 22)

Insert two, paragraph 19, offers a definition of the second law of thermodynamics, ties this definition to the preceding discussion of entropy in a closed system, and suggests the eventual result of both as the heat death of the universe—adding the crucial qualifier that "It is by no means certain, however, that the Universe can be considered as a closed system" in the sense that would lead inexorably to its heat death. Even if the universe as a whole may tend to run down, Sarah tries to create "a local enclave" of order in which "there is a limited and temporary tendency for organization to increase":

> 50. Sarah Boyle imagines, in her mind's eye, cleaning and ordering the whole world, even the Universe. Filling the great spaces of Space with a marvelous sweet smelling, deep cleansing foam, deodorizing rank caves and volcanoes. Scrubbing rocks. (HD, 26)

While maximum entropy seems both very real and very inevitable in the closed system of Sarah Boyle's fragmenting life, Sarah strives to create an enclave of order, a zone of possibility, in which life can find a home. Zoline's story makes clear the heroism with which Boyle struggles against entropy, and in so doing makes much more concrete and less sentimental the process at the heart of Campbell's "Twilight." "To ward off fumey ammoniac despair," Sarah has written in lipstick on the lid of a diaper bin a reminder that "the nitrogen cycle is the vital round of organic and inorganic exchange on earth," offering its "sweet breath of the Universe," as a counter to heat death.

Zoline's story lacks the "big machines" of Forster and Campbell, offering instead only a malfunctioning vacuum cleaner Sarah fixes with a kick, and its concern with entropy seems so intensely personal as to make us forget its species-wide implications. Nevertheless, this narrative both clearly alludes to the megatext of science fiction and offers a whole series of pointillist perspective shifts of the kind so common in SF. Furthermore, this story's original publication in *New Worlds* magazine in 1967 clearly signalled to its readers that it would operate according to assumptions and values quite different from—if not actually opposed to—those of Campbellian genre SF. Chapter five will explore the New Wave aesthetic in greater detail, but some of its salient features included the use of mainstream and experimental narrative techniques, interest focused on the soft sciences such as psychology, brooding concern with apocalyptic disasters and entropy, etc. Editor Michael Moorcock had made *New Worlds* a showplace for New Wave fiction, and Zoline's story clearly invoked the emerging megatext of New Wave concerns and practices. But traces of an older SF aesthetic also reappear throughout "The Heat Death of the Universe." It's hardly accidental that the birthday cake for one of Sarah's children comes in the shape of a rocket and launching pad, nor is it insignificant that the color of Sarah's blue eyes is described by rejecting earlier nature metaphors in favor of a color cooked up by chemists. And despite its ostensibly microcosmic view of Sarah's life, her thinking tends ever toward the macrocosmic, particularly as she repeatedly considers her children not in sentimental terms but in terms of the species implications of their bodies and manners. Even that Frosted Flakes box becomes the occasion for a science fictional new way of seeing:

5. If one can imagine it considered as an abstract object, by members of a totally separate culture, one can see that the cereal box might seem a beautiful thing. The solid rectangle is neatly joined and classical in proportions, on it are squandered wealths of richest colors, virgin blues, crimsons, dense ochres, precious pigments once reserved for sacred paintings and as cosmetics for the blind faces of marble gods. (HD, 14)

Later, Sarah tries to imagine a view of world culture different from that of California and decides that it can't be done before "we reach the statistically likely planet and begin to converse with whatever green-faced, teleporting denizens thereof." More specifically, Sarah's invocation of Duchamp and the Dada aesthetic seems the clear antithesis to Campbell's "scientific method aesthetic," and her interest in one of her childrens' toys, "Baba, the wooden Russian doll which, opened, reveals a smaller but otherwise identical doll which opens to reveal, etc., a lesson in infinity at least to the number of seven dolls," can almost be seen as a parody of Campbell's "big number" of seven million years in "Twilight." However, whether or not Zoline intended "The Heat Death of the Universe" as a specific rejoinder to Campbell, the story clearly subverts expectations about the appropriate subjects for SF, just as it also subverts larger societal expectations about "the notion of woman as stable centre of family life," managing, as Sarah Lefanu says, to express "the vistas of emptiness hidden behind the slogan 'a woman's work is never done.'"[36]

So oblique is Zoline's interrogation of the second law of thermodynamics and so subtle are her allusions to SF that Mark Rose describes the story at the outset of his *Alien Encounters* to ask the question: is it science fiction? Acknowledging that "The Heat Death of the Universe" is "an interesting piece of fiction, and one that clearly gains resonance and impact by having been published in a context of science-fiction expectations," Rose is nevertheless unable to specify a definition of science fiction that will anticipate Zoline's story. He uses this difficulty not to exclude the story from SF, but to suggest the limitations of approaching SF through definitions. Persuasively arguing that the question of whether Zoline's story is or is not SF is simply beside the point, Rose suggests a view of genre I find compelling: "A literary genre is not a pigeonhole but a context for writing and reading—or, in Claudio Guillen's suggestive phrase, 'an invitation to form.' Instead of thinking of science fiction as a thing, a kind of object to be described, it is perhaps more useful to think of it as a tradition, a developing complex of themes, attitudes, and formal strategies that, taken together, constitute a general set of expectations" (Rose, 4). By implication, SF—and other genres—entails complex and unpredictable interactions among writers, audiences, and established but flexible conventions.

Against Definitions

Science fiction is the literature that considers the impact of science and technology on humanity. That's my working definition of SF, one inherited from Joe Haldeman and Joan Gordon. Science fiction is "the narrative use of science to create myths allowing novel points of view to the imagination;" this is the definition Paul Alkon advances, although he quickly notes that his definition is normative rather than descriptive and would exclude many works commonly thought of as SF (Alkon, 7). Attempting to be less normative and more inclusive, James Gunn organizes his fine *The Road to Science Fiction* anthologies around the definition:

> Science fiction is the branch of literature that deals with the effects of change on people in the real world as it can be projected into the past, the future, or to distant places. It often concerns itself with scientific or technological change, and it usually involves matters whose importance is greater than the individual or the community; often civilization or the race itself is in danger.[37]

Each of these and of the dozens of other frequently cited definitions of SF has its strengths, but each also projects a view of the field in which "true" SF reflects one set of values and assumptions, while seeming-SF stories that do not share these values and assumptions must be judged "not-SF," or at least poor SF. Each definition works for the old and new generally agreed upon "classics" of SF, but each one grows less satisfactory as we move out from that agreed upon center, reminding us of Damon Knight's comparison of SF to the Indian Ocean, a body of water with no natural boundaries. Equally inefficient, but much more fun, is Brian Aldiss's definition of SF as "Hubris clobbered by nemesis," or an early fan's specification that SF was "fiction that states that what did not happen yesterday will not necessarily not happen tomorrow." The truth is I do not know of any satisfactory definition of SF or even of one that might distinguish the science fiction of Zoline's "The Heat Death of the Universe" from the No-Frills *Science Fiction* I described at the outset of this chapter.

The genre that starts with *Frankenstein*, sees E. E. "Doc" Smith's rollicking 1928 space opera *The Skylark of Space* as one of its twentieth-century turning points, develops through the sophistication of Harlan Ellison and Ursula K. Le Guin, and manages to include the often conflicting values and concerns of writers as diverse as Robert Heinlein and Joanna Russ, J. G. Ballard and John Campbell, Octavia Butler and Stanislaw Lem, Howard Waldrop and Nancy Kress covers so much territory that it seems to me to need description rather than prescription, a map more than a definition. And indeed, mapping metaphors offer a useful introduction to the problem of defining such a disparate field of literature. Using a metaphor that also reminds us that science fiction now has much more than just a literary dimension, David Hartwell compares the task of defining SF to defining Los Angeles: "No two people agree on what Los Angeles does and does not include; the postal service has a different concept from the phone company; the state, county, and city governments can't agree; certainly the people who live there don't know whether L.A. means downtown plus Century City or everything from the mountains out to the beach, including the Valley" (Hartwell, 116). However, Hartwell quickly adds: "At the same time, it's no problem at all going to Los Angeles; one seldom arrives at the wrong city."

That does seem to be the case with science fiction: no two people agree on exactly what it should or should not include, but we have a pretty good idea of the kinds of territory it covers and the kinds of experiences we can expect in those territories. Ursula K. Le Guin has the right idea when she muses that the very "non-definability" of science fiction may be one of the genre's essential qualities (NBSF, 21). For, unlike other popular genres, science fiction depends more on violating the protocols of genre than on maintaining them. There may be something in the relationship between science and science fiction and the advances we now expect as a norm of science that explains the restlessness of science fiction when considered as a formal genre. Perhaps it is the case that just as the "science" in science fiction must usually depart in some way from the "limitations" of known science, and must also move forward as advances in science reshape our sense of what is not yet possible (and not yet impossible), the science fiction story should be thought of as part of a genre-in-the-making that must continue to escape the fixing stasis of definition.[38] Campbell's "Twilight" was seen as such a departure from his earlier stories as to mandate publication under a pseudonym, and Zoline's "The Heat Death of the Universe" could hardly be a more radical departure from the SF we associate with Campbell, and no definition seems likely to encompass radical shifts such as these in the past of SF, much less anticipate the genre's future mutations.

On Being Read by Science Fiction

What sets SF apart from other popular genres and from mainstream literature is that its readers and writers share a sense of participation in an agenda. Certainly not the old pro-science agenda proposed by Hugo Gernsback nor the pro-scientific-method agenda pushed by Campbell, this agenda does not call for adoption of a specific set of beliefs, much less direct action, but it has to do with the very broad assumption that science fiction is not just a literature of ideas or of "thought-experiments" but also somehow points to or promotes better thinking. Within the semblance of the SF story this search for better thinking often involves what John Huntington discusses as "the myth of genius" and usually has as a goal "the achievement of nonpolitical power" (Huntington, 45). Which is to say that the "agenda" of SF is more epistemological than ideological. This "better thinking" may concern preparing for the future, or may concern innovative approaches to problem solving, or may just be a complication of stereotypes of otherness. "Of all the forms which the quest for knowledge takes in modern sf," notes Peter Nicholls, "by far the most important, in terms of both the quality and the quantity of the work that dramatizes it, is conceptual breakthrough" (ESF, 254). The importance of SF as a vehicle for gaining new perspectives not available through other literary forms has been detailed by Paul Alkon for SF before 1900, and we might think of the conceptual breakthrough as a primary site for privileging new perspectives in literature since 1900.

Roughly analogous to the paradigm shifts through which science has evolved, the conceptual breakthrough in an SF story usually involves the challenging and then the overthrowing of an established paradigm, offering in its place an often radically new way of thinking. "Such an altered perception of the world," continues Nicholls, "sometimes in terms of science and sometimes in terms of society, is what SF is most commonly about, and few SF stories do not have at least some element of conceptual breakthrough." This is particularly easy to see in many of the stories collected in *The Science Fiction Hall of Fame, Volume I*. It is important to add that the idea of the conceptual breakthrough is not confined to what happens within an SF story, but can also be applied to the act of reading SF. To illustrate this process we need only remember how it takes a shift of perspective to see Zoline's "The Heat Death of the Universe" take its place in the SF megatext. Indeed, particularly during the first 50 or so years of this century, conceptual breakthroughs or radical perspective shifts have been claimed to be important effects of reading SF, apparently on the basis of the assumption that reading stories about perspective shifts somehow promotes similar activities in the minds of readers. "Mimsy Were the Borogoves," an *SF Hall of Fame* story by Lewis Padgett, can be seen as a kind of wishful blueprint for this process, as its story of children who "graduate" into a superior form of alien thinking called "x logic" and thus disappear into a different way of thinking dramatizes a powerful and pervasive fantasy to which many SF readers consciously or unconsciously subscribe.

"When I finish a science-fiction yarn," wrote a 1935 reader of *Wonder Stories*, "I feel overwhelmed with thoughts that surge in my brain." Citing this and other letters written by early SF fans, Brian Stableford suggests that a "sense of 'breaking through' to a new way of seeing the world (and oneself)" is common at least at some point in the experience of SF readers (Stableford, 72–73). Judging this perspective shift "one of the most vital elements in the expectations of the science fiction reader," Stableford explains: "It is a breakthrough to new concepts, which allow a new interpretation of the perceived world by setting 'today' in a new context which extends far beyond yesterday and tomorrow to hitherto unsuspected imaginative horizons." Or, to put this another way, the conceptual breakthrough so important to so many SF stories can be thought of as taking place on any or all of three different levels: as a conceptual breakthrough experienced by characters in the story, as a conceptual breakthrough encouraged or demanded by the story before it can make sense for the reader (Stableford's "gestalt shift"), and as the even more amorphous, but no less real, belief that the repeated act of reading SF (being an SF reader or fan) itself indicates a kind of breakthrough—a refusal to be satisfied by the mundane. "One reads science fiction," claims Robert Sheckley, "in order momentarily to transcend the dull quality of everyday life" (Stableford, 95).

In the highly appreciative essay from which I've taken my title for this last section of my first chapter, William J. Schafer implicitly supports the understanding of reading SF as a kind of personal breakthrough. Citing Thoreau's description of reading as "the process of being read, as finding your fate in your capacity for interpretation of yourself," Schafer recounts his experience of "being read" by SF:

> As I ingested reams of sf, I was eaten by it too, in mutual communion. As if by transubstantiation or the process by which our food replaces us, cell by cell, as we consume it, I was taken over by ideas and events in stories, the basic substance of my self replaced by passages of Ray Bradbury, William Tenn, Robert Heinlein, Henry Kuttner, A. E. van Vogt, C. L. Moore and scores of others. . . .[39]

SF was the first literature, notes Schafer, that demanded his active participation, and the partnership "between the lonely imagination of the writer and the lonely imagination of the reader" set reading SF apart and made of it "a dialogue, a dialectic, that enveloped me—a voice erupting into my private imagination to utter a thesis, which by its own power evoked from me an antithesis, a reaction to the posed premise" (Schafer, 390).

Schafer's emphasis on the sense of partnership involved in reading SF supports Samuel Delany's view of SF "as a tool to help you think." Delany continues that "like anything that really helps you think, by definition it doesn't do the thinking for you."

> It's a tool to help you think about the present—a present that is always changing, a present in which change itself assures there is always a range of options for actions, actions presupposing different commitments, different beliefs, different efforts (of different qualities, different quantities), different conflicts, different processes, different joys. It doesn't tell you what's going to happen tomorrow. It presents alternative possible images of futures, and presents them in a way that allows you to question them as you read along in an interesting, moving, and exciting story. (Delany 1984, 34)

What Delany tries to explain, what Schafer hints at, and what all the critical theory in the world cannot deliver is the sheer affective wallop of reading and being read by SF, the sense that you are a part of an enterprise with an agenda, a way of seeing the world as a problem to be solved or an opportunity to be taken, but most of all as an excuse for thinking, for endless speculation fueled by the simple words "what if. . . ."

Chapter Two

FROM THE STEAM MAN TO THE STARS

There is today a field called "human engineering," and when the first School of Human Engineering is opened, John W. Campbell will be entitled to the deanship; I doubt that the full extent of his influence, once or twice removed (through his own writing and that of the authors he attracted to what amounted to a "movement" in those early years of Astounding-and-Unknown), will ever be fully tabulated. Campbell did not originate the ideas; he did not stimulate the emergence of the field; he was one of its earliest and most productive engineers.

Judith Merril

Power, transportation, star ships, medicine, long life—never mind the individual predictions. The most significant single fact today is that ninety percent of all the scientists who ever lived in all history are alive right now—and working—and producing. We are doubling our knowledge every few years and the rate keeps going up. Predictions? Make your own. Pay no attention to the predictions of almost all of the professional scientists; by nature they are very conservative in their predictions and they have almost always been wrong—on the short side. The important fact is not what they *expect*—but the fact that they are alive and working. To get a better notion of the scale of the changes in the next few decades take the very wildest stuff being printed as fiction in science fiction magazines—then *square* it!

Robert Heinlein,
XIXth World Science Fiction Convention, Seattle, 1961

"Picture this. A Navy officer walks the deck of a ship, coughing, late at night in the 1930s. Suddenly an arm snakes around his neck, a needle plunges into his buttocks—" The speaker is a fictional ex-Senator William Proxmire, longtime NASA critic and opponent of government spending for the space program. The story is Larry Niven's "The Return of William Proxmire."[1] And the Navy officer would be a young Lieutenant jg Robert A. Heinlein, gunnery officer on the USS *Roper* in December, 1933—shortly before his medical discharge for tuberculosis. The needle would contain the antibiotics necessary to cure Heinlein's TB and the hypodermic would be administered by a time-travelling William Proxmire, determined to keep Heinlein well and in the Navy, thus precluding his career as a science fiction writer. "Over the past forty years or so," explains Niven's Proxmire to the theorist who will build the time machine Proxmire needs, "I've talked to a great many people in science and in the space program. I kept hearing the name Robert Heinlein. They were seduced into science because they read Heinlein at age twelve. These were the people I found hard to deal with. No grasp of reality. Fanatics" (278).

Proxmire arranges funding for the time-travel project just so he can try to derail the greatest career twentieth-century science fiction has seen. He returns to the ship, finds Heinlein, and simply tells him that the hypodermic will cure his cough. Heinlein, being Heinlein, readily accepts the prospect of a time traveller from the future who wants to give him a shot—actually a spray hypo—takes the shot, and the future does change. The change, however, is not at all what Proxmire expected, and he returns to a future in which science fiction has become speculative fiction (the term championed by Heinlein), the literature of the possible; the manned space program has been taken away from NASA and given to the Navy; and space stations, Moon bases and a nearly completed Mars base exist. Moreover, in what is Niven's most pointed and predictably conservative touch, Proxmire returns to a world in which "Admiral Heinlein doesn't let the Soviets build spacecraft."

Twentieth-century SF abounds with time travel stories, some of the best known of which were written by Robert A. Heinlein. Many of these stories follow the convention of Ray Bradbury's "A Sound of Thunder," in which a time-travelling tourist on a carefully planned dinosaur hunt accidentally kills a butterfly and thus changes the future into a world where Germany rules the U. S., so Niven's premise that a small change in the past might lead to radical and sweeping changes in the future is something of a commonplace in modern SF. What is extraordinary in Niven's story is its faith that Robert Heinlein was such an exceptional individual that his life would have changed the future no matter what his occupation. And who knows, Niven may be right. The same memorial volume that includes Niven's "The Return of William Proxmire" also includes the citation read in 1988 when Heinlein was posthumously awarded the NASA Distinguished Public Service Medal:

> In recognition of his meritorious service to the Nation and mankind in advocating and promoting the exploration of space. Through dozens of superbly written novels and essays and his epoch-making movie *Destination Moon*, he helped inspire the Nation to take its first step into space and onto the Moon. Even after his death, his books live on as testimony to a man of purpose and vision, a man dedicated to encouraging others to dream, explore and achieve. (Kondo, 217–18)

What is certain is that Robert A. Heinlein did more than any other figure in the twentieth century to popularize science fiction, to move it from the pulps to major slick magazines and novel best-seller lists—in short to give SF the cultural prominence it now enjoys. In a field now swollen with success stories, major writers, and significant innovators, Heinlein still stands out along with Isaac Asimov and Arthur C. Clarke as first among giants, and much of the credit for creating the publishing environment in which great success was possible must go to Heinlein's and Asimov's early editor, John W. Campbell. James Gunn identifies Heinlein as the man who sold the genre of SF to the public, and historians of science fiction, if they agree on nothing else, seem to agree that Heinlein and editor John Campbell exerted the crucial influence that made it possible for SF to be what it is today. It was Heinlein's fiction that so effectively caught the public imagination from the late 1940s through the best-seller and college-campus-cult status of his 1961 novel, *Stranger in a Strange Land*, but it was

Campbell's *Astounding* in which Heinlein first began to publish and it was Campbell, building upon and refining precepts laid down by SF's first great editor—Hugo Gernsback—who laid the foundation for the popular reception of SF.

Together, Campbell and Heinlein created modern science fiction, although it has long since escaped their control. And together they were directly and indirectly responsible for launching in the 1950s America's sudden fascination with science fiction film: Heinlein's juvenile novel *Rocketship Galileo* was the rough basis for Irving Pichel's *Destination Moon* (1950), a film for which Heinlein also served as a technical advisor, and Campbell's "Who Goes There?" was made into the classic Howard Hawks/Christian Nyby film, *The Thing from Another World* (1951), remade in 1982 by John Carpenter as *The Thing*. While the relationship of SF literature to SF film is both complex and controversial, Heinlein and Campbell were instrumental in cementing in the public's mind the link between the two media—extending a linkage previously made in 1936 through the association of H. G. Wells with the Alexander Korda film *Things to Come*.[2] It is also the case that both men came under increasing criticism late in their careers and following their deaths for their often controversial views. However, before we can begin to understand the importance of Heinlein and Campbell to SF after 1900, we need to return briefly to the nineteenth century and to the early years of the twentieth to remind ourselves of the American roots of modern SF. While it is by no means the case that science fiction was appearing only in the United States during this time, it was the period when the shaping of the genre largely passed into American hands.[3] Nor is it the case that science fiction was appearing only in dime novels and boys' papers, but my discussion will focus primarily on this specialized line of development that exerted significant influence, for better or for worse, upon early genre SF.

Frank Reade Jr., Tom Swift, and the Invention of the Edisonade

Nineteenth-century American literature brimmed with stories that might be called science fiction or scientific romance. Bruce

Franklin claims in his important *Future Perfect: American Science Fiction of the Nineteenth Century* that "There was no major nineteenth-century American writer of fiction, and indeed few in the second rank, who did not write some science fiction or at least one utopian romance."[4] Certainly the history of American science fiction can proudly point to works by Hawthorne, Irving, Melville, and Poe and to best-selling blockbusters by Edward Bellamy and Mark Twain, but the most influential precursors of modern American SF were by writers long excluded from the American canon, writers who churned out dime novels and boys' papers at a prodigious pace. As Franklin has elsewhere noted, the dime novel was "the dominant literary form in America" between the Civil War and World War I, with hundreds of millions of copies helping to create a mass audience. And one distinct dime novel formula, the invention story, leads directly from Edward Ellis's *The Steam Man of the Prairies*, published in 1868, through the adventures of young inventors and scientists such as Frank Reade, Frank Reade Jr., Jack Wright, Great Marvel's inventors, Frank Edison, Electric Bob, and finally Tom Swift to the pulps, culminating in Hugo Gernsback's *Amazing Stories*—the birthplace of genre SF. To be sure, there were other SF formulas such as future war and lost-race–lost-world stories, there were tremendously influential individual writers such as Wells and Edgar Rice Burroughs, and there were other publishing outlets, most notably mass magazines such as *The Strand, Munsey's Magazine, Pearson's Magazine, McClure's Magazine, Argosy Magazine,* and *All-Story Magazine,* all of which published science fiction from the 1890s through the 1920s, but it was in the dime novel invention stories that American SF found its first great audience and its clearest line of development.[5]

This succession of dime novels and boys' papers largely mirrored Jules Verne's fascination with fabulous inventions and gadgets, although clear evidence exists that Verne was in turn influenced by dime novels. In focusing on the youthful genius who invented whatever was necessary to foil evil, slaughter Indians, win a bet or contest, and make a fortune, these stories codified what has become a mainstay of science fiction narratives: the edisonade. Given its name by John Clute, the edisonade has joined the robinsonade—the narrative of Crusoe-like solitary survival—as one of twentieth-century SF's most frequently invoked formulas.[6] In what is surely one of the most snippish entries in the *Encyclopedia of Science Fiction*, Clute defines the edisonade as "any story which features a young U. S. male inventor hero who uses his ingenuity to extricate himself from tight spots and who, by doing so, saves himself from defeat and corruption and his friends and nation from foreign oppressors."[7] There is in Clute's discussion of the edisonade a not-so-subtle indictment of a large strain of American SF, but there is also an important recognition of the fact that the boy inventors from American dime novels through Tom Swift and well into the early years of magazine SF invoked not only the image of Edison the inventor, but also that of Edison the self-promoting entrepeneur. This myth of the independent scientist-inventor who was also a successful businessman flew in the face of the realities of early twentieth-century corporate industrial reality, as Andrew Ross has recently observed, but it provided one of the strongest assumptions in the economic worldview advanced by early SF.[8] Even while edisonade stories were celebrating the individualist exploits of lone researchers, Edison himself was turning Menlo Park into an "invention factory" staffed by teams of workers, and large corporations such as Eastman Kodak and General Electric were industrializing research in their large laboratories.

But the myth behind the edisonade may be even more important for the writing of SF than for its stories, since early science fiction writers and editors, particularly Gernsback and Campbell, also appropriated that myth for the invention of science fiction, suggesting often quite bluntly that the writer of SF was engaged in a kind of quasi-scientific enterprise consisting of thought experiments and possibly leading to discoveries. The myth of Edison thus became science fiction's take on the Prometheus and Faust myths and served to valorize the SF writer in a way parallel to the Romantic myth of the hero-artist and its Modernist successor. Better than any other literary form, the edisonade also responded to America's need for a new mythology appropriate to a technological age. That science and technology could materially change the future was the extended message of the series of exhibitions and World's Fairs staged in Philadelphia in 1876, in Chicago in 1893, in Buffalo in 1901, and in St. Louis in 1904. In buildings devoted entirely to electricity, manufacturing, or transportation, these exhibitions dramatically announced to the American public that technology could change the future, that telephones, typewriters, electric power—that machines from dynamos to automatic dishwashers—would change not only industry but the home, marking a significant departure from the way things had been. At the World's Columbian Exposition in Chicago in 1893 electricity commanded center stage: the huge grounds were lit by outdoor electric lights, and in the Electricity Building inventions by Edison and Tesla suggested the power and the utility of electric energy. Built in great part from attractions and ideas taken from these international expositions, Coney Island presented the public its first mechanical wonderland, featuring outlandish emblems of the erector set world that was fast displacing the world of nature in the American psyche. And these dramatic concentrations of technology were accompanied by popular magazine articles in publications ranging from *Scientific American* (which devoted a feature each year to detailing the machinery behind new rides at Coney Island) to *Ladies Home Journal*.

In such a technologically infatuated environment, inventors and engineers became not only new symbols of progress and efficiency in the material world but also exemplars in the aesthetic world, particularly in American literature. Engineers and inventors began to figure more prominently in popular fiction, particularly in children's magazines such as *St. Nicholas*, but also in general magazines such as *Literary Digest, Collier's*, and the *Saturday Evening Post*. Boys could hope to grow up to be engineers, but one could imagine becoming an inventor at any age, since, as Thomas Edison frequently pointed out, specialized education was not a prerequisite for becoming an inventor. Accordingly, the idea of the boy inventor not only responded to the spirit of the times but also had a special populist appeal: any boy could be one. And here the myth behind the edisonade comes full circle for SF, where one of the most powerful myths of the science fiction community is that any fan can become an SF writer. For this reason, the edisonade seems doubly significant for the understanding of the twentieth-century development of American SF.

By the turn of the century, the edisonade was already a well-established formula. Twain's *A Connecticut Yankee in King Arthur's Court* presents in Hank Morgan a clearly Edison-like character, and the book's apocalyptic ending pointedly reminds us of Edison's vague, but often repeated, claims that he could, whenever necessary, produce electrical superweapons.[9] Ironically enough, one of the most literal of the early edisonades was not American, but French, as Auguste de Villiers de l'Isle-Adam made the protagonist of his 1886 novel *L'Eve future* (*Tomorrow's Eve*) not an Edison-like inventor but Thomas Alva Edison himself.[10] Garrett Serviss also drafted "The Wizard of Menlo Park" for duty in his *Edison's Conquest of Mars* (1898), a kind of crude sequel to and gung-ho refutation of Wells's *War of the Worlds*, in which Edison's superweapons make short work of the Martians. Other late-nineteenth and early-twentieth-century novelists utilized thinly disguised Edison-surrogates in a range of future war books.

As the American frontier closed, dime novels (somewhat misleadingly named, since they usually ran only 32 pages and cost five or six cents) celebrated the bloody adventures of Western heroes but also played an interesting role in the transition in public consciousness between the Romantic worldview in which pioneers and cowboys were America's mythic heroes and the modern, machine-dominated worldview in which engineers and inventors took their part in the new mythology of what Cecelia Tichi has dubbed the "gear-and-girder" world.[11] These two worldviews briefly intersected in a string of dime novels, starting in 1868 with Edward Sylvester Ellis's *The Steam Man of the Prairies*, published as *American Novel #45* in the Beadle dime novel series. Possibly based in part on an earlier claimed invention of an ambulatory two-cylinder rotary steam engine called the Newark Steam Man, Ellis's steam man was a robot-like humanoid-shaped steam engine that could run 60 miles an hour while pulling a cart behind it in which its inventor, Johnny Brainerd, could ride.[12] The young inventor and his friends take their steam man from St. Louis to the western frontier, where it proves useful for chasing buffalo and terrorizing Indians, all in the interest of gold mining. In 1876, the year of both the great Philadelphia Centennial Exposition and Custer's "Last Stand," Ellis's novel was successfully reprinted under the new title of *The Huge Hunter; Or The Steam Man of the Prairies*, winning enough attention that rival publisher Frank Tousey decided to try a knock-off version.[13] Tousey commissioned Harry Enton, who closely copied Ellis's novel, renaming the young inventor Frank Reade and relocating him to New York but giving him a nearly identical steam man and titling Reade's adventures *The Steam Man of the Plains*. First published in the Tousey-owned boys' paper *The Boys of New York*, Enton's story was republished several times (as had been Ellis's *Steam Man of the Prairies* before), and its success led Tousey to commission three sequels—*Frank Reade and His Steam Horse* (1876), *Frank Reade and His Steam Team* (1880), and *Frank Reade and His Steam Tally-Ho* (1881). These novels featured a progression of armaments in steam-drawn vehicles and consequent damage to Indians, but *Frank Reade and His Steam Tally-Ho* also took the edisonade turn of using the invention to secure entrepeneurial business success.

When Enton balked at publishing further Frank Reade novels under the Tousey house pseudonym of "Noname," the Frank Reade series was passed along to the legendary Luis Senarens, "the American Jules Verne," who wrote between 1,500 and 2,000 dime novel stories during his prolific career. Senarens, in turn, passed along the inventive genius from Frank Reade to his son, Frank Reade Jr., and began a new string of 179 adventures in 1882 with *Frank Reade, Jr., and His Steam Wonder*. Long on prophecy, longer still on pure adventure, and distinctly short on scientific explanation, Senarens's fiction clearly anticipates genre SF, and his work was undoubtedly known to many of SF's first pulp readers. While the typical Senarens work did not contain enough pure scientific exposition to meet Gernsback's desiderata for SF, it is interesting to note that Gernsback did publish in *Amazing* two features about Senarens, championing him as "the American Jules Verne."

Some of the inventions and ideas Senarens described in this series were clearly lifted from the writing of Jules Verne, but, as Moskowitz has pointed out, Verne also borrowed from Senarens and even sent Senarens a letter of praise.[14] Following the success of the Frank Reade Jr. series, Senarens launched a second series of young inventor stories featuring the exploits of Jack Wright in novels such as *Jack Wright and His Electric Flyer; or, Racing in the Clouds for a Boy's Life*. Tousey later published a Jack Wright invention story in every other issue of the *Boys Star Library*. At the same time, competing publishing house Street & Smith began publishing its version of the boy inventor story, built around a protagonist named Tom Edison Jr. and written by a suggestively named "Philip Reade." Another Street & Smith series featuring Electric Bob soon joined the edisonade parade.

Frank Tousey, publisher of the Frank Reade Jr. series, countered with a weekly magazine entirely devoted to invention stories, *Frank Reade Library*—identified by Sam Moskowitz as technically "the first regular periodical completely devoted to science fiction" (120). Before ceasing publication in 1898, *Frank Reade Library* filled its 191 issues both with new Frank Reade Jr. stories and with republications of all of the Frank Reade stories originally published before 1892. Edisonades or invention stories usually also featured other aspects that are firmly part of SF tradition. Once the electric airships and submarines in these stories had been invented, they needed someplace exciting to go, so geographical adventure also became part of the formula. And often the exotic locales led to the discovery of lost races, so dime novels exploited a number of patterns that would be frequently repeated in the pulps and in early genre SF. To name just one obvious inheritor of the edisonade tradition, A. E. van Vogt employed many of its features and more than a little of its feel in his rambunctious fiction.

Dime novels and boys' papers remained popular until the last few years of the nineteenth century, but they became less profitable as efforts to censor them increased. Noted SF bibliographer Everett F. Bleiler has pointed out that dime novels were curiously insulated from the influence of other forms of turn of the century science fiction, apart from the obvious influence of Jules Verne's gadget stories and H. Rider Haggard's lost-race stories. And yet, he also concludes that their influence on later SF has been undervalued (ESF, 336). While these stories have proved deservedly ephemeral, they firmly established the edisonade as one of science fiction's earliest formulas, and, along with their longer-lived successors, the Stratemeyer Syndicate's Great Marvel and Tom Swift novels, did much to prepare the audience that Gernsback would target with *Amazing Stories* in 1926.

As the dime novel publishing phenomenon (one informed estimate is that *billions* of dime novels were printed, since Horatio Alger stories alone accounted for over 250 million copies) waned in the first years of the twentieth century, supplanted by pulp magazines targeting a wider adult audience, the edisonade took one more important turn—into boys' novels published by Edward Stratemeyer. In 1906, having already established several successful boys' series such as The Rover Boys and having edited

Good News, a weekly boys' magazine published by Street & Smith, Stratemeyer founded his own publishing syndicate and decided to launch three new lines of books built around modes of transportation. Railroad Ralph books would focus on train adventures, the Motor Boys books would feature automobiles, and the Great Marvel series would be built around airship stories. The Great Marvel series advance the edisonade beyond the relatively familiar adventures and inventions in the Frank Reade Jr. stories, and also have more in common with later science fiction than do the Tom Swift novels of 1910–1941. As Francis J. Molson has recently reminded us, "Great Marvel was the first American series devoted exclusively to science adventure. It shares with the Tom Swift books the honor of being the longest running and sustained of early science fiction series."[15] And it was the Great Marvel series that moved the invention story–edisonade into hard covers.

Of course, Great Marvel was not nearly as successful as was the Tom Swift series, and it is those books we most remember as the apotheosis of the edisonade. An ad reprinted in the back of an early Tom Swift book makes clear its underlying market assumption: "Every boy possesses some form of inventive genius. Tom Swift is a bright ingenious boy and his inventions and adventures make the most interesting kind of reading." Stratemeyer tapped Howard R. Garis to write the Tom Swift series, this time under the house name of Victor Appleton. Possibly hedging his bets against the possibility that Great Marvel would prove too fantastic to secure a lasting audience, Stratemeyer designed the Tom Swift series much more conservatively, featuring more "reasonable" inventions and avoiding the sensational antagonists of the dime novels. In 1910 *Tom Swift and His Motor-Cycle* was the first of the five Tom Swift books published that year, the other four featuring respectively Tom's motor boat, his airship, his submarine, and his elecric runabout. *Tom Swift and His Motor-Cycle* introduced Tom, his inventor father, and Eradicate Simpson, their black servant. A motorcycle, even when rebuilt and improved by young Tom, is a fairly tame invention, and the plot of this novel centers on Tom's using the motorcycle for getting one of his father's inventions to the patent office. Indeed, E. F. Bleiler claims that the early Tom Swift novels are "really economic parables" more than invention stories (Bleiler,

1989: 112). The strong economic subtext in the series is not surprising, considering that Stratemeyer was not only a close friend of Horatio Alger Jr.'s but also had authored an Alger-like "success" series of "Bound to Win" stories and had even ghosted 11 unfinished Alger manuscripts after Alger's death. With this economic turn, the edisonade codifies another consistent feature of early genre SF: a preference for the small businessman-entrepeneur over corporate interests, a focus that would feature prominently in many of Robert Heinlein's stories and novels.

The series was a great success, with the exploits of Tom Swift running through 40 titles between 1910 and 1941. By 1931, over six and a half million copies of Tom Swift novels had been sold, and Stratemeyer's daughter reports that in all its editions the first Tom Swift series sold 20 million copies.[16] While the general tone of these books remains well known, having been extended into the space age by the Tom Swift Jr. series, it is important to mark the role Tom Swift played in laying a foundation for the success of American SF. The series firmly established the edisonade as a basic cultural myth and intrigued new generations of boy readers with a combination of science and engineering information and speculation that would be at the core of genre SF.

Only two more important manifestations of the edisonade need mentioning, but these two novels, Hugo Gernsback's *Ralph 124 C41 +: A Romance of the Year 2660* (1925) and E. E. "Doc" Smith's *The Skylark of Space* (serialized in 1928, published as a novel in 1946) carried the tradition of the edisonade into space opera and were hugely influential in shaping twentieth-century SF. Gernsback's story, published in 12 installments in his own primarily nonfiction magazine, *Modern Electrics*, retained the "can-do" optimism and technophilia of the boys' invention story but made its protagonist, Ralph 124C41+, not only a man, but a near superman, one of the 10 best brains on Earth. Moreover, Ralph is nearly matched by strong villains, first by the rival human Fernand 600 10, who abducts Ralph's girlfriend, Alice, and takes her into space, and then by the giant Martian Llysanorh', who takes Alice from Fernand, and kills her just as Ralph reaches the Martian's spaceship. Going far beyond anything previously seen in an edisonade, Ralph then uses his genius to preserve Alice's body until they can return to Earth, where he revives her in his laboratory. What makes Ralph's story so remarkable, however, is not any single marvelous invention but a veritable catalogue of future technology. Eric Rabkin, who anthologized a representative excerpt from *Ralph 124C 41+* in his very useful *Science Fiction: A Historical Anthology*, comments on how frequently Gernsback's implicit predictions hit the mark, particularly with his diagram for an "Actinoscope," a device very much like radar.[17]

The edisonade reached its apotheosis and shaded into space opera in E. E. "Doc" Smith's *The Skylark of Space*, first published in *Amazing Stories* in 1928, where it was heralded by the editor as "the greatest interplanetarian and space flying story that has appeared this year."[18] Its title reminiscent of the invention- and locale-specifying dime novel title such as *The Steam Man of the Prairies* and of Great Marvel titles such as *The Wonderful Cruise of the Electric Monarch*, Smith's novel featured the interstellar travel of a spaceship, the *Skylark*, powered by a discovery made by the prototypical edisonade hero Richard Seaton. Reflecting one "advance" in the edisonade formula, Seaton is not an independent researcher but works in Washington in a government research laboratory devoted to rare metals. Reflecting another "advance," superscientist Seaton has an equally talented superscientist antagonist, the evil but strangely honorable Marc C. ("Blackie") Duquesne. After Seaton accidentally discovers a solution containing a mysterious element X that releases the atomic power of copper, he leaves the Rare Metals Laboratory, where only his colleague Duquesne believed in the potential of his discovery, and develops a spaceship powered by his new propulsion system in a private company funded and organized by his friend Martin Crane—a "multimillionaire explorer-archaeologist-sportsman" who also just happens to be a good engineer and a "rocket-instrument man second to none in the world." Employed by the unprincipled World Steel Corporation, Blackie Duquesne steals some of the X solution, builds his own spaceship, kidnaps Seaton's fiancée and another young woman in a plan to get more information from Seaton, and accidentally accelerates so far into space that he cannot return to earth. Seaton and Crane pursue Duquesne in the Skylark, rescue him and the two women, and enter into a temporary truce with the evil scientist that enables their combined brainpower to prevail in a series of conflicts on alien worlds.

Smith's novel "brought the edisonade to its first full maturity," claims John Clute in *The Encyclopedia of Science Fiction*, adding that

49

this work created "a proper galactic forum for the exploits of the inventor–scientist–action-hero who keeps the world (or the Universe) safe for US values despite the efforts of a foreign-hued villain" (1123). The prevailing view in most SF histories is that Smith's work was so popular and exciting because it had such a grand scale, as reflected in Sam Moskowitz's reference (1963) to its "marvel of distances and places which strained comprehension," but Joe Sanders argues that Smith's appeal has more to do with presenting a sense of scientific thinking taking place.[19] Certainly, Smith's novel features an endless round of problem solving, and Seaton, Crane, and Duquesne reach their solutions through a rhetoric that foregrounds logic and scientific method in response to "mind-staggering situations." And it should also be pointed out that Smith's story often seems as interested in monetary as in scientific matters. Reflecting the economic concerns of the dime novel but displacing the focus on money with a focus on corporate organization and competition, *The Skylark of Space* goes to some length both to explain the economic value of Seaton's solution ("To break it down to where you can understand it, it means a billion kilowatts per plant at a total amortized cost of approximately one one-hundreth of a mil per KW hour") and to curb Seaton's enthusiasm for finding a small lab with Crane's specifications for organizing their new company as "a stock company, capitalized at one million dollars, with ten thousand shares of stock." Smith's novel may have successfully transported the edisonade into deep space, but it also extended into space the corporate ethic that underlies and/or has given rise to so much American SF. While Smith is better known to contemporary readers for his Gray Lensman series, which may be the apotheothis of space opera, *The Skylark of Space* remains a significant step in the development of the edisonade, as it launched its dime novel concerns into genre SF, where those concerns more than occasionally continued to surface through SF's "golden age" and into the 1950s.

Hugo Gernsback "Invents" Genre SF

That *The Skylark of Space* first appeared in *Amazing Stories* was most appropriate, since this landmark story was published in the first true SF magazine—the birthplace of genre SF, presided over by Hugo Gernsback, SF's first great editor and critic. *Amazing* appeared in the context of several other pulp magazines devoted to a single kind of fiction. Following the general lead of Frank Munsey, who invented the pulp magazine all-fiction format in *Argosy* (1896) and who had tried specializing in one kind of story in 1906 with *Railroad Man's Magazine,* Street & Smith publishers brought out *Detective Story Monthly* in 1915, *Western Story* in 1919, *Love Stories* in 1921, and *Weird Tales* in 1923. Accordingly, genre SF arose in the much larger pulp market that had supplanted dime novels and boys' papers and that would continue to dominate popular publishing into the 1950s. Gernsback may have "invented" genre SF, but the pulp tradition was well established before he entered it. Gernsback, born in Luxembourg in 1885, had emigrated to America in 1903 and had started several magazines—including *Modern Electrics,* in which he published *Ralph 124C 41+,* and *Science and Invention* (which featured a special "Scientific Fiction" issue in August 1923)—before publishing *Amazing Stories* in April 1926. In *Amazing* and its successors such as *Wonder Stories* Gernsback republished fiction by Wells and Verne, new science fiction (or "scientifiction") that fit his prescriptions for a new genre, science articles and quizzes, and his own pronouncements about what SF should be and do. "By 'scientifiction,'" Gernsback wrote in his first editorial, "I mean the Jules Verne, H. G. Wells, and Edgar Allan Poe type of story—a charming romance intermingled with scientific fact and prophetic vision." That "intermingling," he suggested for the "ideal proportion of a scientifiction story should be 75 percent literature interwoven with 25 percent science." Later abandoning the term "scientifiction," Gernsback "invented" the term "science fiction" in an editorial in the June 1929 *Science Wonder Stories;* the term had been used before, but never with the referential specificity supplied by Gernsback. Infatuated with the idea of science and the potentially shaping value of a literature that contained significant amounts of scientific exposition (he even went so far as to suggest that science fiction writers should be able to take out provisional patents on the devices they predicted in their stories), Gernsback saw *Amazing* as a kind of pseudoscientific journal in which the play of new scientific ideas could point toward the improvement of the world, as he most explicitly claimed in a June 1927 editorial:

Not only is science fiction an idea of tremendous import, but it is to be an important factor in making the world a better place to live in, through educating the public to the possibilities of science and the influence of science on life which, even today, are not appreciated by the man on the street. . . . If every man, woman, boy and girl, could be induced to read science fiction right along, there would certainly be a great resulting benefit to the community, in that the educational standards of its people would be raised tremendously. Science fiction would make people happier, give them a broader understanding of the world, make them more tolerant.

In pronouncements such as this, Gernsback codified the didactic element of science fiction already implicit in the works of H. G. Wells and other early writers. As baldly as Gernsback stated his beliefs and as unsophisticated as they are about the affective power of any literature, I should admit that—given a very broad view of "science"—I generally agree with the *sentiment* behind them, as indeed I suspect do most contemporary writers and readers of SF; what Gernsback captured, no matter how crudely, was the sense that this genre was different and that it could make a difference.

While most histories of twentieth-century SF disparage Gernsback's perceived naïveté more than they credit his vision, Andrew Ross has recently reminded us that a cultural consideration of Gernsback produces a perspective very different from a literary one. In the first place, notes Ross, Gernsback, unlike the publishers of other pulp genres, actually lived the values of his magazine and reflected the myth of the edisonade in its creation as well as in its content. Specifying that the roots of the Gernsbackian story lay "in the 'invention hero' dime novels like the *Frank Reade Weekly Magazine*, the ham-radio culture, and the popular boy-inventor culture of the turn of the century," Ross concludes:

... Gernsback's own life story was exemplary of the starring role cast for the freelance inventor in the popular formulae he established as the generic "hard science" core of SF. In an age of collective corporate management, Gernsback's hands-on ownership and editorial role in the "invention" and early production of SF was a throwback to the myths of the individualist inventor-entrepeneur a la Edison of an earlier era.[20]

In the second place, Ross points out that Gernsback's "naive" faith in the power of science was shared by a wide range of professionals of his time, including—to name just a few—Herbert Hoover, Theodore Roosevelt, Thorstein Veblen, and Lewis Mumford, as well as by the European left. "To see this widely shared social fantasy as a naive example of blind faith in technological progress is not good enough," claims Ross, who terms this view "part of our own naive response to history," and he argues instead that "we are obliged to substitute for the given wisdom about SF's 'uncritical technophilia' a more historically nuanced account of its place in a context better described as *critical technocracy*" (105). Finally, Ross argues that even the flat, didactic, unsophisticated-seeming prose that marked Gernsback's approach to SF has an ideological, if not a literary, rationale:

> At the core of the Gernsback formula . . . was a populist principle that science could be explained and understood by everyone, and that its name would not be associated with exclusive rhetorical idioms or with obfuscatory accounts of the object world by overcredited experts. For Gernsback, scientific language was the universal language of progress that ought to be accessible even to those without a college degree. Indeed, the straightforward prose of early SF clearly contrasts with the rich American argot of local dialects found in the Western and hard-boiled genres. (110–11)

Whether or not Ross's revisionist approach to Gernsback proves persuasive within the SF community, it is an important reminder that the "history" of SF has been a largely anecdotal construct, frequently shaped to particular ends and infrequently contextualized in the larger culture.

Whatever the prevailing literary opinion of Gernsback, it seems clear that he advanced prescriptive guidelines for the writing of science fiction, helped organize clubs of fans to discuss its reception, helped foster the popular tradition of science fiction criticism in which writers and readers critiqued the genre, and, in short, marked the formal emergence of the genre. In recognizing that there existed a group of fans "pretty well oriented to this sort of literature" and in giving them a place to react and interrelate in the "Discussions" section of *Amazing* (and later in helping to organize the Science Fiction League), Gernsback proved instrumental in the development of SF "fandom," surely one of the phenomena that most distinguish SF from other literatures. Perhaps almost as important, Gernsback selected the artist Frank R. Paul to do the covers and interior illustrations for *Amazing*, and Paul's streamlined vehicles and cities and bright red and yellow colors were hugely influential in shaping popular notions of what the future would look like. Over the years and for a series of magazines Paul painted over 175 SF covers, codifying a tradition of the importance and influence of art unmatched in any other literature.

As Gary Westfahl, Gernsback's most effective champion, has argued in a series of persuasive articles, Gernsback "made it possible to believe in SF."[21] Westfahl's conclusion that Gernsback should receive credit for giving SF "characteristic content, a characteristic form, and characteristic purposes," as well as for being "the first true critic who offered a complete theory of the genre's nature, purposes, and origins" and thus "standing up and declaring that SF existed as a genre," seems compelling to me. It flies in the face, however, of the disparaging—and sometimes ridiculing—judgments of many SF writers who would more likely agree with the view of Malcolm J. Edwards in *The Encyclopedia of Science Fiction* that while Gernsback "gave the genre a local habitation and a name," he also "bestowed upon his creation provincial dogmatism and an illiteracy that bedevilled US SF for years" (491). Anyone strongly interested in the history of SF would be well-served by closer attention to both sides of this argument—not so much for what it teaches about Gernsback as for what it reveals about the competing assumptions and agendas in the larger discussion of the history and nature of science fiction. A useful middle ground is supplied by James Gunn, who makes few claims for the literary merit of the fiction Gernsback promoted but who stresses the importance of Gernsback's efforts to create an enabling phenomenology for SF:

> Gernsback provided a focus for enthusiasm, for publication, for development. He may not have shaped modern science fiction . . . but he provided a place for science fiction to be shaped.
>
> Looking back on the place, it may have been a ghetto, but it was a golden ghetto, a place of brotherhood and opportunity and wonder. Before Gernsback there were science fiction stories. After Gernsback, there was a science fiction genre.[22]

John W. Campbell and the "Astounding" Era

Almost a corollary to the disparaging of Gernsback by SF writers (some of whom had trouble getting him to pay for their stories and who referred to him as "Hugo the Rat") is the lionizing of John W. Campbell, editor of *Astounding Stories* (renamed *Astounding Science-Fiction* in 1938 and *Analog* in 1960) from 1937 to his death in 1971. Under Campbell's editorship the careers of such well-known SF writers as Isaac Asimov, Lester Del Rey, Robert A. Heinlein, Theodore Sturgeon, A. E. van Vogt, L. Sprague de Camp, L. Ron Hubbard, Clifford D. Simak, Jack Williamson, Henry Kuttner, and C. L. Moore were started, solidified, or given resurrecting boosts as Campbell insisted on higher writing standards for the genre and injected idea after idea for which his writers became famous. Isaac Asimov, for instance, credited Campbell both for the idea that produced his classic "Nightfall" and for working out the famous "Three Laws of Robotics." Suggesting Campbell's method, Theodore Sturgeon recounted that the editor would challenge his writers with assignments such as: "Write me a story about a man who will die in twenty-four hours unless he can answer this question: 'How do you know you're sane?'" or "Write me a story about a creature that thinks as well as a man but not like a man."[23]

Every history of SF tells the Campbell story, none more enthusiastically and more forgivingly of Campbell's later excesses than James Gunn's *Alternate Worlds*, with its chapter "The Astounding Editor: 1938–1950," where Gunn treats not only Campbell, but also the four authors most associated with his success: Isaac Asimov, Robert Heinlein, Theodore Sturgeon, and A. E. van Vogt. Campbell's tenure as SF's most influential editor has been most thoroughly studied by Albert I. Berger in *The Magic That Works: John W. Campbell and the American Response to Technology.*[24] However, perhaps the most useful and balanced overview of Campbell's role is to be found in the chapter on "The Victory of American SF" in Edward James's *Science Fiction in the 20th Century*, where James considers not only the extent of Campbell's influence but also whether or not that influence stemmed primarily from Campbell's skill as an editor or from external considerations such as the fact that he could offer writers better pay than could other magazines.[25] James also considers some of the ways in which Campbell may have been a negative influence on SF, particularly near the end of his career when his views of the genre became so rigid as to exclude exciting new writers, his views of science shaded into a troubling fascination with pseudoscience such as L. Ron Hubbard's Dianetics, and his racial views approached bigotry.

Campbell's strengths and weaknesses are the subject of a critical debate far too broad for me to do more than mention. Suffice it to say that from 1937 to 1949, with the appearance of The *Magazine of Fantasy and Science Fiction*, edited by Anthony Boucher and J. Francis McComas, and to 1950 with the appearance of *Galaxy Science Fiction*, edited by H. L. Gold, American science fiction was dominated by Campbell's magazine and his beliefs about the genre. Those beliefs shared the core assumptions of Gernsback but expanded the notion of science to include "soft sciences" such as sociology and anthropology as well as shifting the prevailing SF paradigm of science from a Darwinian focus on biology to a focus on physics. Campbell took Gernsback's faith in reason over emotion—a faith that valorized a monolithic view of science—and sharpened it to stress both the scientific method and the pure power of thinking. "The business of science fiction is to predict the probable trends of the future," declared Campbell, sounding not very different from Gernsback, who proudly announced as a motto for *Amazing*: "Extravagant Fiction Today— Cold Fact Tomorrow." Like Gernsback, Campbell saw science fiction as having a vital connection to science. When in 1960 Campbell finally realized his long-held goal of excising "astounding" from the title of his magazine, renaming it *Analog*, his reasoning clearly revealed his belief that science fiction was, in fact, a kind of science. After explaining that "an analog is a system which behaves in a manner similar to some other and less manipulable system so that it is easier and more convenient to study," Campbell declared: "Science fiction is, very strictly and literally, analogous to science facts. It is a convenient analog system for thinking about new scientific, social, and economic ideas—and for re-examining old ideas."[26] While stressing the importance of the science in SF, however, Campbell also insisted that its "human story" must be most important, explaining in a 1947 "symposium" organized by Lloyd Arthur Eshbach:

> In older science fiction, the Machine and the Great Idea predominated. Modern readers—and hence editors!—don't want that; they

want stories of people living in a world where a Great Idea, or a series of them, and a Machine, or machines, form the background. But it is the man, not the idea or machine that is the essence.[27]

He more specifically explained this "new" narrative demand:

> In older science fiction—H. G. Wells and nearly all stories written before 1935—the author took time to bring the reader up to date as to what had happened before his story opened. The best modern writers of science fiction have worked out some truly remarkable techniques for presenting a great deal of background and associated material without intruding into the flow of the story. (cited in Gunn, 170)

Under Campbell's guidance, science fiction stories in *Astounding* were to devote much more attention to the sociology and psychology of the future (or past) than to its technological or scientific newness. "An idea is important only in how it reacts on people, and in how people react to it," he cautioned would-be writers. "Whether the idea is social, political, or mechanical, we want people involved in and by it" (94). After stressing the importance of "patient and detailed analysis" and "style" ("a thing that is six stages more tenuous and about one tenth as definable as a ghost, and yet makes the difference between a 'nice idea, too bad he can't write' story and a bell-ringing, smash-hit yarn"), Campbell concluded: *Astounding*'s policy is free and easy—anything in science-fiction that is a good yarn is fine by us" (100). Summing up his view of the way Campbell freed SF from its most limiting pulp traditions, Isaac Asimov has written:

> What, specifically, did Campbell do? First and foremost, he de-emphasized the nonhuman and nonsocial in science fiction. Science fiction became more than a personal battle between an all-good hero and an all-bad villain. The mad scientists, the irascible old scientist, the beautiful daughter of the scientist, the cardboard menace from alien worlds, the robot who is a Frankenstein monster—all were discarded. In their place, Campbell wanted businessmen, space-ship crewmen, young engineers, housewives, robots that were logical machines.[28]

Asimov divides science fiction into three broad categories: adventure SF, gadget SF, and social SF. The subdivision of science fiction he finds "sociologically significant" (and the kind he

writes) is, of course, "social science fiction," "that branch of literature which is concerned with the impact of scientific advance
upon human beings," and says that if Gernsback is the "father of
science fiction," then surely Campbell deserves credit as "the
father of social science fiction."

Robert A. Heinlein Discovers the Future

Campbell's "creation" of modern science fiction was accomplished through his partnership with an exceptional stable of
"modern" SF writers, the most popular and influential of whom
was Robert Anson Heinlein. Tuberculosis had ended Heinlein's
naval career in 1934; he had first tried his hand at writing science
fiction in response to a contest ad in *Thrilling Wonder Stories* in
1939 (after writing the story—"Life-Line"—he decided to send it
to Campbell), and by 1941 he was the indisputable "Dean of
American SF writers," commanding the top per-word rates (one-
and-a-half cents per word) from the leading SF magazine (in
which his stories also appeared under the names of "Anson
MacDonald" and "Caleb Saunders," "Lyle Monroe" being the
pseudonym reserved for lesser pieces published in other magazines). Although Heinlein came to the writing of SF after a lifetime of reading it, starting with Frank Reade dime novels, Tom
Swift stories, and the science fiction published in Gernsback's
Electrical Experimenter, he was a relative rarity in that he began
writing as a mature and experienced man of 32, with a good
education and a profession other than writing in his background. Even though from 1939 through 1942 his writing
appeared exclusively in the pulps, Heinlein made it clear from
the outset that his goal was to free himself from this market.
And, following his civilian war service, he did just that, starting
in 1947 with several sales to the *Saturday Evening Post* and,
between 1947 and 1959, with a very popular series of 12 novels
aimed at juvenile boys and published by Scribner's. At the same
time as he was writing his juveniles he continued to write serialized fiction for *Astounding*, *Galaxy*, and the *Magazine of Fantasy
and Science Fiction*, including *The Puppet Masters*, which was published as a novel by Doubleday in 1951. When Scribner's turned

down his 13th novel in the juvenile series, *Starship Troopers*, he moved to Putnam's and there published a series of very successful and influential novels, including *Stranger in a Strange Land* (1961), *The Moon Is a Harsh Mistress* (1966), and *I Will Fear No Evil* (1970). He continued to publish novels, several of which became best-sellers even though they were disappointments to many Heinlein fans and critics, until his death in 1988. In championing an aggressive space program in his fiction, essays, and speeches, Heinlein, suggests his most interesting critic, Bruce Franklin, "was perhaps more than any other single person, responsible for the popularization in America of the concepts of space travel and for the commitment to undertake it."[29] Focusing only on his impact on SF, James Gunn calls Heinlein "the indispensable science fiction writer of his time."

What seemed to make Heinlein's stories so immediately popular with the readers of *Astounding* was his ability to *assume* the future in his stories, to imply it with casual references to gadgets and discoveries without bothering to offer explanations for each novum. In this sense, he almost perfectly fulfilled Campbell's desire for stories "that would be written for a magazine of the twenty-fifth century," offering a future that felt "lived-in." For example, it was Heinlein's genius to at once make the future almost boring in terms of its "newness," but exciting in terms of its challenges and potential, a technique shown in his 1947 story "Space Jockey." Furthermore, Heinlein—possibly reflecting his great admiration for the attempt of H. G. Wells to provide an "outline" of past history, and following but scaling down the vision of Olaf Stapledon—wrote his stories within a larger framework of a general outline of the history of the future in which they appeared, giving each story a location within larger historical periods and developments and a relation to other stories set in this future. Campbell published the chart showing this "outlined and graphed history of the future," plotting characters, dates, or major discoveries, in the May 1941 *Astounding*. This idea of "future history," also developed in the "Foundation" stories of Isaac Asimov, was to become a staple of modern SF, creating an important part of the enabling megatext for readers and other writers alike.

For the first three years of his writing career, when his best stories appeared almost exclusively in *Astounding*, Heinlein and

Campbell formed a close friendship, exchanging correspondence about the nature of Heinlein's stories and of SF writing in general, as well as about numerous other mutual interests. It is tempting to conclude that the veteran writer and successful editor Campbell served as an important mentor for the novice writer (and Heinlein's widow acknowledges that "Robert learned much about the art of writing from John"), but it seems more likely that Campbell built many of his new writing standards around the work he received from Heinlein—a slightly heretical proposition considered by Ed James in *Science Fiction in the 20th Century* and by the Panshins in *The World Beyond the Hill*. Heinlein later credited Campbell with "markedly" influencing only one of his stories, "Sixth Column," which was a reworking of an idea Campbell persuaded him to try to develop. Always a bit combative, the relationship between Campbell and Heinlein cooled during World War II, and Heinlein's remarks about his former editor grew increasingly resentful after that. In one sense, Heinlein simply outgrew Campbell, since after the war he became the first SF writer to place his stories in nongenre, upscale magazines ("the slicks") such as *The Saturday Evening Post*, the first to publish a highly successful series of juvenile novels with a major publishing house (Scribner's), and the first SF writer to see a novel on the *New York Times* best-seller list (*Stranger in a Strange Land*, in 1962).

Whether or not Heinlein significantly influenced Campbell's view of SF, his example and his pronouncements about the genre had a huge impact on fellow and succeeding writers and on generation after generation of readers. Just as surely as he charted the future, Heinlein mapped the territory of SF in terms that continue to be repeated today. In a 1947 essay, "On the Writing of Speculative Fiction," Heinlein divided the field into gadget and human-interest stories (his allegiance obviously to the latter) and decreed that the human-interest story could be developed through three main plots: boy-meets-girl, the Little Tailor ("about the little guy who becomes a big shot, or vice versa"), and the man-who-learned-better ("the story of a man who has one opinion, point of view, or evaluation at the beginning of the story, then acquires a new opinion or evaluation as a result of having his nose rubbed in some harsh facts").[30] Even more influential was Heinlein's specification for the "Simon-pure science fiction story":

1. The conditions must be, in some respect, different from here-and-now, although the difference may lie only in an invention made in the course of the story.
2. The new conditions must be an essential part of the story.
3. The problem itself—the "plot"—must be a *human* problem.
4. The human problem must be one which is created by, or indispensably affected by, the new conditions.
5. And lastly, no established fact shall be violated, and, furthermore, when the story requires that a theory contrary to present accepted theory be used, the new theory should be rendered reasonably plausible and it must include and explain established facts as satisfactorily as the one the author saw fit to junk. It may be far-fetched, it may seem fantastic, but it must *not* be at variance with observed facts, i. e., if you are going to assume that the human race descended from Martians, then you've got to explain our apparent close relationship to terrestrial anthropoid apes as well. (Eshbach, ed., 17)

To this list, Heinlein added the qualifier that he has violated all of his own rules, invoking Kipling's maxim that "There are nine-and-sixty ways / Of constructing tribal lays / And every single one of them is right." Nevertheless, even today, if you can find a discussion of the nature of SF that does not significantly correspond to Heinlein's five precepts, odds are it will be at pain to refute one or more of them—such is the lasting synthesizing power of his view.

Perhaps even more lasting has been Heinlein's sense of the mission of science fiction, best articulated in his "The Discovery of the Future," delivered as the Guest of Honor Speech at the Third World Science Fiction Convention, in Denver in 1941. This was the address in which Heinlein claimed that "science fiction, even the corniest of it, even the most outlandish of it, no matter how badly it's written, has a distinct therapeutic value because *all* of it has as its primary postulate that the world *does* change."[31] Heinlein's emphasis in that speech, given at a time when world war seemed imminent to him, was on the prophylactic value of SF, which, he believed, so prepared its readers for dramatic change in world situations that it gives them an edge for surviving. "WE stand a chance," ominously intoned Heinlein, "for I am very much afraid that a great many people of the type who laugh at us for dealing with this stuff, will not be able to hang on" (Kondo 158).

Heinlein flattered his audience at the 1941 World Science Convention by assuring them that "statistically" science fiction fans "are extremely precocious—quite brilliant," confidently adding "I've had enough data on it to know" (Kondo, 159). What set them apart, he explained, was their commitment to *scientific method*, which he quickly distinguished from the practices followed in the laboratory:

> Since I have to define it in terms of words, I can't be as clear as I might be if I were able to make an extensional definition. But I mean a comparatively simple thing by the scientific method: the ability to look at what goes on around you. Listen to what you hear, observe, note facts, delay your judgment, and make your own predictions. That's all there is, really, to the scientific method: to be able to distinguish facts from non-facts. (159–60)

A fact, continued Heinlein is "anything that has happened before this moment," while "anything after this moment is a nonfact." Stressing the need to maintain distinctions between fact and nonfact, as well as between fact and fiction, Heinlein promised his audience that the scientific method could not only help them distinguish between facts and nonfacts but also help them keep from getting their "teeth smashed in." And, following the clear line of Edison, if not of the edisonade, Heinlein reassured his audience that "the use of the scientific method does not depend on any formal education in science":

> It is an attitude and point of view and not a body of information. You need have no formal education at all to use the scientific method in your everyday life. I am not disparaging the body of scientific information that has been gathered by specialists or the equally enormous body of historical and sociological data that is available. Unfortunately, we can't get very much of it. But you can still use the scientific method, whether you've had a lot of education or not, whether you've had time to gather a lot of personal data or not. (162)

While Heinlein does not quite identify science fiction with the scientific method, the implication and import of his comments are clear: more than a literature, SF is an education; more than an attitude toward stories, it is an attitude toward life; more than anything as trivial as a genre, it is a vital mission.

The connections Heinlein saw between "scientific method" and science fiction grow even more clear when we consider a January 1942 argument he had with Campbell. Following the attack at Pearl Harbor, Campbell had apparently written to Heinlein, criticizing what he felt was the stupidity of the U. S. Navy high command that had failed to anticipate such an attack. After expressing his exasperation at the way Campbell tended to insulate his thinking in matters not related to science from those that were, Heinlein complained:

> So far as I have observed you, you would no more think of going off half-cocked, with insufficient and unverified data, with a respect to a matter of science than you would stroll down Broadway in your underwear. But when it comes to matters outside your specialties you are consistently and brilliantly stupid. You come out with some of the goddamndest flat-footed opinions with respect to matters which you haven't studied and have had no experience, basing your opinions on casual gossip, newspaper stories, unrelated individual data out of matrix, armchair extrapolation, and plain misinformation—unsuspected because you haven't attempted to verify it.[32]

(Ironically, not only would these charges be even more appropriate if made against Campbell late in his career, when he became obsessed with championing such causes as Dianetics and such concepts as psionic power; they would also fit well if made against Heinlein's own thinking late in his career, when, as many commentators have noted, he began to treat his own opinions as if they were facts.)

In what sounds as if it were the ultimate insult he could imagine, Heinlein acknowledged that most people—such as his milkman—were guilty of holding similarly uncritical opinions, adding:

> But I don't expect such sloppy mental processes from you. Damn it! You've had the advantage of a rigorous training in scientific methodology. Why don't you apply it to everyday life? The scientific method will not enable you to hold exact opinions on matters in which you lack sufficient data, but it can keep you from being certain of your opinions and make you aware of the value of your data, and to reserve your judgment until you have amplified your data. (*Grumbles*, 33)

Starship Troopers: Heinlein's "Good" War

I detail this correspondence for the light it casts on Heinlein's commitment to his version of the scientific method, on the relationship between Campbell and Heinlein, and on the dogmatism that emerges from and has occasioned so much criticism of Heinlein's *Starship Troopers*. The problem with this fetishizing of the scientific method, of course, is that it is ultimately a commitment to belief masquerading as science, to a methodology that rests on objective rhetoric but on subjective application. It is a most extreme form of SF's confidence in the knowability of the universe—in scientific certainty that may take work to achieve but that remains a reachable goal. Between the lines of Heinlein's critique of Campbell lies the dogmatism that leads in *Starship Troopers* to the presentation of Heinlein's opinions on moral issues with the rhetorical swagger of mathematical certainty. That 1959 novel won Heinlein the second of his four Hugo Awards and proved immensely popular, but it also became his most controversial work, opening its author to charges even from within the SF community that he was a fascist and militarist.

Starship Troopers opens with a rhetorical strategic feint as it follows the experience of Mobile Infantryman Juan "Johnnie" Rico through a gripping battle between humans and the "skinnies," humanoid allies of the "bugs" in a future interstellar war.[33] The battle is of no particular strategic importance, nor does Rico display in it a degree of courage or ingenuity beyond that expected of any trooper in his unit. The rhetorical point of the battle scene is to establish a sense of action and excitement that might encourage Heinlein's reader to enlist for the duration of what will soon turn out to be a very ponderously preachy book. The scene introduces the idea of a future elite fighting force that uses the technology of massive powered body armor to maximize the importance of the individual in a war against a "hive" species adapted by evolution to "total communism." At the same time, the Mobile Infantry (M. I.) armored suit maximizes the importance of the individual fighting man in a future where super-weapons might be expected to have made the infantryman quite obsolete. One of Heinlein's many dogmatic assumptions in this novel, however, is not only that the single soldier will never be obsolete, but also that the single soldier of the future will maintain an essential kinship with soldiers of the distant past: Rico's nerves at the outset of the battle are compared to those of Greek "old-timers as they climbed into the Trojan Horse," and M. I. drill sergeants improbably instruct their recruits to read "Horatius at the Bridge" or "The Death of the *Bon Homme Richard*" to better understand their potential. Indeed, Heinlein's first chapter reference to the Trojan Horse acquires ironic significance in this book, which at first seems to be about warfare but is in fact a utopian view of both a future soldier state and a "perfect" military.

After its action-packed first chapter, *Starship Troopers* backtracks to its real concern: the depiction of a masculinist fantasy future society where the franchise is held only by veterans of federal service, where the difference between the soldier and the civilian is cast as a moral one, where only veteran soldiers can teach the required high school course in History and Moral Philosophy, and where the ideal society has given rise to the ideal fighting force. Chapter two is a flashback to the events leading up to Rico's surprise enlistment in the M. I., and chapters three through nine then detail the rigors and philosophical indoctrination of basic training. Chapter ten follows Rico to his first unit, noting almost parenthetically that while he had been in basic the Terran Federation had entered into "The Bug War," part of a historical process so inevitable, Heinlein suggests, that "the historians can't seem to settle whether to call this one 'The Third Space War' (or the 'Fourth') or whether 'The First Interstellar War' fits it better" (104). Picking up where the action of the first chapter stopped, chapter eleven follows Rico, now a corporal, through a chain-of-command-clarifying fight with another corporal, to a brief respite on an R & R planet, and finally to his decision to extend his M. I. enlistment to career status. Rico's entry into Officer Candidate School in the next chapter allows Heinlein another round of indoctrination lectures and a more thorough presentation of the table of organization of his ideal military force (only three percent officers—the lowest percentage in any army of record, everyone fights, etc.), and into Rico's first battle as a temporary officer, in which, once again, Heinlein's protagonist performs competently but not heroically or brilliantly, and finally returns to his first outfit as a commissioned officer. The final chapter comes full circle, showing Rico's nerves as he waits for a combat drop like that which opened his story, the difference being that the time has advanced far enough for Rico now to command his old unit and for his father, who in the second chapter had bitterly opposed his decision to enlist, to have become his platoon sergeant.

In between Rico's first and final combat drops, Heinlein gives rhetorically weighted voice to an array of maddening sociological, psychological, and philosophical assumptions. His most effective rhetorical ploy presents Rico's first person narrative in the "aw shucks" wondering voice of Huck Finn, a voice that passes along the lectures of Rico's many "teachers" as received truth rather than opinion. A brief listing of these "truths" would include the assumptions that war is always inevitable, that the imperial expansion of humanity through the stars is a biological imperative, that morality is a science (making Heinlein's views "facts"), that the ultimate reason for fighting in a war is to defend women, that the "noblest fate that a man can endure is to place his own mortal body between his loved home and the war's desolation," that military violence can be "selective" and "controlled," that juvenile delinquency and crime stem from the absence of corporal punishment (notably public flogging), that the military is a better functioning "family" than is its nuclear counterpart (weakened by mothers who cannot understand), that military law should supersede civil codes, that soldiers possess more "civic virtue" than do civilians, and that full citizenship should be granted only to those who have volunteered for a term of federal service (technically including service other than in the military, but slanted so heavily toward military service that this option gets completely lost in the martial rhetoric of *Starship Troopers*).

On the other hand, Heinlein's polemic contains elements that might be seen as progress in the development of science fiction. The protection of women may be cast as the "ultimate reason" M. I. troopers fight, but Heinlein grants women superior reflexes and mathematical skills that make them better spaceship pilots than men. Likewise, Samuel R. Delany, who was very troubled by the book, acknowledges his gratified surprise when he realized that Heinlein's protagonist, a Filipino whose native tongue was Tagalog, was a person of color, an almost unheard of development in SF to that point. While Heinlein's description of the M. I. armored suits may be wistful from a military standpoint, it does not fetishize technology, and the emphasis on individual fighting men (most of whom die or suffer severe wounds) may be seen as a more "responsible" than the "planet-busting" super-weapons so routinely invoked in earlier (and later) space opera. On several occasions, Rico gets to show off his common sense in handling personnel and equipment issues, but he is certainly not presented as any kind of mental whiz, and not only does Heinlein's novel not fetishize "brain power," but it also contains a populist dig at "the intelligent elite" in its account of a failed "Revolt of the Scientists": "It fell flat on its foolish face of course. Because the pursuit of science, despite its social benefits, is itself not a social virtue; its practitioners can be men so self-centered as to be lacking in social responsibility" (143). And finally, while *Starship Troopers* certainly does glorify the military, it does not exactly glorify war (and is certainly not, as the *Encyclopedia of Science Fiction* would have it, "a tale of interstellar war that transforms its protagonist from a pacifist into a professional soldier"), focusing on the "thrill" of duty and honor rather than that of violence and conflict. Samuel Delany is much more accurate when he criticizes the work for presenting war as a—if not the—viable field for personal growth.[34] This equation of military service with growth is emblemized by the declaration of Rico's father, who could join the military only after his son's enlistment and his wife's death in a Bug attack: "I had to perform an act of faith. I had to prove to myself that I was a man. Not just a producing-consuming economic animal . . . but a man" (136). And it is in this respect that Heinlein's utopia is a masculinist fantasy, based on what it means "to be a man." So unconcerned with man as a "producing-consuming economic animal" is Heinlein that, apart from a perfunctory dismissal of a caricatured "Marxian theory of value," Heinlein's utopia has virtually nothing to say about economics.

That a number of inconsistencies, if not outright contradictions, run through Heinlein's novel may stem in part from its odd status as a quasi–juvenile novel. Heinlein later claimed that it was not a juvenile, but "an adult novel about an eighteen-year old boy":

I have so written it, omitting all cleavage and bed games, such that Miss Dalgliesh (his editor at Scribner's) can offer it in the same list in which she has my other books, but nevertheless it is not a juvenile adventure story. Instead I have followed my own theory that intelligent youngsters are in fact more interested in weighty matters than their parents usually are. (*Grumbles*, 95–96)

Heinlein's juvenile novels are much less likely to "talk down" to his younger audience than are many, if not most, such works, and many adult readers have read his juveniles without realizing that they were not the intended audience, yet *Starship Troopers* would seem to violate Heinlein's own standards in this respect. While it concerns "weighty matters," it presents Heinlein's opinions about those matters through a series of lectures by authority figures—all clearly adults—to the 18-year-old Rico. Moreover, these lectures are camouflaged not only as truth, but as indisputable "science," offering Heinlein's audience not something to think about but something simply to accept. All of Heinlein's values are presented as part of a "scientific theory of morals," based on a strongly Darwinian view of the survival instinct—a view that constructs survival for humanity in exactly the same terms as for wild animals. Rico's teachers stress again and again that their philosophy is an "exact science," not "wishful thinking," and is accordingly "mathematically verifiable." Rico, for example, is ordered to bring to class "a written proof, in symbolic logic," of his M.I.- (and Heinlein-) sanctioned view that a single unreleased military prisoner is sufficient "moral" reason to start or resume a war (141–42).

Somewhat similarly, Heinlein not only outlines his plan for a "veteranocracy" in terms that completely abandon his commitment to change, structuring instead a civic utopia that is "revolution-proof" since all potential revolutionists will have been co-opted under this system and made a part of the ruling system. Heinlein the libertarian, and confirmed anti-authoritarian in so many of his works, here presents in authoritarian rhetoric no less than an ode to military authoritarianism—with the vague suggestion that these military principles somehow translate to the running of a perfect polis. This polis seems to rest primarily on the author's belief that crime can be averted by more parental spanking and occasional public flogging, an assumption "mathematically proved" through an analogy to the training of puppies (91–93). And, once this corporally cultivated respect for law has been instituted, Heinlein apparently assumes that all laws will be just, that the polis will always be right. What is finally so maddening about *Starship Troopers* is simply that in it Heinlein seems to have added a new plot possibility to the options of boy-meets-girl, the Little Tailor, and the man-who-learned-better: Heinlein's fourth story type can only be called "the man who who knows it all," and the last 20 years of his writing career would see this story type almost exclusively. Brian Aldiss perfectly captures this method: "Don't listen to all these experts with their jargons and explanations, Heinlein seems to be saying, it's as simple as this—and we are given a cartoon, an old folk-saying. And that is the truth. It is no more complex than that. Whoever says it is is messing with your head, playing a trick on you."[35]

From War Forever to "The Forever War"

Of course, Heinlein is hardly alone among science fiction writers (or writers of every kind) in using his art to posit ex-cathedra pronouncements. And one of the many galling assumptions in *Starship Troopers*, that contact with alien cultures would inevitably lead to war, suggests one of the ways in which SF has managed to be at once a visionary and a blindered literature. Presented as an indisputable truth by one of Rico's instructors at Officer Candidate School, Heinlein's "proof" of the inevitability of interstellar conflict rests on the perception that species survival is integrally bound to population pressure:

> ... it may be verified by observation that any breed which stops its own increase gets crowded out by breeds which expand. Some human populations did so, in Terran history, and other breeds moved in and engulfed them.
> Nevertheless, let's assume that the human race manages to balance birth and death, just right to fit its own planets, and thereby becomes peaceful. What happens?
> Soon (about next Wednesday) the Bugs move in, kill off the breed which "ain'ta gonna study war no more" and the universe forgets us. Which still may happen. Either we spread and wipe out the Bugs, or they spread and wipe us out—because both races are tough and smart and want the same real estate. (147)

This "logic" that justifies not only imperialism but also genocide and that starts from the assumption that war is a scientific given has appeared throughout the history of SF and is one of the genre's most troubling features.

Bill the Galactic Hero (1965), Harry Harrison's heavy-handed satire on *Starship Troopers*, directly mocks Heinlein's imperial imperative—along with most of his other assumptions about the glory of military service—and can be seen as part of a much larger long-running dialogue in SF about violence and warfare (as distinguished from the large number of apocalyptic SF works about the aftermath of nuclear war). Once implicit, this dialogue in recent years has become both explicit and much more intro-spective. Anticipating or siding with Heinlein are prominent sto-ries and novels such as Fredric Brown's *Science Fiction Hall of Fame* entry "Arena" (1944) and A. E. van Vogt's *War against the Rull* (1959). Opposing Heinlein's view are stories such as Murray Lein-ster's "First Contact" (1945), Barry Longyear's "Enemy Mine" (col-lected in *Manifest Destiny* (1980) and made into the 1985 film), and several powerful stories collected in the *Norton Book of Science Fic-tion*, including Lewis Shiner's "The War at Home," Connie Willis's stunning "Schwarzschild Radius," Pamela Sargent's "Gather Blue Roses," Kim Stanley Robinson's "The Lucky Strike," and John Kessel's "Invaders." And no discussion of the assumptions of *Star-ship Troopers* should proceed far without referring to Joe Halde-man's Hugo and Nebula Award-winning *The Forever War* (1975). Haldeman's fine novel has been incorrectly called a rebuttal to *Starship Troopers*, but it is more a realistic correction, sharing some of Heinlein's gusto for the military and for duty and courage, but, in line with Haldeman's experience as a Vietnam veteran, pre-senting the soldier as the most marginalized rather than most cen-tral member of society and noting the fact that Earth's economy becomes totally dependent on sustaining the war. Moreover, even the sacrifices of Haldeman's soldiers, no matter how coura-geous or honorable, are shown to be essentially meaningless, as the reason for their war proves to be nothing more than a sense-less misunderstanding: "The 1143-year-long war had been begun on false pretenses and only continued because the two races were unable to communicate."[36] And treading a compli-cated line between Heinlein's and Haldeman's works is Orson Scott Card's *Ender's Game* (1985), which both represents the military as immorally manipulative and makes thrilling and fun the "basic training" that prepares Ender for the genocide he commits while thinking he is only playing a war game.

More explicitly, three recent anthologies have intensified SF's examination of its assumptions about conflict and war. Almost triumphantly agreeing with Heinlein is *There Will Be War* (1983), edited by J. E. Pournelle, an aggressive conservative who, along with his coauthor Larry Niven, used the example of an alien invasion in *Footfall* (1985) to lecture readers on the need for the neutron bomb. A mixture of fiction and pro-military articles, *There Will Be War* has spawned a series of sequel collections, strongly reminiscent in tone and apparent propagandistic purpose of the "future war" books of the turn of the nineteenth century. Obviously opposed to the *There Will Be War* sensibility is *There Won't Be War* (1991), edited by Harry Harrison and Bruce McAllister. Finally, there is *When the Music's Over* (1991), edited by Lewis Shiner, which expands its focus to include stories not just about war, but also about violence. Written in response to Shiner's challenge to come up with a story "in which conflict— any kind of conflict—was resolved without violence," this anthology also demonstrates its editor's belief that avoiding violence in SF can be seen "not as a limitation, but as an invitation to new possibilities, a chance to open our fiction, as well as our minds, to new ways of thinking."[37] Discussing both of these latter volumes in a review in *Foundation*, Farah Mendlesohn has observed that their single-issue focus on peace has unfortunately led to ignoring issues seen as "peripheral," such as the marginalization of "women and ethnic, religious and sexual minorities."[38] I mention her well-taken point not to tax these anthologies for their shortcomings (like Mendlesohn I find *When the Music's Over* the far more satisfying and thought provoking of the two) but to suggest the distance SF and SF criticism have come in the attempt to understand violence and war in a century where history has proved sadly inimical to such an effort. Just as surely as science fiction has played some role in the construction of the myth of the superweapon in the twentieth century, it may now be taking tentative steps toward contributing to myths of peace in the twenty-first century.

Chapter Three

SCIENCE FICTION OUTSIDE GENRE SF

To try to lift the curtain of mystery over these roads, to speak of scientific achievements yet to come as realities, and in this way to lead the reader to the most advanced outposts of science—such are the tasks of science fiction, as I see them. But they do not exhaust the aims of Soviet science-fiction: its philosophy is to serve the development of the imagination and creative faculty of our people as an asset in the study of social life; and its chief aim is to search for the new, and through this search to gain an insight into the future.

Ivan Antonovich Yefremov

First Contacts

The *Llanvabon*, a spaceship from Earth, is exploring the Crab Nebula in Murray Leinster's classic story "First Contact" when it unexpectedly encounters another spaceship from a previously unknown race, apparently also engaged in study of the region.[1] Cautious but amiable contact between the two ships reveals that the aliens are quite human-like oxygen breathers who see in the infrared spectrum and communicate telepathically. Neither ship can determine the location of the home world of the other, since both are on remote exploratory missions. The problem, as both the captain of the Earth ship and the captain of the alien ship agree, is that neither ship can risk letting the other return to its world with information of the existence and location of another race of intelligent creatures. Even though the benefits from such contact are clear to both captains, both fear that knowledge of the location of either home world might inevitably lead to treacherous military attack, explained by Darwinian logic:

> The possibility of an enormous spurt in the development of both, by peaceful contact and exchange of their separate technologies, would probably appeal to them as to the man. But when dissimilar human cultures are in contact, one must usually be subordinate or there is war. But subordination between races arising on separate planets could not be peacefully arranged. Men, at least, would never consent to subordination, nor was it likely that any highly developed race would agree.... If the alien ship now approaching the Llanvabon returned to its home base with news of humanity's existence and of ships like the Llanvabon, it would give its race the choice of trade or battle. They might want trade, or they might want war. But it takes two to make trade, and only one to make war. They could not be sure of men's peacefulness, nor could men be sure of theirs. The only safety for either civilization would lie in the destruction of one or both of the two ships here and now. (317–18)

Aliens and humans seem to think pretty much alike, which is precisely the problem, as both races justify their paranoia and suspicions as "strictly logical." The more humans and aliens find they have in common, the more humans ascribe their own motivations to the aliens. Fortunately, both ships arrive at the same solution, and each race uses bomb-carrying crewmen who visit each other's ships to blackmail the other captain into simply swapping spaceships after removing all signs of the location of their respective home planets and rendering each ship incapable of following the other. In this way, each race can be informed of the existence of the other, can learn much about the other from the technology and artifacts of the other's ship, and a future rendezvous in the Crab Nebula can be arranged if it is desired by both planets.

Published in 1945 and containing a topical reference to "the sneaking brutal ferocity of a Japanese," Leinster's story is most noteworthy for its peaceful solution to the "inevitable dilemma" of alien contact; in the context of genre SF its nonviolent resolution surely represents more the exception than the rule. So it is somewhat ironic that "First Contact" would be the SF story cited in Soviet science fiction writer Ivan A. Yefremov's far-future novella, *The Heart of the Serpent*, as a telling example of what was so wrong with ancient capitalist thinking—and, by extension, with American genre SF.

Yefremov, author of *Andromeda* (1958), the best-known work of Soviet SF in the years immediately following the lifting of repressive Stalinist limits on SF, uses his first-contact story to contrast enlightened communist principles of universal brotherhood with the old capitalist forms of social thought that had led to works such as Leinster's "First Contact." Whereas Leinster's story poses the problem of allaying mutual distrust, Yefremov's poses only the problems humans and aliens face as they try to cooperate. In Yefremov's story, set in a far future when communist principles have become universal, the starship *Tellur*, on a mission of discovery that will span some 700 earth years, happens upon an alien vessel. Moot Ang, captain of the *Tellur*, prepares his crew for this first contact by shocking them with the "ridiculous apprehensions" of the characters in Leinster's story, an example of "the writings of those who sought to defend the old society, proclaiming the inevitability of war and the eternal existence of capitalism."[2] Ang and his crew members criticize many of the scientific and linguistic assumptions in "First Contact," but what they most reject is the assumption that beings who could conquer space would not have evolved past the point of war and conflict. As one crew member explains:

> Human beings cannot vanquish space before they have achieved a higher mode of life when there are no more wars and when each individual has a high sense of responsibility to all his fellow-men!
> In other words—humanity has been able to harness the forces of Nature on a cosmic scale only after reaching the highest stage of the communist society—there could be no other way.... And the same applies to any other human race, if we mean by this the higher forms of organized, thinking life. (66–67)

Accordingly, this "first contact" can only be a chance for the universal brotherhood of a perfected society to be extended to thinking beings from other worlds. Moreover, even before they meet these beings, the crew of the *Tellur* knows they will not only be rational (their thinking based on mathematical and dialectical logic), but also "beautiful." "Any thinking being from some other world that has been able to reach the Cosmos must be just as perfect and universal as the humans of our Earth, and hence just as beautiful. . . .There can be no thinking monsters, no mush-room men, no octopus-men!" (52–53). And indeed, although the aliens met by the *Tellur* come from a flourine-based planet and display some physical differences such as having unjointed, four-fingered hands and gray skin, they are immediately perceived as physically beautiful—and desirable—by the crew from Earth. Although some form of call from another of the aliens' ships cuts short the exchange of information between the two crews, a member of the Earth ship supplies the aliens with an idea (only vaguely described by Yefremov) for instituting evolutionary chemical changes that would eventually allow people from the fluorine planet to preserve all their hereditary characteristics while shifting their metabolisms to an oxygen base—making future cooperation between Earth and the unnamed planet even easier and more complete.

Apart from its propagandistic swipe at Leinster's story and its smug satisfaction over the perfection of future communist society, Yefremov's story contains numerous descriptions of future technology and considerable speculation about the nature of a flourine-based life-form. While it contains several characters, they are only rudimentarily differentiated, and their collective view is so strong as to keep them being much more than tag-team spokespersons for Yefremov's very hopeful view of a communist far future. What the story does not contain is any real sense of conflict or drama or narrative drive, being more lecture than story. In its clearly socialist utopian aims, Yefremov's story reflects an aspect of Soviet and Eastern European SF that seems to diverge from the paradigms of most American genre SF. While the American pulp tradition produced aliens so uniformly threatening and monstrous that the term "B. E. M." (for "bug-eyed monsters") could be generally applied to them, Soviet and Eastern European SF almost uniformly presented aliens in first contact stories in a positive light. Indeed, these contrasting first contact stories represent contrasting literary traditions nearly as alien to each other as are the races that first meet within their narratives.

Not only do these stories suggest some of the great differences between American and Soviet–Eastern-European SF—in great part differences determined by political change within the former Soviet Union—but they also can represent an even broader split between American SF and that produced in Great Britain and Europe, particularly in the period between the two World Wars. In this sense, the contrasts between Yefremov's and Leinster's approaches to the first-contact theme can be seen as emblematic of larger contrasts between what is often constructed as the "high" European tradition of SF and its "low" American counterpart. And, while the rhetoric of "high" and "low" literature seems to me generally unproductive, it represents one predictable reaction to the fact that, following World War I, American SF and European SF were produced out of largely differing concerns, for largely differing audiences, and promoted largely differing views of both humanity and technology. Of necessity, this brief attempt to describe twentieth-century SF has been and will continue to be primarily interested in the American-shaped version of the genre. What I will try to do in this chapter, however, is to outline some of the differences between the two traditions and to look more closely at two relatively recent masterpieces from the European tradition—Stanislaw Lem's *His Master's Voice* (1968) and Boris and Arkady Strugatsky's *Roadside Picnic* (1972). Both of these works continue to explore the first-contact theme introduced in the contrast between fiction by Leinster and Yefremov, and, in developing a theme that has remained central to American genre SF, both offer points of comparison as well as contrast. Finally, Lem and the Strugatskys are among the best and most significant writers twentieth century SF has produced.

Two Traditions

Almost every study of science fiction in the twentieth century details an essential difference in "seriousness" or "purpose" between American SF and noteworthy strains of well-known SF from the United Kingdom, Eastern Europe, and the former Soviet Union, usually focusing on SF written from the 1920s through the 1940s—the heyday of American genre SF. Speaking of continental SF, prominent European critic Franz Rottensteiner refers to "features that are uniquely its own," suggesting that those features are "perhaps a matter of philosophy, of seriousness of purpose, as opposed to the irrelevance and playfulness of most American SF."[3] Speaking primarily of the British writers Aldous Huxley, C. S. Lewis, and Olaf Stapledon, but also of European writers such as Karel Čapek and Josef Nesvadba, Brian Aldiss contrasts the implicit seriousness and worth of their writing with what he sees as the bankruptcy of Gernsbackian genre SF, suggesting that the appearance of the American pulps divided SF into high and low streams.[4] Coincidentally supporting such an easy division was the fact that most European SF before 1950 was published in books, whereas in America SF appeared primarily in magazines, and one further result of this difference is that the most celebrated American SF of the time tends to be short stories, while the most celebrated European SF of the period tends to be novels.

Aldiss also calls attention to and tacitly supports the Swedish writer Sam J. Lundwall's charge that the European heritage of SF had been "stolen" by America, "transforming it and vulgarizing it and changing it beyond recognition."[5] What seems to be at stake here is not so much an attempt to describe a European tradition of SF as much as to describe literature that was not "tainted" by the American pulp tradition. Sometimes the political-sociological concern of H. G. Wells will be invoked as one of the aspects of the higher European tradition, as opposed to the gadget-centered interests of Jules Verne, but Verne is also sometimes contrasted with Gernsbackian technophilia. And sometimes it will be acknowledged, as it has been by Franz Rottensteiner, that "average" SF in the European tradition can be quite bad, marked by "a certain clumsiness and technical backwardness."[6]

However, as Edward James has noted, most of the European writers commonly linked to this "European tradition" did not perceive SF as a genre, much less that they were writing in a European strain of that genre. It is clear that a number of prominent European writers did share the broad concerns of H. G. Wells, but they also could be linked to a utopian tradition that influenced Wells himself. At any rate, as James concludes, by the 1950s such a bifurcated view of high European SF and low American SF was pretty much beside the point, since science fiction "had become identified as an American product," with the "victory" of American SF "just one facet of the post-war cultural supremacy of the United States."[7] The British SF writer and critic Christopher Priest seconds James's view of this "victory" with his grumbling acknowledgment that "Modern science fiction is a primarily American phenomenon, and much of the genre is written either by Americans or by authors who adopt the American idiom."[8]

James offers a most useful, evenhanded, and pragmatic overview of the divergence of American genre SF from SF produced outside the genre in the years between the wars in his *Science Fiction in the 20th Century*. Another excellent account of this divergence can be found in Brian Stableford's essay, "Science Fiction Between the Wars: 1916–1939," and subsequent bibliography in Neil Barron's *Anatomy of Wonder 4: A Critical Guide to Science Fiction* (1995). Stableford pegs much of the difference between these two "streams" of SF not just to the Gernsback-engineered rise of the pulps but to more profound causes such as the relatively different impact of World War I on America and on Britain and Europe.[9] The devastating Great War, notes Stableford, left European speculative fiction much less confident and adventurous than its American counterpart, with particularly chilling effect on utopian and future war stories. The "exotic romanticism" and technological optimism of the American pulps then developed in marked contrast with the British tradition, which became "argumentative, pessimistic, and acutely concerned with social issues" (66–67). Moreover, this more serious British engagement with the idea of the future was bolstered by a boom in Britain in speculative nonfiction, with futurological speculation by J. B. S. Haldane and others prompting fictional reactions from Aldous Huxley, C. S. Lewis, and Olaf Stapledon.

Noting similarly influential political and intellectual conditions in France, Germany, and the Soviet Union, Stableford chronicles ways in which key works in the "European tradition" "go beyond the surfaces of particular ideologies to reach more fundamental questions about the nature of the good life and the entanglement of political power and technological instrumentality" (76). Masters of this form would include Yevgeny Zamyatin, whose dystopian *We* (1924) was a strong influence on Orwell's *1984* (1949) (as was Katharine Burdekin's *Swastika Night* [1937]), Karel Čapek with *R. U. R.* (1921) and *War with the Newts* (1936), Aldous Huxley, whose *Brave New World* (1932) has been called by Brian Aldiss "arguably the Western World's most famous science fiction novel," and Olaf Stapledon, whose *Odd John* (1935) and *Sirius* (1944) explored individual encounters with science, while his *Last and First Men* (1930) and *Star Maker* (1937) explored the evolutionary future not only of humanity but of the cosmos itself.

Even when approached as evenhandedly as it is by Stableford and James, this view of a "higher" European tradition of SF perpetuates a widely held view of Gernsbackian pulp SF that may need considerable revision. As I noted in chapter two, Andrew Ross has recently called into question the dismissal of "the Gernsback Continuum" as "a naive example of blind faith in technological progress," choosing instead to reexamine the pulps in the larger context of broader progressive movements based on "critical technocracy."[10] Reacting precisely to the genre "history" I've just been describing, Ross cautions: "In the case of early SF, the conventional historical narrative is often overlaid by prejudices against the North American vulgarization of the high-minded and socially critical European SF tradition created by respectable intellectuals like H. G. Wells, Jules Verne, Aldous Huxley, Yevgeny Zamyatin, Fritz Lang, Olaf Stapledon, and Karel Čapek" (104). Against this narrative, Ross suggests that the pulps represented a larger "positivist religion (shared by left and right alike)"—a "widely shared social fantasy" that was as enthusiastically received by the European left as by American Fordists. "We need to know more," cautions Ross, "about the hallowed place of engineers and scientists in public consciousness in the years of boom and crisis between the wars, the consolidation of the industrial research science at the heart of corporate capitalism, and the redemptive role cast for technology in the drama of national recovery and growth" (103). Ross reminds us that much of the "history" of SF as a genre has been constructed apart from cultural contexts that might significantly change our understanding of the genre in the twentieth century. He also suggests that this "naive" tradition was implicated in the language of nationalistic destiny, as "an embryonic response to the call for the colonization of space, where adventure, as always, was imperialism's accomplice" (112).

A more polemical objection to the view of a "high" European tradition of SF comes from Gary Westfahl, who notes that critics advancing this history past 1920 must "watch their own traditions fade and fall apart, while American science fiction expands and grows stronger to the point that, by 1950 or so, American writers and ideas dominated the world, and the British and European authors were forced to imitate or respond to the American tradition."[11] This is essentially the same claim adopted later by Edward James, but with the difference that Westfahl credits the success of American SF not to international cultural hegemony but to the complete theory of SF offered by Hugo Gernsback and the institutions for critical commentary fostered by Gernsback. While proponents of the "high" tradition of European literature point to the literary skill of its authors, Westfahl argues that literary criticism of SF—criticism that rose from the Gernsbackian tradition—was what led to the dominance of American SF.

A Master's Voice: Stanislaw Lem

While it is important both to recognize that the view of a "superior" European tradition persists both explicitly and implicitly in most accounts of twentieth-century SF and to recognize that this view needs considerable revision and rethinking, my concern in this chapter is not so much with either perpetuating or refuting this construction as it is with simply acknowledging the individual genius of several writers firmly associated with European SF: Stanislaw Lem and Boris and Arkady Strugatsky. And, in looking at these writers I will return to to the theme of first contact with which I began this chapter, a theme developed quite differently in Lem's *His Master's Voice* and in the Strugatsky brothers' *Roadside Picnic*. I have chosen to discuss these works—and this theme—both because they illustrate the highly self-reflexive aspect of twentieth-century SF and because they explore a theme of great fascination to American and European traditions alike.

First-contact stories have always been important to science fiction, in no small part because they explore a fictional novum—the existence of other intelligent life forms in the universe—that many SF writers and readers see as more probability than fiction. If actually realized, this first-contact theme would also go a long way toward justifying the missionary fervor and sense of purpose found in much SF. Moreover, first-contact stories have a particularly self-reflexive aspect, since their interrogation of the alien "Other" takes place in a genre that has itself been "othered" by many critics. Protocols of the first-contact story usually involve problems of "radical translation" that must be solved before communication with the aliens can be established, and this, too, occurs in a genre that requires special reading and interpretive protocols before its "message" can be understood. As the *Encyclopedia of Science Fiction* notes, the first-contact story is perhaps the most common communication scenario in a genre that has been intensely concerned with communication and linguistic issues.

Both "positive" and "negative" twentieth century first-contact stories can trace their lineage to European traditions, since benign aliens were popularized in Camille Flammarion's works *Real and Imaginary Worlds* (1865) and *Lumen* (1887) and by J. H. Rosny Aîné in "*Les Xipehuz*" (1910) and *Les navigateurs de l'Infini* (1925), while the Darwinian view of threatening aliens bent on conquest was firmly established by Wells's *War of the Worlds* (1898).[12] Somewhat ironically, the most influential early positive depiction of an alien who was radically different from humans came from the pulp tradition, as Stanley Weinbaum's "A Martian Odyssey," published in *Wonder Stories* in 1934, presented in the Big-Bird-like Tweel a possibly superior ally from the stars to an Earthman beset by Martian creatures.

First-contact stories can take many forms, ranging from actual meetings to the interception of messages that only reveal the existence or previous existence of other intelligent life-forms. Classic examples of the meeting story include "A Martian Odyssey," "First Contact" (1945), James Blish's *VOR* (1958), Stanislaw Lem's *Solaris* (1961), Naomi Mitchison's *Memoirs of a Spacewoman* (1962), and more ambiguous recent works such as the Strugatskys' *Roadside Picnic* (1972; English, 1977), John Kessel's *Good News From Outer Space* (1989), Gwyneth Jones's *White Queen* (1991), and even possibly Karen Joy Fowler's *Sarah Canary* (1991). Classic examples of the message-from-space first-contact story include Fred Hoyle's *A for Andromeda* (1962), James Gunn's *The Listeners* (1972), and Stanislaw Lem's *His Master's Voice* (1968).

Lem's novel derives its title from the His Master's Voice Project, a Manhattan-Project-like government-sponsored undertaking whose job is to decode a string of neutrino emissions that may be a message from the stars. Lem's protagonist, Peter Hogarth, is a famous mathematician—the subject of some 28 biographies—who has been asked to join the project. But even the above brief description introduces some of the complexity that characterizes Lem's approach to this theme. In the first place, the fact that the HMV project can be compared only to the scientific undertaking that produced the atomic bomb and the fact that the project is located in an abandoned nuclear testing facility in Nevada immediately remind us that such a large scientific undertaking is anything but free from military and political connections. In the second place, while Hogarth is generally recognized as a genius, he is a controversial one who does not restrict his work to his own statistical specialty and who is known more for his doubting than for his vision—which are possibly reasons he was not an original member of the HMV team but was asked to join the project only after it had encountered major obstacles. As well-known as Hogarth is for his work in mathematics, his greatest proof, having to do with statistical determinism of human behavior, has been ignored by specialists in behavior because "none of them wanted that kind of discovery." If Hogarth is to be believed, his "proof" has simply been rejected by the sciences that found it inconvenient or threatening, suggesting that the same fate may well befall theories about the possible message from space that do not fit comfortably with existing scientific knowledge. And, in keeping with this introduction, Lem's novel catalogues problems that seem to have no solutions, chronicling a mammoth scientific undertaking that ultimately fails to make more than very limited sense of the "letter from the stars."

That such a work would come from the Polish writer Stanislaw Lem is only to be expected, since Lem has built his reputation with works that interrogate doubt rather than celebrate discovery and problem-solving. Author of over 30 books—ranging from essays on literature and science to fiction—which have been translated into over 30 languages, Lem may be one of the best-known SF writers in the world, and he is certainly one of the most respected.[13] In works such as *The Star Diaries* (1976), *Memoirs of a Space Traveler* (1982), *Tales of Pirx the Pilot* (1979), *Solaris* (1961),

The Invincible (1973), *The Cyberiad* (1974), *His Master's Voice* (1983), *The Futurological Congress* (1974), *Memoirs Found in a Bathtub* (1973), and *Fiasco* (1986) Lem has established himself as the present-day master of philosophical science fiction and one of SF's greatest satirists, but also as a writer whose variety and innovation resist genre and mainstream labels alike. Austrian critic Franz Rottensteiner (who as Lem's literary agent may be less than totally objective) claims that Lem is the most significant SF writer since H. G. Wells and in the company of Stapledon, Borges, and Čapek, noting that Lem's particular strength lies in presenting the method of science as a philosophy of science—as "critical doubt in action," a process in which science "throws up new questions for any problem solved."[14] Making similar claims for Lem's importance, Darko Suvin presents Lem as a writer who has managed to fuse the stronger sides of the Soviet and American SF traditions. Accordingly, Lem, says Suvin, is "internationally unique because he was the first to continue the fictional tradition of socialist hope and the rationalist 'philosophical tale' while modifying it with new approaches consonant with the modern scientific and cognitive age."[15] From a more general perspective, Suvin, writing for the *Encyclopedia of Science Fiction*, simply notes that Lem is "one of the most significant SF writers of our century, and a distinctive voice in world literature" (711).

Complicating his status, however, is the fact that Lem refuses to think of himself as an SF writer and has written denunciations of SF—particularly American SF—so scathing that in 1976 individuals in the Science Fiction Writers of America (SFWA), through a complicated and controversial series of events, rescinded his honorary membership, awarded only three years before.[16] Somewhat indicative of his view of genre SF is Lem's argument in "Science Fiction: A Hopeless Case—with Exceptions" that SF is largely trash—kitsch:

> Knowing no discretion and no reverence for things inconceivable by the human mind, piling universes upon universes without batting an eyelash, mixing up physics, metaphysics, and trite trash from misinterpreted philosophical systems without end, science fiction is the true embodiment of kitsch, because of the cheekiness of its total ignorance, which even denies the existence of a higher knowledge, toward which it finds no path, and denies it triumphantly and obstinately.[17]

In "Looking Down on Science Fiction: A Novelist's Choice for the World's Worst Writing," the piece whose republication in the SFWA Forum occasioned several extreme responses from outraged SFWA members, Lem attacked the entire structure of genre SF, suggesting that its steady readership—fandom—"is largely made up of frustrated individuals estranged from society" and that "most science fiction is to authentic scientific, philosophical, or theological knowledge as pornography is to love," he specifically singled out the publishing approaches of Poul Anderson and Robert Heinlein for derision (SFS, 127–28).

Considering the widely perceived arrogance of his criticisms of SF, it is not surprising, but somewhat ironic, that Lem's own fiction tends to dwell on the limiting effects of human-centered views of the universe, on the limits of human knowledge, and on the knowability of the universe itself. *Solaris*, perhaps Lem's best-known work, offers unforgettable emblems of these problems in its presentation of an ocean-like sentient life-form that covers most of the surface of the planet Solaris and confounds Earth scientists with unfathomable constructs, including hauntingly life-like phantom characters apparently drawn from the scientists' memories. The strong suggestion of this novel is not only that Earthly academic categories are rendered ludicrous by the living ocean but that the ocean being may ultimately have more in common with human conceptions of God than those of alien life-forms. *Solaris* then presents the familiar structure of a mystery but frustrates that structure by refusing to present any solution, as Lem's protagonist, the scientist Kelvin, can only learn to accept a kind of humbling self-knowledge from his unsuccessful efforts to understand phenomena tied to the ocean. In this resignation in the face of an unknowable power, Kelvin shares much with Peter Hogarth in *His Master's Voice*, with the exception that Hogarth's resignation shades into a faith that transcends his commitment to science.

His Master's Voice opens with a number of very human complications that attend the larger problem of decoding what may or may not be a message from outer space.[18] Even Hogarth's account of his role in the project comes to us through the mediation of a Nabokovian editor who became responsible for the manuscript after Hogarth's death and who admits that he cannot be sure whether a key part of Hogarth's writing was meant to appear as preface or as afterword to the narrative. Such an ultimately unresolvable question in the presentation and interpretation of a manuscript written by a well-known figure in a perfectly known language can only prepare us for the infinitely greater difficulty of ascribing purpose to a message possibly written by unimaginably different aliens in a civilization removed from ours by thousands of years. And, in fact, everything in Hogarth's narrative repeats this caveat as—before he even begins to describe the problem of decoding the message itself—he notes how his 28 biographers have all misunderstood him and how he himself has no certain sense of what his life means. Whatever the impact of Hogarth's "antibiographical" musings, they do support the thesis maintained throughout his account that "one's personal experience in life is fundamentally unconveyable. Nontransmittable" (62), a thesis that can only alert us to the unlikelihood of figuring what might be transmittable from a civilization where "experience in life" must be dramatically alien from that on Earth. By interrogating knowability at the human level Hogarth prepares us for the nearly insurmountable difficulty not just of understanding the neutrino emissions that may be a letter from the stars, but of understanding how enormously difficult that basic undertaking is. In addition to its sustained argument that the universe will not give up its secrets to anthropocentric inquiry, Lem's novel systematically explores the problems of radical translation, offers a critique of the myth of objective science, and roundly blasts many conventions and assumptions of science fiction, as well as offering a narrative of the movement of a great mind from self-absorbed cynicism to a kind of secular faith.

Like Fred Hoyle's and John Elliot's *A for Andromeda* and James Gunn's *The Listeners*, events in *His Master's Voice* follow the recognition that neutrino "noise" from the general direction of Canis Minor and recorded by instruments at Mount Palomar perfectly repeats its pattern every 416 hours, and, therefore, may be not noise but "information"—a message. Unlike those two only superficially similar first-contact stories, Lem's narrative offers no final solution to the mystery of the message, as not only is it never decoded, but its basic nature can never be agreed upon. While Hoyle and Elliot and Gunn all foreground the dedication and selflessness of the questing scientists in their stories, Lem tends to focus on scientific selfishness, turf protection, and bureaucratic inflexibility. In Lem's hands, even the "discovery" of the neutrino pattern results not from the rigorous power of science but from chance. Not only is the neutrino pattern the unexpected by-product of a failed experiment, but it is also a by-product noticed by a pseudoscientist quack, whose loony claim that the message was in Morse code alerted a distinguished scientist to the possibility of pattern only when he happened to pick up and read an article in a Topeka, Kansas, paper left on a train seat. Accordingly, the possible message comes to the attention of science only through a series of accidents, coincidences, and misunderstandings, and through a conflict of odd personalities and manically different intended uses for the neutrino recordings.

After establishing the unlikelihood of the recognition that there may be a pattern to be decoded, Lem turns toward diminishing the genre-based expectation that problems exist to be solved and replacing it with a more profound understanding of the depth and complexity of this particular problem. A series of striking metaphors, all designed to strip the Master's Voice Project of its aura of scientific power, is perhaps Hogarth's first line of defense against the positivist expectations of his readers. "Ants that encounter in their path a dead philosopher," we are reminded, "may make good use of him" (22). Likewise, Hogarth implies that—in accidentally stumbling across the message from the stars—"we did with it no more than a savage who, warming himself by a fire of burning books, the writings of the wisest men, believes that he has drawn tremendous benefit from his find" (27). The message may be a particularly complex Rorschach test designed to elicit the predisposition of human civilization (32), the humans trying to decipher the message may be acting blindly like "pigs trained to find truffles" (61), or their efforts at code-breaking may be ridiculously misapplied, "like a man prepared to study a handwritten letter as if it were a seismogram" (189). The "content" of the message may be as natural and as unintended as sugar in a urine sample, or it may be as artificial as a sugar level in the urine sample determined by conscious ingestion of large amounts of sugar (190). So beyond human conceptualization is the message, Hogarth believes, that it "was the plan of a cathedral sent to australopithecines, a library opened to Neanderthals" (93), and because of his persistent pessimism, Hogarth is accused of trying to sabotage the project.

Moving his comparisons closer in history, Hogarth relates a story from World War II told to him by a Jewish colleague who had first been threatened with and then spared from execution by a Nazi officer acting upon unfathomable motives. When Hogarth confesses that he does not understand the German officer's actions, his colleague explains:

> Although he spoke to us, you see, we were not people. He knew that we comprehended human speech but that nevertheless we were not human; he knew this quite well. Therefore, even if he had wanted to explain things to us, he could not have. The man could do with us what he liked, but he could not enter into negotiations, because for negotiation you must have a party in at least some respect equal to the party who initiates it, and in that yard there were only he and his men. A logical contradiction, yes, but he acted exactly according to that contradiction, and scrupulously. (65)

Neither Rappaport, who tells the story, nor Hogarth glosses this chilling anecdote in any way, but the example of a member of the "master race" so convinced of the inhumanity of his victims casts an obvious shadow over an enterprise in which the likelihood is overwhelming that humans are trying to understand a message from a civilization far in advance of theirs. And Hogarth does return to the consideration of genocide as he considers a kind of fellowship threshold that must separate "higher" from "lower" species in any evolutionary scheme:

> If we learned that for some reason exchanging signals with the Cosmos required the annihilation of Earth's ants, we would certainly think that it was "worth" sacrificing the ants. Now, we, on our rung of development, may be—to Someone—ants. The level of fellowship may not necessarily extend, from the standpoint of those beings, to such planetary vermin as ourselves. (162)

The likely indifference of the civilization that sent the message haunts Hogarth—particularly as he fears that a misinterpretation of the message may actually produce a weapon more terrible than any made by human design.

Hogarth's fear of a misreading that might produce a weapon is seemingly well grounded, as information from three or four percent of the message has been read as a recipe by groups in the project, producing a semiliquid mucus-like substance termed "Frog Eggs" by the biochemist group and "Lord of the Flies" by the biophysicists (because the substance apparently drives houseflies alone into a frenzy when in proximity to them). The colloidal substance produces energy through a kind of cold fusion the scientists cannot completely explain, and immediately inspires a number of theories about its nature and purpose. Some see this substance as a sign that the entire code describes an entire Sender who could be synthesized once the code was completely understood (an idea realized in *A for Andromeda*, where the message, somewhat improbably, leads to the synthesis of a beautiful and dangerous alien woman). Other theories ranged from seeing the substance as some kind of embryo to seeing it as a kind of plasmic brain. "Frog Eggs" would be little more than a curiosity, were it not for the fact that its properties seem to allow for the displacement of energy from the site where an atom is smashed to some remote location—the perfect mechanism for an unstoppable bomb that can be instantaneously sent anywhere on Earth. Such a destabilizing weapon would have a draconian, perhaps terminal, impact on the weapons race between East and West, and Hogarth and several colleagues who first understand this deadly potential implication of the TX effect (tele + explosion) of Frog Eggs enter into a conspiracy to keep the possibility of the superweapon a secret until they have fully tested it. This conspiracy forms the dramatic core of *His Master's Voice*, although it proves unnecessary when further testing reveals that Frog Eggs can be either made into a powerful atomic bomb or delivered to a remote site with pinpoint accuracy, but not both at once, completely precluding its use as a weapon.

Even though its outcome is benign, this episode points out how easily science can be drawn into military concerns and is seen by Hogarth as confirming his sense of self as someone who seeks out evil. Hogarth remains convinced that Frog Eggs resulted from a misreading of the code, and he compares the process that created the substance to putting a program tape from a computer into a player piano and being ecstatic when the computer tape randomly produces a musical phrase (145). Such a radical misreading is compared to the kind of error where someone misreads a kitchen recipe, substitutes "amanita" for "amandine," and consequently poisons all who eat the dish (145). Moreover, such a misreading almost inevitably results from an inquiry process that from its outset had looked for military applications. "We are proceeding," warns Hogarth, "like a man who looks for a lost thing not everywhere, but only beneath a lighted street lamp, because there it is bright" (145). Despite the insistent efforts to misread the message as a blueprint for some kind of weapon, the one indisputable property of the neutrino beam is that it favors life, fostering over millions of years the organization of molecules that are the chemical foundation of life. While the neutrino beam does not create life, it increased the chances of life's forming, thus raising the prospect that the neutrino emissions do not carry a message but constitute a process.

Before the TX effect of the substance is completely discounted, however, its possibility leads to a complete takeover of the HMV project by the military, who, it turns out, had all along been sponsoring a parallel project (dubbed His Master's Ghost), staffed with more-trusted scientists. Scientists from this shadow project are no more successful in decoding the message, but they do provide two of the most persuasive theories about the nature of the message. The first of these theories posits that the message may be a kind of informational umbilical cord that connects cycles of the universe, bringing the basic information from the collapsed old universe into the new universe that is its successor. Accordingly, there is no message to be decoded, since the neutrino string is "only an emission produced by processes that are purely physical, natural, and totally uninhabited, therefore devoid of any linguistic character, of content, of meaning" (181). The second theory (very similar to the assumption at the heart of Gunn's *The Listeners*) is that the message comes from a civilization already dead some 30 billion years, but a civilization so powerful that it undertook to affect the universe that would follow its own by sending a message of information designed to foster life in the new universe. According to these two cyclical theories: "The signal either was a natural phenomenon, a 'last chord' of a dying Universe, hammered out by a 'fissure' between world and antiworld onto a neutrino wave; a deathbed kiss planted upon the front of the wave—or else it was the last will and testament of a civilization that no longer lived!" (187–88).

Hogarth's own view, finally, is that the message was indeed sent by a superior civilization—one so superior that it crafted the message in such a way that it could not be misinterpreted by those not yet advanced enough to use its information wisely. However, to call this opinion a "view" is to misrepresent what becomes for Hogarth an unshakeable article of faith. That the Senders could devise a message that would resist the pointed efforts not only of humanity but also of other not-yet-mature civilizations throughout the universe convinces Hogarth that the Senders had attained a degree of perfection far beyond that of mere biological systems. In sensing "their greatness," Hogarth begins to understand "what a civilization could be based on, and what a civilization could be" (194), and his belief in the absolute superiority of the Senders becomes for him "the only equivalent available to me of holiness" (196). Unable to solve the mystery of the code, Hogarth finds equanimity in the faith that the message was not a mystery to be solved or a test to be passed in scientific or technological terms, but a letter that can only be read by civilizations adequately advanced in all respects:

> And so: the Senders had in mind certain beings, certain civilizations, but not all, not even all those of the technological circle. What sort of civilizations are the proper addressees? I do not know. I will say only this: if, in the opinion of the Senders, that information is not fitting for us to learn, then we will not learn it. I place great confidence in Them—because They did not let me down. (198)

The proud genius who is haunted by his very human propensity for seeking out "evil" is finally moved not just by the liberating superiority of the Senders but by the implication of their precautions—that "at one time They were—or, who knows, perhaps still are—like us" (194).

While my account of *His Master's Voice* has focused heavily on its interrogation of knowability and on its relentless critique of anthropocentric thinking, I should note that Lem also laces his narrative with criticisms of science fiction itself. Of course, the degree of complexity he assigns to the breaking of the code is something of a rebuke to SF first-contact stories in which communication problems are easily overcome, and his refusal to offer a technological solution to the mystery of the code also flies in the face of SF convention. However, Lem's criticisms are often explicit, as Hogarth repeatedly identifies theories about the instrumentality of the message (message as prelude to invasion or even as "helpful" obstetric intervention for the birth of a new society) with the reading of too much science fiction. More explicitly, he rejects the tendency of these sensational theories to reflect science fiction's propensity for imagining the alien in terms of human society, "primarily in its American version" (99). Yet Lem provides his strongest denunciation of SF in Hogarth's description of the disappointment felt by his colleague Rappaport when he turned to science fiction for inspiration:

> One day I found him amid large packages from which spilled attractive, glossy paperbacks with mythical covers. He had tried to use, as a "generator of ideas"—for we were running out of them—those works of fantastic literature, that popular genre (especially in the States), called by a persistent misconception, "science fiction." He had not read such books before; he was annoyed—indignant, even—expecting variety, finding monotony. "They have everything *except* fantasy," he said. Indeed, a mistake. The authors of these pseudo-scientific fairy tales supply the public with what it wants: truisms, clichés, stereotypes, all sufficiently costumed and made "wonderful" so that the reader may sink into a safe state of surprise and at the same time not be jostled out of his philosophy of life. If there is progress in a culture, the progress is above all conceptual, but literature, the science-fiction variety in particular, has nothing to do with that." (106–7)

This, like so many of Lem's attacks on SF, contains much that is accurate and deserved as well as much that is arrogant, unfair, and misleading, but as a list of characteristics Lem's fiction is scrupulously crafted to avoid, Hogarth's most pointed critique is an effective reminder of the power and achievement of *His Master's Voice* and of the irrefutable contribution of Stanislaw Lem to the genre he finds so disappointing.

The combination of Lem's ego with his logic-chopping certainty gives his writing about SF an imperiousness that is frequently hard to take, no matter how thought-provoking. One of his most curious essays, "About the Strugatskys' *Roadside Picnic*," first published as the afterword to the 1981 Polish translation of the novel, praises the Strugatskys, two brothers then Russia's most celebrated SF writers, for "transcending the science fiction tradition" and surpassing the canon established by Wells," then attempts to graft Lem's view of the Senders developed in *His Master's Voice* onto the Strugatskys' quite different first-contact story.[19] *Roadside Picnic* starts from the assumption that aliens visited Earth some 20 years in the past, leaving six well-defined Zones in which mysterious artifacts and phenomena can be found, most of which seem to refute "natural laws" and, indeed, to challenge the very notion of causality upon which Earth science is built. Like some triumphant detective, Lem announces his "hypothesis" that the alien visitation at the heart of *Roadside Picnic* was "no landing after all" but "an automatically piloted space probe" that accidentally broke up and hit the Earth in the six Zones of the Strugatsky narrative. Reprising Hogarth's faith in the wisdom of the Senders in *His Master's Voice*, Lem argues that "the Zone's peculiarity is most simply explained by the foresight of the senders, who, unable to eliminate the possibility of an accident, therefore took care that its consequences would be kept within bounds" (273).

As interesting as is Lem's preoccupation with "preserving the mystery" of the alien visitors, his analysis seems to miss the Strugatskys' clear emphasis not on the alien "other" but on the Zones as a terrible window into the human condition, both under capitalism and under technology divorced from moral considerations. While not responding specifically to Lem, Boris Strugatsky implicitly critiques Lem's focus when he complains: "I am quite offended that people always talk to me about the future, about aliens, about the plurality of worlds, all kinds of such rubbish, as if the Strugatskys existed totally isolated from the present day."[20] And, even more tellingly, Arkady Strugatsky would seem to target the Lem of *His Master's Voice* for criticism when he insisted in an 1987 interview:

> We simply don't need extraplanetary intelligence in itself, and never have needed it. When something extraterrestrial appears in one of our books, it's only there to show the reader that we can't put our hope in them. It doesn't matter whether they exist or not; one must always rely on oneself.[21]

To begin to understand the import of the apparent difference between Lem's and the Strugatskys' approach to first-contact stories, and to prepare the way for a closer look at *Roadside Picnic*, we need briefly to describe the context of Russian SF in which the Strugatsky brothers so clearly and so effectively write.

Russian SF

SF in Russia (since almost all Soviet SF came from Russia, I will usually simply refer to Russian SF) has roughly paralleled American SF since the 1890s, although with the notable difference that political developments in Russia and in the Soviet Union have largely dictated the nature of the genre at any given time. Marxist-Leninist SF, as shaped by prevailing political power in the Soviet Union, built on a strong tradition of Russian utopian and dystopian fiction, represented by Nikolai Chernyshevsky's utopian socialist *What Is to Be Done?* and Dostoyevski's *Notes from Underground*. Vladimir Mayakovsky's *The Bedbug* (1928; trans. 1960) and Yevgeny Zamyatin's *We* (1924) are the two early-twentieth-century classics in this tradition, and Zamyatin's dystopia is one of the great works in the history of SF. Likewise, Mikhail Bulgakov's *The Heart of a Dog* (1925) has been belatedly recognized not only as a classic satire on Soviet practice but also as a subtle investigation of the Frankenstein theme. Darko Suvin observes that the strength of the Russian tradition lies in its "blending the rationalist Western European strain of utopianism and satire with the native folk longings for abundance and justice."[22] Suvin's discussion of "Russian SF and Its Utopian Tradition" in his *Metamorphoses of Science Fiction* provides the definitive overview of Russian SF, and my summary draws heavily from him, as well as from Patrick L. McGuire's essay on Russian SF in the third edition of *Anatomy of Wonder*.[23]

Major periods or stages in Russian SF would be socialist pre-revolutionary works, 1920s SF focused largely on interplanetary adventure and somewhat parallel to American pulp SF of the period, Stalin-era SF during which the genre was crippled by Stalinist limitations, Sputnik-era SF in which the genre was resurrected, Brezhnev-Kosygin retrenchment in the 1970s, and the postperestroika era of the 1980s to the present. Suvin holds that SF really began to flourish in Russia only in the 1920s, energized as it was by "a revolutionary regime committed to industrialization and modern science as a means for achieving utopian mastery over man's destiny" (252). The spaceflight speculations of Konstantin Tsiolkovsky fueled much of the interest in SF in Russia during the 1920s, and Alexei Tolstoy's *Aelita* (1922) and *Engineer*

Garin's Death Ray (1926) were among the most popular novels of the period. The 1920s also saw the proliferation of what has been termed the "Red detective story," thrillers in which communists and capitalists struggle for control of some superweapon. Indeed, Suvin notes that some 155 SF novels were published in Soviet Russia between 1920 and 1927, a number that becomes more significant when he contrasts it with the fact that between 1930 and the magazine publication of Yefremov's *Andromeda* in 1957 there were no significant works of Russian SF.

The modern history of Russian SF can be thought of as beginning in 1956, when the Twentieth Congress of the Soviet Communist Party loosened Stalin's system of control of history and literature, and the opportunity to write less politically circumscribed SF was immediately boosted by the technological triumph of the Sputnik satellite in 1957. The resulting surge in SF attracted a new audience among the young and the intelligentsia that Suvin estimates was "probably as large if not at times larger than its American counterpart" (265). With the publication in 1957 of his far-future, visionary utopian novel *Andromeda*, Ivan Yefremov became the first leader of modern Russian SF, leading a "new wave" that actually returned Russian and Soviet SF to its classical utopian and socialist vision. In combining grand visions with a cast of characters who evolve through their mistakes and failures as well as successes, in stressing the need for personal creativity as a counter to entropy, and in advancing strong female heroines, Yefremov, suggests Suvin, may have created the "first utopia in world literature which successfully shows new characters creating and being created by a new society, that is, *the personal working out of a collective utopia*" (269). When the utopian confidence of what Suvin calls the "Yefremov era" in Soviet SF began to fade in the mid-1960s, what might be called the "Strugatsky era" began, as Arkady (who died in 1991) and Boris Strugatsky became the most popular and influential SF writers in the Soviet Union.

What is most important here for the understanding of SF as a genre is to recognize some of the ways in which Russian SF has been shaped by directives and limitations quite unlike any explicit influences on the development of American genre SF. For example, Patrick L. McGuire notes of preperestroika Russian SF that "many of the conventional situations of science fiction are 'impossible' under dialectical materialism, and so many of the favorite Western rationalizations are forbidden by censorship" (448). Moreover, as Istvan Csicsery-Ronay has explained, the "central role that a clearly defined philosophy of science plays in Soviet Marxism" has accounted for significant differences between Russian and Western SF because science was held to "prove" Marxism-Leninism, making Marxist-Leninist political practice "the only scientific approach to reality."[24]

More specifically, "cold stream" SF, dictated by the Stalinist "theory of limits," dictated that Russian SF should "solve only technological problems of the nearest future, and that it should not attempt to go beyond such limits, for only thus will it remain based on socialist realism" (Suvin, 264). Accordingly Russian SF during the rule of Stalin and for some time afterward was prohibited from any significant extrapolation and limited to serving as a propaganda shill for state-planned technology. McGuire explains:

> On top of the rules for "socialist realism," which applied to all litera-
> ture, science fiction was expected to follow a so-called near-target
> rule; it said that SF might utilize scientific developments only slightly
> in advance of reality. Ideally, indeed, it should do no more than to
> anticipate the practical application of technology now at the labora-
> tory stage. Moreover, even within these limits the officially spon-
> sored spirit of the times strongly discouraged any evocation of a
> "sense of wonder." Denunciations for "cosmopolitanism" or "mysti-
> cism" lay in wait for the writer at every step. (446)

"Warm stream" SF, including that written by the Strugatsky brothers, rejected the theory of limits. "Instead of a wretched 'close range' SF, which stayed within the limits of the scientific-popularization essay and celebrated the technological accomplishments of the near future," explains Arkady Strugatsky, "a kind of SF came along that was concerned with wide social and philosophical conclusions" (Gopman, 2). While the "theory of limits" had been substantially abandoned by the time the Strugatsky brothers began publishing in 1959, their writing struggled against its institutional successor during the Brezhnev 1970s—what Arkady Strugatsky describes as "a featureless, grey SF," explaining that "the greyer it is, the safer and quieter and the more convenient for the editor's smooth career" (Gopman, 3–4).

The Strugatsky Brothers: "Tomorrow Will Be"

Early Strugatsky works were broadly in the Yefremov tradition, featuring future history set in an optimistic time of full communism, but by the mid-1960s their utopian optimism had dimmed, reflecting growing disillusionment with Khrushchev-style communism. The cheerful confidence of *Space Apprentice* (1962), in which a young space welder stumbles into a chance to accompany and learn from the wise and humane Inspector General of the communist organization responsible for administering space exploration and development as he tours his sector, gives way to the anguished investigation of a classic no-win situation in *Hard to Be a God* (1973), in which an observer from Earth discovers that, whatever he chooses to do to intervene in a feudal world's brutal development, the consequences both for himself and the world are morally disturbing. In works such as *The Second Invasion from Mars* (1968), *Monday Begins on Saturday* (1965), *Tale of the Troika* (1968), and the *The Snail on the Slope* (1966–1968) the Strugatskys turned to ever darker satires to explore the moral implications of the extreme bureaucratization and politicization of science and of cognitive ambiguities that seemed to have no solutions. Noting this trajectory, Darko Suvin writes in the *Encyclopedia of Science Fiction*: "Over their career, the brothers moved from a comparatively sunny vision in which utopia could be aimed at in the near future to a sense that the tensions between utopian ethics and the inscrutable overwhelmingness of stasis were in fact irresolvable" (1174). Their concern with contradictions and paradoxes in human nature and their criticism of some aspects of Soviet life, however, never constituted a total rejection of "socialist hope," nor were the Strugatskys ever dissidents or anti-Soviet, even though their *The Ugly Swans* was suppressed in 1968 for its perceived criticisms of the future. Yet, as Boris Strugatsky insists in a 1990 interview with Alla Bossart, "an optimist is not someone who thinks that tomorrow will be better than today" but someone who says that tomorrow "will be," that "the future will exist" (72).

Whether the future exists apart from the present or has been already "used up" in the present is one of many questions raised by *Roadside Picnic*, one of the Strugatskys' most powerful and most troubling novels. Establishing the political context for this

1972 work, Istvan Csicsery-Ronay identifies it as "a fable of the despair of the '60's intelligentsia facing the complete destruction of the reform movement, which was betrayed—as the fable has it—not so much by the Brezhnev regime as by the moral-spiritual conditions which made that regime possible."[25] Csicsery-Ronay adds that, while the Strugatsky brothers were deeply disappointed by limits on the scientific elite under Brezhnev and were showing the influence in their work of writers such as Kafka who stressed the struggle with insurmountable obstacles, their concern in *Roadside Picnic* was not with specific political conditions so much as with "the convergence of Eastern and Western ennui, the fruit of global acquiescence to purely material satisfactions and the abdication of all higher moral purposes—the victory of 'realism' over utopian idealism" (21).

At the center of this novel is the contested explanation for six discreetly bounded Zones scattered in a line across the Earth. These Zones contain mysterious artifacts—"full empties," "itchers," "hoops," "pins," "so-sos," "rattling napkins," "black sprays"— that seem to be products of an advanced technology. The original purposes for which these objects were designed are unfathomable to Earth scientists, but military and industrial applications have been discovered for many of them, making them extremely valuable commodities. Scientific expeditions into the Zones bring out some of these artifacts, but the Zones are best exploited by a group of "stalkers," who smuggle objects out of the Zone to be sold on a lucrative black market. One of these stalkers, Red Schuhart, is the novel's protagonist, as we see him during three different periods, each of which is marked by a dangerous and disastrous foray into the Zone. Red, the uneducated "honest man," provides most of our perspective on the Zone, but his views are augmented by and contrasted with those of Pilman, a famed scientist, and Noonan, a plump and pink consummate bureaucrat.

The Zones also display physical phenomena and processes that defy Earthly understanding of natural law—directed gravity in "mosquito mange"; a "meatgrinder," a space in which a human body is simply twisted and torn apart; shadows that stretch toward the Sun; reanimated corpses; a deadly colloidal gas called "witches' jelly." Furthermore, the Zones affect humans living near them in ways no one can understand: plagues decimated inhabitants immediately surrounding the Zones and blinded many with a loud noise; when inhabitants of Harmont, a Canadian town where one of the Zones is located (the one Zone that is the focus of *Roadside Picnic*), who were alive at the time of the visitation, move away they seem to carry with them a kind of disaster effect that leads to high numbers of deaths of those around them; the Zones also seem to display a mutagen effect on children of the stalkers, who are afflicted by strange mutations, as eventually are the stalkers themselves.

Several explanations for the mysterious phenomena associated with the Zones have been advanced. No agents of the visitation were ever seen, but it has been suggested that the Zones represent an advance wave for alien contact, offering Earth the tools to make a giant technological leap and construct a device to return the alien signal. Another hypothesis is that invisible aliens reside in the Zones and are preparing humanity for the future, and, of course, some hold the view that the Zones constitute some form of invasion. However, the hypothesis privileged by the Strugatskys' title is that unknown aliens simply stopped on Earth for a picnic , leaving the Zones as a kind of cosmic litter. Pilman, a Nobel Prize-winning physicist who provides one the novel's three most sustained points of view, details this hypothesis:

> "A picnic. Picture a forest, a country road, a meadow. A car drives off the country road into the meadow, a group of young people get out of the car carrying bottles, baskets of food, transistor radios, and cameras. They light fires, pitch tents, turn on the music. In the morning they leave. The animals, birds, and insects that watched in horror through the long night creep out from their hiding places. And what do they see? Gas and oil spilled on the grass. Old spark plugs and old filters strewn around. Rags, burnt-out bulbs, and a monkey wrench left behind. Oil slicks on the pond. And of course, the usual mess— apple cores, candy wrappers, charred remains of the campfire, cans, bottles, somebody's handkerchief, somebody's penknife, torn newspapers, coins, faded flowers picked in another meadow."[26]

In Pilman's view, humanity is reduced to making sense of unfathomable detritus; when a use does seem to be found for some object or process from the Zones, it is a case of "hammering nails with microscopes."

Where Pilman's graphic analogy breaks down, however, is that the animals, birds, and insects left in the wake of a human picnic feel none of the moral and psychological devastation of humans in the wake of the alien visitation. Whatever is not known about the aliens and the Zones, what is known is that they have given rise to a Hobbesian world in which "bloodsucking" capitalists, gangsters, and shady representatives of the military-industrial complex maintain an exploitative world built on the human misery of the stalkers, who are forced by economic hopelessness to return again and again to the Zone, even as its dangers maim and kill them. The animals, birds, and insects in Pilman's analogy will not compete to profit from the litter of the picnic, will not doom each other to lives redefined by the commodification of artifacts left by the picnic, will not base economies on the dream of deriving unlimited wealth from the Zone, only to lock workers—stalkers, construction workers, chauffers—into the mean and disillusioning lower end of those economies. Meeting with his black market contacts to sell "swag" he has brought back from the Zone, Red Schuhart recoils from the human implications of the economic system that has sprung up around the Zone:

> Redrick got out on the eighth floor and walked down the thick carpet on the corridor, cozily illuminated by hidden lamps. It smelled of expensive tobacco, French perfumes, the soft natural leather of stuffed wallets, expensive ladies of the night, and solid gold cigarette cases. It reeked of everything, of the lousy fungus that was growing on the Zone, drinking on the Zone, eating, exploiting, and growing fat on the Zone and that didn't give a damn about any of it, especially about what would happen later, when it had eaten its full and gotten power, and when everything that was once in the Zone was outside the Zone. (68)

For Red, the corridors of power and plenty which he can visit only to sell his swag are already taking on an alien quality as strange as that found in the Zone; indeed, "everything that was in the Zone" has started to creep "outside the Zone," giving a peculiarly human dimension to its violent terrors.

Pilman's voice is given prominence by the Strugatskys' structure: an interview with him introduces the novel, and, while three of the novel's four other sections focus on Red Schuhart, the third section, presenting the point of view of Richard Noonan, a bureaucrat, features a lengthy conversation between Noonan and Pilman, in which Pilman offers a philosophical overview of the visitation. Despite his impressive credentials, Pilman proves to be a surprisingly passive scientist, displaying a detachment in the opening interview and an abstractness in his conversation with Noonan that make him seem more alien than human. Unlike the idealistic and utopian-minded scientist Kirill, Pilman is a skeptic, but, also unlike Kirill, Pilman is cautious enough to avoid the Zone's dangers, so his skepticism lives, while Kirill's utopianism dies in a careless accident. In his interview, Pilman seems blithely determined to specify what science has not been able to do in the 30 years since the visitation. Only the fact of the visitation itself seems of great importance to Pilman, since it proves that humanity is not alone in the universe. Declining to speculate about smaller specific discoveries connected with the Zones, Pilman also refuses to discuss the human problem of the stalkers, claiming that it, too, is not within his competence. When pressed about what his precise competence might be, Pilman implies that his work has primarily to do with keeping unauthorized information from escaping the Zones, recasting science in a containing rather than exploratory role.

Pilman's barroom conversation with Noonan, an official administering the Zone, but also with black-market ties to the military-industrial complex, is less guarded, but no less dissatisfying. When asked how the processes started with the visitation will end, Pilman shrugs that it may be a matter of luck whether or not "in pulling these chestnuts out of the fire, we may pull out something that will make life impossible not only for us, but for the entire planet" (99). As Csicsery-Ronay has pointed out, the inscrutability of the visitation and its aftermath has robbed the Pilmans of the world of their assumptions, leaving them "no science to do" and leaving Pilman, who will "of necessity become an experimental metaphysician" (27), concerned with surviving. Accordingly, concludes Csicsery-Ronay, Pilman "represents the irremediable alienation of cognition and theory from the active, irresponsible life of the post-Visitation world" (27). Abstracted from the human implications of the visitation and "not mired in the mud of life," Pilman has become such an intellectual observer that he offers no hope of providing moral authority in the postvisitation world.

Nor does Noonan, the bureaucrat, offer any hope for improving the postvisitation world. Ostensibly responsible for supplying equipment to the institute studying the Zone, Noonan is actually playing both the legal and illegal sides of the Zone-driven economies. In his unofficial and often illegal capacity he has been working to gain control of the stalker economy by breaking up the gangs of stalkers who do not deal only with him and by trying to corner the market on swag from the Zone. Noonan also has darker ties either to powerful organized crime or to the corporate structure of the military-industrial complex, which wants Zone discoveries for its own research and profit. A self-described "practical person," an organizer and administrator—the consummate bureaucrat—Noonan is an affable and decent enough individual, but he is ready to make almost any compromise to prosper in safety as a middleman in transactions pertaining to the Zone. Contemplative about human nature, Noonan is nevertheless an amoral manager who sees problems associated with the visitation largely in an organizational light. When he tells Guta, Red's wife, to remember that "there's nothing in the world that can't be fixed" (114) he does so purely in mechanical or bureaucratic terms, as unaware of the limitations of his vision as he was when discussing "the decline in morality" with the madam who ran the prostitutes at his club. If Pilman has been forced to become a metaphysical survivor, Noonan has become the ultimate economic and organizational survivor, concerned with effective managing rather than with morality.

That leaves Red to provide some kind of moral center for the Strugatskys' very troubled world, and he does, although in a way that is deeply problematized by the novel's ending. Red endures the dangerous and disillusioning life of a stalker to support his wife, Guta, and their mutated child, Monkey, who is slowly regressing to an animal-like existence. From the outset of the novel, it is clear that Red bitterly resents the "bloodsucking" social and economic system that supports the mean stalker economy. Like the Russian scientist Kirill, his idealistic mentor at the International Institute of Extraterrestrial Cultures, Red clings to the belief that the Zone can have a positive effect on humanity.

Angrily responding to a government official who is encouraging those living near the Zone to emigrate to other areas, Red insists:

"You're absolutely right. Our little town is a hole. It always has been and still is. But now it is a hole into the future. We're going to dump so much through this hole into your lousy world that everything will change in it. Life will be different. It'll be fair. Everyone will have everything that he needs. Some hole, huh? Knowledge comes through this hole. And when we have the knowledge, we'll make everyone rich, and we'll fly to the stars, and go anywhere we want. That's the kind of hole we have here." (36)

Red's words reflect the pure idealism of Kirill, but in attempting to fuel that idealism Red leads Kirill into the Zone on an official collecting trip that leads to Kirill's death. Curiously enough, Red's utopian notion of a "hole into the future" closely matches Pilman's pragmatic assessment of the visitation and Zone as "primarily a unique event that allows us to skip several steps in the process of cognition" (100). For Kilman, the Zone is a value-free opportunity, "like a trip into the future of technology."

Perhaps uniquely among stalkers, Red is known for his loyalty, even in the face of extreme danger in the Zone. During his second trip into the Zone during the novel, he risks his life to carry out one of the most despicable of his fellow stalkers, Buzzard Burbridge, who has lost his legs to the effects of witches' jelly. This second trip was undertaken to secure money for the care of Red's wife and child, and when it goes wrong, Red realizes that he has been sold out by one of his middlemen and abandons his scruples about military uses of Zone products, selling some of the potent witches' jelly, prohibited in legal research, to an illegal research facility. Agonizing over his decision to provide the witches' brew to military researchers who "can kill us all with this thing," Red despairs: "Every man for himself, only God takes care of everybody. I've had it" (81).

Red's third and final trip into the Zone takes place after he has spent several years in prison and after the regression of his daughter has become nearly complete. Buzzard Burbridge, whom Red saved on the second trip, had promised him then a map that would lead him to the Zone's most fabled object—a golden ball reputed to answer all wishes. Out of desperation, Red now thinks that the ball offers his daughter her only hope of returning to normalcy, and so he agrees to try to reach the golden ball, accompanied by Burbridge's son, Arthur. As Red and Arthur make their way toward the quarry where they expect to find the ball, Red's thoughts become more and more bitter and more and more politically reflective. The physical challenges and threats of the Zone strike him as metaphors for his life: "My whole life is like this. I'm stuck in filth and there's lightning over my head" (136). "Where have you seen a good system?" he thinks. "When have you ever seen me under a good system?"

The unspecified "you" of the above comment refers to Noonan, who had chided Red for not fitting in and going with the flow regardless of the merits or faults of the system in which he lives. Increasingly, however, during Red's third trip into the Zone "you" comes to stand for everything that has oppressed Red, the system itself. "God, its just one long brawl!" (144) he anguishes, as he determines to think his life through—to understand his condition and his options. Thinking is not something Red is used to, but he realizes that he needs to find the words to explain his situation to himself. One of the most troubling aspects of his life he must deal with stems from his grimly pragmatic knowledge that he has brought Burbridge's quite likable and decent son with him only to use him to spring the deadly "meatgrinder" phenomenon that "guards" the golden ball. Red, who has been characterized by his visceral determination to save lives in the Zone, does nothing to stop the trusting Arthur as he runs to his death in the meatgrinder. Arthur's final excited words reflect the utopianism of the dead Kirill, as he encounters death while joyfully shouting: "[H]appiness for everybody!... Free!... As much as you want!... Everybody come here!... There's enough for everybody! Nobody will leave unsatisfied!... Free!... Happiness!... Free!" (143). At best, it seems as if Red has decided to sacrifice Burbridge's child so that he might save his own; at worst, it seems that he may have sunk into the animalistic bloodsucking immorality he had so long opposed. When Red reaches the ball, his frustration at not having the right words with which to think about his situation only increases, and the last words in *Roadside Picnic*, addressed to the ball or God or something are:

> "I am an animal, you see that. I don't have the words, they didn't teach me the words. I don't know how to think, the bastards didn't

let me learn how to think. But if you really are . . . all-powerful . . . all-knowing . . . then you figure it out! Look into my heart. I know that everything you need is in there. It has to be. I never sold my soul to anyone! It's mine, it's human! You take from me what it is I want . . . it just can't be that I would want something bad! Damn it all, I can't think of anything except those words of his . . . 'HAPPINESS FOR EVERYBODY, FREE, AND NO ONE WILL GO AWAY UNSATIS-FIED!'" (145)

Red's final inarticulate anguish can be interpreted either as the bleakest of endings or as a small sign of hope. We have no way of knowing whether the "wish machine" will grant his utopian plea or, for that matter, whether it might—in the tradition of fairy tales and of systems theory—grant the wish, only to accompany it with unexpected and terrible "side-effects." That Red seems to have sacrificed some of his personal integrity to reach the ball may be a sign of his unworthiness or it may be a sign of the need to reach utopian goals through complicated and painful choices. That the "golden ball" turns out to be copper-colored is also a troubling hint that this particular fairy tale may not come true. There is evidence, however, to suggest that Red's quest through-out the novel has uniquely prepared him for this moment and left it to him to utter humanity's most fervent wish. He may not have arrived at the eloquence of a Kirill or the technical sophisti-cation of a Pilman, but as Csicsery-Ronay concludes, "he appears to be the last man capable of restoring spiritual content in the age of absolute demoralization" (33). "Left alone with Red's wish," Csicsery-Ronay continues, "the reader must also participate in Red's exit into the ball, out of the narrative and into personal commitment or moral death." What is clear is that only Red can redeem the Zone left from the visitation, somehow using his own troubled awakening to transform its barrenness into another of SF's zones of possibility.

The question of the meaning of Red's final wish argues for *Roadside Picnic*'s status as great literature, as does the book's com-plicated restructuring of the fairy tale paradigm, but the Stru-gatsky brothers also use this novel to broach a number of issues more specific to SF. The most basic of these is the interrogation of the myth of technology, metonymically invoked by the magical artifacts left behind by the unseen visitors. One reason, argues Csicsery-Ronay, why the visitors do not need to be seen is that we already see them whenever we look in the mirror—"they are us: they are our image of our own future" (30). He explains:

> One reason why the Visitors are absent is that the Visitation itself is an image of the scientific-technological explosion, a process that has increasingly come to seem "subjectless"—an impersonal, indifferent, objective evolution blindly operating according to its own runaway feedback, autonomous of the human desires that created its conditions. The dangers the extraterrestrial artifacts pose to human society are clearly the same as those posed by the irrational military and commercial use of contemporary terrestrial technology. (29)

In this sense, Pilman's theory of the roadside picnic, says Csicsery-Ronay, "refers not so much to the landing of extraterrestrials as to the way humanity in the contemporary world uses its own technology—as if it, too, were an alien species that might wish at some future time to fly from a blasted zone of its own making." Of course, in its critique of a blind worship of science and technology, *Roadside Picnic* can also be seen to join the tradition of self-reflexive works of SF that interrogate the genre's own assumptions. When Red admits to Noonan, "I sort of fell behind science a bit" (118), he reminds us that sometimes such a distancing can provide a vital new perspective.

Other Earth Traditions: First Contact Begins at Home

While Lem and the Strugatskys are arguably the most important SF writers outside of the genre tradition of American and British SF, it is important to remember that neither they nor the tradition of "socialist hope" from which their writing emerged can adequately suggest the range of SF written in other countries. The most comprehensive introduction to foreign-language SF remains the third edition of Neil Barron's *Anatomy of Wonder*, which contains excellent overviews of German, French, Russian, Japanese, Italian, Danish, Swedish, Norwegian, Dutch, Belgian, Romanian, Yugoslav, and Hebrew SF. In addition to these countries, SF in the People's Republic of China, Australia, and Canada deserves attention and can be sampled in Wu Dingbo's and Patrick Murphy's *Science Fiction from China* (1989), Peter McNamara's and Margaret Winch's *Alien Shores: A Landmark Collection of Australian*

Science Fiction (1994), and David G. Hartwell and Glenn Grant's *Northern Stars: The Anthology of Canadian Science Fiction* (1994). Hartwell and Grant's anthology pairs nicely with David Ketterer's excellent study *Canadian Science Fiction and Fantasy* (1992). Other anthologies that suggest some of the variations in world SF are Donald A. Wollheim's *The Best from the Rest of the World: European Science Fiction* (1976), Darko Suvin's *Other Worlds, Other Seas: Science-Fiction Stories from Socialist Countries* (1970), Brian Aldiss and Sam J. Lundwall's *The Penguin World Omnibus of Science Fiction* (1986), and David G. Hartwell's *The World Treasury of Science Fiction* (1989).

Perhaps most glaringly missing from my own truncated account of "world" SF is a consideration of SF in Japan, where cyberpunk has become a significant cultural as well as a literary-critical phenomenon. In a number of influential essays, Takayuki Tatsumi, Japan's foremost scholar of cyberpunk, offers excellent insight into the ways in which Japanese popular culture and cyberpunk have intertwined. Of particular interest are his overview of cyberpunk in *Hayakawa's SFM*, his "Graffiti's Rainbow" columns in *Science Fiction Eye,* and his "The Japanese Reflection of Mirrorshades" in Larry McCaffery's *Storming the Reality Studio.* A strong sample of Japanese SF not limited to cyberpunk can be found in John L. Apostolou and Martin H. Greenberg (eds.), *The Best Japanese Science Fiction Stories* (1989).

Chapter Four

COUNTERCULTURES OF SCIENCE FICTION—RESISTING GENRE

That was my problem then and it's my problem now: I have a bad attitude. In a nutshell, I fear authority but at the same time I resent it—the authority *and* my own fear—so I rebel. And writing science fiction is a way to rebel. . . . And so I write. I want to write about people I love, and put them into a fictional world spun out of my own mind, not the world we actually have, because the world we actually have does not meet my standards. Okay, so I should revise my standards, I'm out of step. I should yield to reality. I have *never* yielded to reality. That's what science fiction is all about.

Philip K. Dick, "Now Wait for This Year"

One can wonder why a literature that prides itself on exploring alternatives or assumptions counter to what we normally believe has not been more concerned with the roles of women in the future. There are two possible answers, although neither excludes the other. Either science fiction is not as daring or original as some of its practitioners would like to believe, this being more a worthy ideal than a reality; or this literature, designed to question our assumptions, cannot help reflecting how very deeply certain prejudices are ingrained—despite its sometimes successful efforts at imaginative liberation from time and place.

Pamela Sargent, from her introduction to *Women of Wonder*

Countertraditions

Following a spaceliner disaster, a small group of survivors land on an uncharted and barely habitable planet. The group immediately begins planning for a long stay, even going so far as to initiate a pseudoscientific breeding program to provide a second generation dedicated to building "civilization" on the new planet. One of the group, however, a woman, refuses to accede to the fantasy of survival and colonization, pragmatically noting that once emergency food is exhausted the planet offers them no sources of nourishment. She simply wishes to be left out of the group's plans, choosing to die on her own terms. When the group refuses to allow her dissent, she kills the others to maintain her independence and then, eventually, commits suicide.

Following the assembly of a group of elite psionic-talented professionals who contract with commercial organizations to counter the psionic powers employed against them by other businesses, a bomb seems to kill the owner of the anti-psi service and his senior employee sets out to track down those responsible for the murder. The employee is aided by his dead former employer, whose consciousness remains at least temporarily accessible in a kind of half-life. But the material world around the employee seems to be reverting to the past, slipping from 1992 back to 1939, and survivors of the bomb blast start aging and dying at a vastly accelerated rate. As the employee fights against a voracious entropy that threatens to dissolve his world and end his life, he gradually discovers that *he* may be the one who died in the bomb blast, that his employer may have been the survivor, and that the employer may be the one accessing his former employee's consciousness. The novel that began with the effort to find a murderer has turned into a question of who in fact was murdered, and the answer to that question depends on whether the employee's reality or that of the employer holds sway for the reader. What seemed to be a "who done it" has inexorably been swallowed by an ontological "what is it"; questions about events in reality have devolved into questions about the nature of reality itself.

Neither of the above scenarios "works" in the way a reader of SF before 1960 would be likely to recognize. Neither features the positivism of early genre SF, neither invokes a sense of celebratory wonder, neither valorizes science or technology, and neither presents a world in which problems can be understood, much less solved. Clearly, if these two stories are accepted as science fiction, then our understanding of science fiction must be expansive or flexible enough to envision a genre that encompasses its own antithesis, the inversion of its ostensible values and assumptions. And, indeed, that is the case, as these crude summaries are of Joanna Russ's *We Who Are About To . . .* (1977) and Philip K. Dick's *Ubik* (1969), two celebrated novels by two of modern SF's most influential writers. To understand the importance of Dick and Russ, both individually and as representatives of other writers who share their rejection of genre assumptions, it is necessary to understand some of the ways in which SF since 1900 has generated and grown from developments that call into question or deconstruct its basic assumptions and formulae.

Science fiction has always been an oppositional literature, at least in part. At its most basic level, in relying on alternative or hypothetical propositions about reality, science fiction challenges the hegemony of realist literature, although it relies on realist techniques to glove its fantastic elements with the rhetoric of rationality. On a slightly more ideological level, science fiction consistently opposes limitations on knowledge and the prevailing limitations of science, suggesting always that more can be discovered, more can be known, more can be done. Challenging prevailing wisdom and received ideas is the modus operandi of most SF stories, and the genre has long prided itself on the radical parallax that seems an indispensable aspect of science fiction thinking. Utopian and dystopian SF works regularly interrogate political and social norms, frequently, if not usually, advancing a generally libertarian philosophy that mistrusts authority in all its official guises. And yet, for all its trappings of iconoclasm, SF in the twentieth century has also been uncritically supportive of far too many totalizing systems of belief and has blithely accepted far too many cultural constructions as immutable aspects of reality.

While questioning particular systems of authority, SF, for the most part, has been strongly invested in accepting the authority of science at some ultimate level—the idea that while individual SF stories may bend the "laws" of science, those laws still constitute reality. That there is some form of objective reality and that such a reality is knowable are propositions underlying the vast majority of SF stories. And, while many features of that objective reality have been questioned by SF, several others have been accepted as so "natural" as to be almost physical laws, inescapable "cold equations." As Jenny Wolmark has recently pointed out, the frequent if not pervasive assumption in SF narratives has been that "meanings are assumed to be both fixed and universal," ironically aligning "the literature of change" with an essentialism that denies change in "human nature."[1] The relations between the sexes and the construction of gender are perhaps most noteworthy in this respect, with much of twentieth-century SF able to imagine almost anything *but* significantly different gender roles and sexual stereotypes, able to embrace any change but that in the traditional relationships between men and women. "For all its speculation on the consequences of scientific development," concludes Sarah Lefanu, "science fiction has been notably silent on the concomitant subject of social development, particularly as regards the personal and political relationships between women and men."[2]

Accordingly, one of the most significant developments in twentieth-century SF has been the appearance of writers and writing that insist on turning the lens of change on SF itself, on its confidence in a knowable and objective reality, and on its ostensible confidence in the immutability of gender relations. This "countertradition" has become stronger as the century has progressed. Indeed, it may by now have supplanted the objective and essentialist positions it challenged, particularly since the lessons of quantum physics more and more seem to support a worldview that embraces indeterminacy as a basic principle. Certainly the list of contemporary writers who would be strongly associated with this "countertradition" would be quite long, including a large number of both British and American New Wave writers, a large number of SF's women writers, and even a number of "hard SF" writers such as Gregory Benford. My concern in this chapter, however, is with two of the most influential sources of this countertradition—Philip K. Dick, for his tireless assaults on the comfortable assumption of an objective reality, and Joanna Russ, as one important representative of the large and growing number of feminist SF writers who, starting in the 1960s and 1970s, used science fiction to question the "naturalness" of sexual difference and the ways in which that difference was socially constructed. Indeed, it might be argued that, without the interventions of Dick's sometimes maddening and always troubling writing and without the increasingly incisive deconstructions of gender in feminist SF, the genre would not have maintained much, if any, cultural authority in a post-Campbellian world. At any rate, no understanding of science fiction since 1900 would be complete without recognizing the importance of the contributions made by Philip K. Dick and by women and feminist writers such as Pamela Sargent, James Tiptree Jr. (Alice Sheldon), Joanna Russ, Ursula K. Le Guin, and Octavia Butler.

Philip K. Dick and the Breakdown of Reality

No single career better emblemizes the strengths and the weaknesses of twentieth-century SF than that of Philip K. Dick. Heinlein may have been the writer singly most responsible for selling the genre to the public, but Dick was the writer who pointed the way to the genre's full potential for cultural authority. In over 40 novels and more than 100 short stories he helped turn SF's extrapolation away from technological and scientific issues toward the human and social implications of those issues, away from the consensus ideology of the future associated with Campbellian SF and toward the more oppositional, more critical stance of contemporary SF. Many of his works were written so hastily and under such commercial pressure that they contain glaring inconsistencies and unmistakable signs of careless writing. However, even Dick's weakest stories often contain stunningly revelatory moments, while his strongest works, including *The Man in the High Castle* (1962), *Ubik* (1969), *Do Androids Dream of Electric Sheep?* (1968) (renamed *Blade Runner* after the 1982 movie), *The Three Stigmata of Palmer Eldritch* (1965), and *VALIS* (1981), are among the most powerful produced in SF or in any other modern literary mode. That literary critic Fredric Jameson would refer to him as "the Shakespeare of science fiction" begins to suggest the special status Dick has achieved within the field.[3] And, that Dick is not better known as one of the major postwar American novelists suggests the persisting stigmatizing power of being associated with science fiction.[4]

111

Dick provided a transition between the social satire fore-grounded in 1950s SF such as Pohl's and Kornbluth's *The Space Merchants* and the almost exclusively interior-focused writing of the New Wave, with the noted SF writer and Dick critic Kim Stanley Robinson claiming that "single-handedly he may have wrought as many changes in the nature of the genre as did all of the New Wave."[5] *The Encyclopedia of Science Fiction* rates Dick as one of the two or three most important writers in twentieth-century U.S. science fiction, and critics such as Stanislaw Lem and Darko Suvin, who generally have nothing kind to say about genre SF, single Dick out as the writer of genius who somehow manages to rise above the limitations of the genre. Indeed, Thomas M. Disch, one of America's most distinguished SF writers, who rivals Lem in his scathing criticism of much of the genre, states that his rule-of-thumb test for determining how well other readers' views of SF match his own is simply to find out whether they "know—and admire—the work of Dick."[6] All of Dick's champions acknowledge that his writing is frequently flawed (Disch notes that Dick is "capable of whole chapters of turgid prose and of bloopers so grandiose you may wonder, momentarily, whether they're not just his little way of winking at his fellow-laborers in the pulps"), but they also acknowledge that his finest works achieve a haunting, unsettling quality rarely found in literature of any sort.[7] Ursula K. Le Guin once called Dick our "home-grown Borges," and indeed, it is hard to read Dick without being reminded much more of Borges and Kafka and Nabokov than of Heinlein, Clarke, and Asimov.

Dick either introduced to genre SF or most effectively fore-grounded the serious contemplation of the nature of evil, the serious contemplation of morality, the serious contemplation of death, metaphysical speculation, and an obsession with ontology. These issues had previously appeared in SF, but only in the service of rationalizing plots and advancing action, as something to be assumed rather than interrogated. Trying to capture the essence of Dick's originality, Brian Aldiss, writing in his *Trillion Year Spree*, notes of his writing:

> We can never be certain what is ground-level reality, and yet we never tire of these webs of maya—of illusion. What *is* unwavering in Dick's work is his moral sensibility. He recognizes and portrays the

actuality of evil: a kind of being, lacking in empathy, sympathy or any sense of common humanity—be that being android, psychotic junkie, autistic, paranoid or fascist. (330)

Dick unabashedly embraced the icons and tropes of science fiction, but consistently redirected his readers' concerns from the scientific and technological aspects of those tropes and icons to their political and metaphysical implications. "And yet Dick is a science fiction writer," concludes Le Guin, "not borrowing the trappings to deck out old nonsense with shiny chromium fittings, but using the new metaphors because he needs them; using them with power and beauty, because they are the language appropriate to what he wants to say, to us, about ourselves."[8]

For John Campbell (Don A. Stuart) in "Twilight," entropy served to emphasize the immutability of physical law and as an excuse for imagining a future in which incredibly advanced technology remained as a tribute to human ingenuity. For Pamela Zoline in "The Heat Death of the Universe," entropy became real as a psychological condition, a universal law given a very specific application. For Philip K. Dick, however, entropy is neither physical nor psychological, but moral, emblemizing evil and offering the most important challenge to human courage. For him, SF was simply the best way to get at the fundamental questions of existence, and he consistently found ways to refocus the literature of rationality and order on the breakdown of order at all levels of being. And, while nothing in the above paragraph even hints at it, Dick's fiction is also usually humorous, and frequently outlandishly funny.

While the above themes have been uniformly noted by Dick scholars, what has not been given much attention is the fact that these themes also function self-reflexively to question the nature of writing itself. Indeed, had Dick not so firmly grounded his novels in the traditions of genre SF, he would almost certainly have been seen as an important member of the metafictional movement of the 1960s. Dick's novels question reality-building and the difference between originals and imitations in ways with obvious implications for fiction writing. Even more explicitly, his *The Man in the High Castle* implicates art in the construction of reality, featuring a novel-within-the-novel that presents a history much closer to our own than the alternate history of the frame novel, while also offering a detailed investigation of aesthetics. As Dick has explained, one of his purposes in writing such a fiction was to show how the subjective world of one powerful person can infringe on the world of another person, thus exerting the greatest power one human being can exert over others. Of course, this "greatest power one human can exert over others" is precisely the power of effective novelists whose literary semblances momentarily displace the referential reality of their readers.

Another of the reasons for Dick's importance is that he was arguably the first genre SF writer whose works invited and rewarded analysis driven by theory that was not SF-related. While Dick was, in one sense, a prototypal 1960s novelist, whose novels reflected the drugs, antiauthoritarianism, and counterculture paranoia of his time, Dick's novels also raise most of the salient issues of postmodernism, consistently foreground basic aesthetic issues, and support a strong critique of capitalism. Carl Freedman has argued that "the defining characteristics of Dick's fictional worlds are commodities and conspiracies," and Dick's fascination with economic reality usually suggests that commodities and conspiracies are inextricably related.[9] In a rambling letter to the FBI, Dick denounced Peter Fitting for attempting to impose a Marxist reading on his works, but Fitting's claim that Dick's work subverts the repressive system of capitalism in general as well as the ideological assumptions of the representational novel remains highly persuasive.[10]

Brian Aldiss may slightly overstate the case when he claims that all of Dick's novels "are one novel, a fatidical *A la recherche du temps perfide*," but it is hard not to think of a general "Dickian Universe" as more important than the particulars of his individual works (Aldiss, 329). Comparing Dick to Dickens, Le Guin has observed that the impact of both lies in the "powerful personal psychic imprint" of their works more than in plot or character (Le Guin, 34). Three main and interrelated themes are explored again and again in Dick's writing: the multiple and subjective nature of reality, the distinction between human and machine, original and simulacrum, and—at the end of his career—the explicit search for god. His best known novel, *The Man in the High Castle*, and perhaps his most enigmatic, *Ubik*, both question the nature of reality by presenting semblances in which what Dick's characters think is reality seems instead to be a fiction or pseudoworld constructed by some other person or entity whose own "reality" seems likely to be yet another construct. These reality constructs or alternate realities may be the product of art, technology, advertising, or, in the case of *The Three Stigmata of Palmer Eldritch*, of mind-altering drugs. For Dick, as Norman Spinrad reminds us, "in a very real sense all realities are altered realities, one from another."[11] All of Dick's works are concerned with distinguishing between "the spiritless ersatz and the humanly real," but this theme finds its most dramatic emblem in the distinction between human and machine or human and android, a distinction brilliantly explored in *Do Androids Dream of Electric Sheep?* And, while all of Dick's works can be read as part of a search for the numinous, his final novels, *VALIS* and *The Divine Invasion*, literalized the metaphysical questioning of earlier works, presenting an overtly religious search for divinity.

Aldiss describes the "multidextrous" Dickian ur-novel as "elegant, surprising, and witty, spilling out disconcerting artifacts, scarecrow people, exiles, street-wise teenage girls, Fabergé animals, robots with ill-consciences and bizarre but friendly aliens" (329). Focusing on Dick's protagonists, Norman Spinrad observes that all "are not really movers and shapers but find themselves placed in a central role that requires from them heroism of one kind or another. And they are all real people with real jobs that mean something to them and with real and troubled personal lives and relationships of one kind or another" (207). John Huntington offers a similar list of motifs in which Dick seems intensely invested in work after work: " . . . the difficult or broken marriages; the high expectation for the effect of art and holy books; the ambiguous, authoritarian father figures who most often appear as corporation executives; the harried everyman figures trapped in compromises; entropic decline; and—everywhere—imitations, fakes, people or things which are not what they seem."[12] And part of the deception of Dick's novels is that their science fictional aspects are never more than a means to an end, never the object of inquiry into or speculation about science or technology, but always a vehicle for more-basic questions. What is unique in Dick's fiction, as Kim Stanley Robinson has observed, is not the novum or icon or element that makes each work science fiction, but the odd and frequently excessive-seeming combination of these elements. Ironically, as Michael Bishop sums up an oft-observed phenomenon in Dick's writing, "the ambiguity and intentional irreality of Dick's fictional universes imbue them, para-doxically, with an off-center *life-likeness*."[13] Furthermore, Robinson claims that as a general rule, Dick "reverses the value of any element that was given a simplistic positive value in the Golden Age" (32–33), a practice most dramatically evident in Dick's description of the madly evil Nazi teleology in *The Man in the High Castle* in terms that could easily apply to that of golden age SF.

The Man in the High Castle offers a compendium of most of the familiar features of Dick's novels, with the exception that its characters are richly drawn, certainly among the most fully developed in all of Dick's writing, if not, as Robinson has claimed, among all of science fiction. Set in an alternate world where Germany and Japan have won World War II, this novel opposes the evil of the Nazis to the surprisingly benign and philosophical Japanese. The United States has been divided into three zones, with the West coast occupied by the Japanese and the East by the Nazis, with a collision between these two powers growing imminent. The Nazis pursue outer space and racial genocide with equal fervor and success, having colonized Mars, while using nuclear weapons to kill most of the population of Africa. Against this backdrop of sweeping events, Dick's characters are markedly insignificant: Mr. Tagomi, a Japanese trade official in San Francisco, is a low-level bureaucrat, Robert Childan is an obsequious and petty rare artifacts dealer, Frank Frink is a Jewish artisan, his ex-wife Juliana is a waitress. Although the lives of these characters briefly intersect with those of a German officer plotting against the Nazi regime and a Nazi assassin, their actions do not make much difference to the world at large. What these characters do accomplish, however, is a kind of courageous dignity in their own lives, illustrating Dick's central concern with people who are weak, even "losers," who nevertheless manage to survive.

In the central Rocky Mountain zone between the two occupiers lives "the man in the high castle," the novelist Abendsen, who in fact does not live in a high castle and who may not be responsible for the striking premise of his suppressed novel, since he wrote it with the assistance of the I Ching (just as Dick claims to have written *Man* with the I Ching's assistance). While this novel presents a history that is closer to that we know, it also contains significant differences, leaving the reader to consider no fewer than three realities: the reader's, that of the semblance of *The Man in the High Castle*, and that of the semblance of *The Grasshopper Lies Heavy*. Moreover, these three realities interpenetrate in several ways, including a moment in *Man* when one of its focus characters seems to meditate into a kind of fugue state in which he "sees" not the occupied San Francisco of Dick's semblance but the polluted and freeway-marred San Francisco that would be most familiar to Dick's readers. Mark Rose calls attention to the fact that Dick's *The Man in the High Castle* so recontextualizes history within layers of fiction as to question "the very idea of tangible, objective history" and, in so doing, "becomes a self-reflexive meditation not only upon the alternate history as a form but implicitly upon all science fiction narratives concerned with the meaning of time."[14]

Although *The Man in the High Castle* is undoubtedly Dick's best known novel (even though the movie *Blade Runner* effectively invokes some of the issues central to *Do Androids Dream of Electric Sheep?*), and the only one of his novels to win a Hugo award, the book I want to examine most closely is *Ubik*, a novel considered by some a masterpiece and by others "that magnificent but flawed novel," or a "heroic failure." The diversity of responses here is understandable, since *Ubik* reveals the uniquely indeterminate extreme of Dick's relationship to his readers. *Ubik* offers, as Michael Bishop so diplomatically puts it, a narrative "not necessarily reducible to a single comprehensive diagnosis" (141). Its title refers to an enigmatic substance that functions in the narrative as a kind of universal reality rehabilitator, a principle of stability and permanence, an antidote to entropy. Sometimes treated as a product, a kind of universal commodity, in satiric advertisement copy at the beginning of each chapter, Ubik appears in the narrative as an aerosol spray that can reverse the reversion of time and slippage of reality that so threaten the characters in this novel. And yet, as a final "ad" makes clear, Ubik the product functions metonymically for the most fundamental and vital of all processes:

> I am Ubik. Before the universe was, I am. I made the suns. I made the worlds. I created the lives and the places they inhabit; I move them

here, I put them there. They go as I say, they do as I tell them. I am the word and my name is never spoken, the name which no one knows. I am called Ubik, but that is not my name. I am. I shall always be.[15]

Of course, within the universe of a work of fiction, Ubik also perfectly describes the writer, and many of the questions about the nature of reality confronted by Dick's characters in this novel are also questions about the nature of fiction that confront Dick's readers.

The novel is set in the future of 1992, just over 20 years beyond the time of its writing. This future is distinguished by two major departures from conventional reality: a state between life and death has been discovered, a time when the consciousnesses of the cryonically preserved deceased can be technologically contacted. People in this half-life can communicate with the living, but only for a limited time, as their consciousnesses "run down" like depleted batteries, and/or the deceased inexorably "move" toward rebirth in a new womb, apparently confirming the process specified in the *Tibetan Book of the Dead*. As one of Dick's characters acknowledges, this "half-life experience was real and it had made theologians out of all of them." The second change suggests a world in which psionic talents, people with several distinct kinds of parapsychological powers, have been commodified, incorporated into the business world in ways that their talents can further corporate success. Psionic talents, however, fall into two major categories: some talents can make things happen or predict the future, while a second group can only counter or nullify the talent of the first. This second group of talents, called inertials, has been employed by "prudence organizations," who contract with companies to insure that other companies will not gain a competitive advantage by employing psi talents. The leading psi organization is owned by Hollis, while the leading prudence organization is owned and led by Glen Runciter. As the novel opens, Runciter's organization is scrambling to figure out where Hollis's top operatives have disappeared to, assuming that they have been secretly assembled somewhere for a major project.

There is a third respect in which the world of *Ubik* is significantly different, insofar as commodification has accelerated to the point where practically everything, including front doors to apartments, has become coin-operated. This by-no-means-fantastic extrapolation is crucial to Dick's narrative both in formal terms and as a clue to its ultimate interpretation. It is significant to note that the obsessive foregrounding of Joe Chip's money troubles creates a level of economic reality that remains unchanged throughout the varying and contesting levels of reality in the novel; whether he is alive or in half-life, Joe Chip never has enough money, and it is only when he is given a free lifetime supply of the reality-maintaining Ubik that he gains any sense of equilibrium.

The action of the novel seems to divide into two parts, the first consisting of events leading up to Runciter's inertials' being lured to the moon, where they and Runciter are the victims of a humanoid bomb trap set for them by Hollis. Following the bomb blast the events of the novel become harder to follow as the reality of each event tends to be undermined or supplanted by the suggestion that reality is constantly being manipulated. Of course, in a novel where so many seeming dualities are confused, if not deconstructed, by Dick's writing, it is probably a mistake to assume that the events of the novel can so neatly be divided in two. Although life and death have been blurred by the concept of half-life and past and present have been blurred by the new psionic talent of Pat, a mysterious girl who attaches herself to Runciter's top assistant Joe Chip, a remarkable number of dualisms seem to organize this narrative. Psionic talents have been dualized as positive and inertial and psionic organizations have been reduced to the competition between those headed by Hollis and Runciter; and the Runciter organization has been constructed as the result of teamwork first between Glen Runciter and Ella, his wife who assists him from half-life, and then between Runciter and his top field tester of psionic talent, Joe Chip. Yet each of these seemingly fixed dualisms begins to break down in some way as Dick's story progresses.

One plausible description of the action of *Ubik* would be to say that Runciter's and his anti-psi agents are lured to the Moon by Hollis and there some or all are all killed by a bomb and some are all are gotten into cold-pacs soon enough to preserve their consciousnesses in half-life. At first it seems that Runciter is the only one to die in the blast and that Joe Chip and the others return him to Earth where he can be placed in the same half-life morato-rium as his wife. However, the reality of the survivors soon seems to be regressing to earlier times, and one by one they seem to be aging and dying at a fantastically accelerated rate. Gradu-ally, the possibility occurs to these survivors that they may have been the casualties in the bomb blast, that they may be in cold-pac half-life, that Glen Runciter may have been the only survivor, and that Runciter is now trying to contact them. When a message to Joe Chip, ostensibly from Runciter, appears as graffiti on a bathroom wall, this hypothesis seems to be confirmed. The mes-sage, however, raises new questions through both its unusual location and its unusual form: "Jump in the urinal and stand on your head. I'm the one that's alive. You're all dead" (120). In fact, by the time Runciter seems to manage to appear to Joe Chip, it is as clear as anything ever becomes in *Ubik* that Runciter only the-orizes that he is alive and Joe dead, and his theory fails to explain a number of odd phenonomena. And, by the novel's end, one of the initial signs that Runciter was outside the cold-pac trying to communicate with the half-live Joe Chip—the appearance of Runciter's profile on Joe's money—has been completely inverted, as Joe's profile begins to appear on Runciter's money.

In this fashion, the reader is left with no way of confidently determining what the baseline semblance of the novel really is—whether Joe Chip has been living (or half-living) in a pseudo-world "reality" essentially controlled by Runciter, whether Runciter has been living (or half-living) in a pseudoworld "real-ity" essentially controlled by Joe, or whether both are living (or half-living) in a pseudoworld "reality" structured by the conflict between the protective half-life consciousness of Runciter's wife Ella and the malicious and devouring half-life consciousness of a teenager named Jory. Further complicating our attempts to make sense of this jumble of competing "realities" is the presence in the novel of an enigmatic young woman, Pat Conley, who may have been planted in Runciter's organization by Hollis. Pat has the unique antitalent of being able to recast the present by tinkering with alternate possible futures as they existed in the past. She clearly shifts the present at least twice in the novel, and there is no way of determining whether or not she changes events at other times. Moreover, the novel swells with absurd and incon-gruous elements that would make "sense" only if part of the strange logic of a dream. Characters wear outlandish costumes such as a "tweed toga, loafers, crimson sash and a purple airplane-propeller beanie" and react to events in an incomprehensible manner. When what seems to be the wealthy industrialist who has hired the Runciter inertials to rid his company of psionic infiltrators suddenly floats to the ceiling, Runciter's reaction is so calm as to be insane:

> "I've heard of this," Runciter said to Joe. "It's a self-destruct humanoid bomb. Help me get everybody out of here. They just now put it on auto; that's why it floated upward" (167).

An insistent foregrounding of ominous elevators, a preoccupation with coins and money, and a number of small inconsistencies also seem more compatible with the peculiar illogic of dreams than with any familiar logic of reality.

Accordingly, there is no way in which any interpretation of the events of this novel can persuasively rule out other possibilities. This may be the result of sloppiness and inconsistency on Dick's part, a possibility supported by the presence of sloppy and inconsistent writing in enough of his other works and noted by even his staunchest supporters. However, in a wonderfully ironic, even Dickian paradox, the structuring principle of *Ubik* is clearly one that would have been violated by consistency and logical relationships; in a novel stressing the multiplexity of reality the presentation of events that can be reconciled in a single view of reality would itself be a supremely careless act. Far more likely is Norman Spinrad's explanation that Dick's plots are deliberately contradictory in order to maintain the indeterminacy at the heart of his novels (Bishop, 138).

John Huntington offers an even more intriguing rationale, suggesting that the hectic pace and structure of Dick's writing may result in part from Dick's attempts to follow A. E. van Vogt's formula for introducing a new idea every 800 words. Dick has himself claimed: "A lot of what I wrote, which looks like the result of taking acid, is really the result of taking van Vogt very seriously" (cited in Huntington, 154). And what Dick seems to have taken most seriously is precisely what many readers of van Vogt most criticize—his loose ends, his unexplained puzzles, a sense of mystery in the universe.

This fascination with and allegiance to van Vogt has prompted Thomas M. Disch to quip that, in a sense, Dick's *Solar Lottery* "is van Vogt's best novel." If van Vogt's mechanical shifts and reversals every 800 words in *The World of Null-A* gave Dick a glimpse of the numinous, Dick's not quite so programmatic reversals and contradictions in *Ubik* give his readers fits but also free them in some ways from ideologically normalized expectations, much as does the cut-up method employed by William Burroughs. As Huntington reminds us, "the absence of conscious intent does not thereby render the thought of the narrative trivial." "In fact," he concludes "it may well be argued that it is precisely this freedom from controlling rational structures—especially insofar as such structures are really ideologically-weighted conventions—that gives Dick's writings their value" (159). Trapped in what Huntington explains as "the enigma of authenticity" in the act of his own writing as well as in the semblances of his fictions, Dick's search for the authentic led him to some of the most experimental writing in postwar American fiction. That literary critics focused on the "mainstream" by and large failed to notice this is understandable; that SF critics were so slow to catch on is less easy to forgive.

What does seem clear is that certain principles remain constant in the Dickian universe, even if reality is subjective and ever-changing. Regardless of who is actually alive and who dead, the half-life pseudoworld of *Ubik* is characterized by two conflicting processes, one a deterioration of reality, "a going-out-of-existence," the other a replenishment, "a coming-into-existence." The first process, one of inexorable decay, gives us Dick's view of entropy, and it seems that entropy and evil are very similar, if not coterminous, in Dick's value system. The second process, the struggle against entropy, is emblemized by the mysterious product Ubik, but in a world that has been hypercommodified, Dick's association of "good" with a product makes little sense. Instead, Ubik seems more likely a convenient emblem for the essential human courage that fights against entropy throughout the novel. John Huntington offers the most eloquent overview of the inherently contradictory nature of Dick's writing when he concludes: "Seeking wisdom, we find a wiseguy; but just when we are ready to treat his novels as only a game, they radiate profundity" (Huntington, 159).

Feminist SF and the
Breakdown of Patriarchal Assumptions

Even though the first work of modern science fiction, *Frankenstein*, was written by a woman and even though feminist analysis best explains its haunting strengths, women characters figure in that novel only as victims. The early history of science fiction does not change this picture much: women play no significant roles in Verne's fiction, and the closest thing to a major female character in Wells is Weena in *The Time Machine*. Moreover, when women have figured in early science fiction they have invariably been used to reinforce patriarchal stereotypes, as is the case in "Helen O'Loy," where a "female" robot proves her humanity by choosing to die with her human husband. Other unfortunate examples are only too easy to find, whether they illustrate out-and-out misogyny or somewhat less extreme masculinist values. In his *Skylark of Space*, for example, E. E. "Doc" Smith casually explains of one of his male protagonists: "As for women, Crane frankly avoided them, partly because his greatest interests in life were things in which women had neither interest nor place, but mostly because he had for years been the prime target of the man-hunting debutantes and the matchmaking mothers of three continents." Or, consider the assumptions underlying this description by A. E. van Vogt in *War Against the Rull*: "She seemed to be in her early thirties and she had blue eyes and a good-looking face and figure, but there was an unfeminine firmness in her expression that detracted from what would otherwise have been great beauty." Somewhat more oblique, but perhaps most telling of all of the attitude toward women assumed in early genre SF, is the example of Murray Leinster's "First Contact," in which a male crew member from Earth finally convinces himself that the aliens "are just like us" because he has spent two hours exchanging "dirty jokes" with his male alien counterpart.

When Joanna Russ faulted SF in the early 1970s for not challenging assumptions about gender roles, Poul Anderson dismissed her complaint with the patronizing "explanation" that "women have not been relevant" to SF and "the frequent absence of women characters has no great significance, perhaps none whatsoever."[16] Anderson's response may have illustrated an extreme even within the ranks of male SF writers (Philip K. Dick, for example, immediately took issue with Anderson's claim), but any overview of the genre during the first 50 or 60 years of the century will reveal few significant and/or significantly developed female characters, fewer still women SF writers, and little or no effort within the genre to speculate about gender or sexual roles.

And yet, for all that can be said about what SF failed to do in its early years, it should also be noted that the genre has had a relationship with women that may further distinguish SF from other popular genres. After scrupulously cataloguing many of SF's "maltreatments" of women, Eric S. Rabkin concluded his essay for Marleen Barr's *Future Females: A Critical Anthology* (1981) with the mitigating claim that SF had significantly improved a record it was not entirely to blame for in the first place. "Rather than continuing the cry of outrage over past failures," he suggested, "it is time to recognize that science fiction has been and continues to be a leading voice in the chorus for cultural change."[17] Whether or not we agree with all of Rabkin's propositions, his 1981 comments are consonant with the fact that in the 1990s SF has emerged as perhaps the most rewarding venue for feminist speculation and has been singled out by a number of feminist critics as being particularly well-suited for interrogations of gender roles and gender construction. Indeed, the reciprocal relationship between SF and feminism has been doubly rewarding: just as SF has proved to be a "zone of possibility" for feminist discourse, feminist concerns have created important "zones of possibility" within the genre's narratives, accounting for perhaps the most important single development in SF since the 1970s.

Women and SF: Histories and Theories

Conjunctions and prepositions pose the first difficulty for anyone who wishes to discuss the relationship between women and SF. Women "in" SF stories (or, as Joanna Russ once insisted, claiming there were no women in SF, "images of women in SF"), SF "by" or "for" women, women "as" aliens or as "the other," women "and" feminism, the construction of gender in SF stories—all of these intersections and unions merit more consideration than the scope of this study will permit. Accordingly, my discussion of some of the ways in which SF has been heavily dependent upon women writers for its contemporary forms will concentrate on writers and works that, while not necessarily "feminist" in any rigorous sense, have opposed or modified the genre's heavily masculinist tendencies. Fortunately, a growing number of anthologies of SF by women and critical studies of the relationship between feminism and SF offer the reader ample insights into the importance of women to the evolution of the genre.

While a few women writers such as C. L. Moore, Leigh Brackett, Katherine MacLean, Marion Zimmer Bradley, Margaret St. Clair, and Andre Norton had established successful careers in SF before the 1960s, it is fair to say that only during the late 1960s and early 1970s did women emerge as a significant force in the genre. The only story by a woman chosen for the *Science Fiction Hall of Fame* anthology, for example, was Judith Merril's "That Only a Mother" (1948), which sentimentally foregrounds a mother's all-encompassing love for a daughter horribly deformed by radiation. More subversive and threatening protofeminist stories such as C. L. Moore's "Shambleau" (1933) and "No Woman Born" (1944) were published before the 1960s but were few and far between. Probably the most dramatic sign of the emergence of a body of SF that was clearly feminist came in 1975 with the publication of Pamela Sargent's *Women of Wonder*, a collection of SF stories "by women about women." Sargent's fine lengthy introduction to this anthology, "Women and Science Fiction," codified the contributions of earlier women writers to the genre and called attention to the "new generation" of 1970s women SF writers.

Her expansive analysis offered a history of women SF writers who "wrote like men," who "wrote like women" insofar as they presented sentimental and domestic semblances in which female characters assumed only familiar cultural roles, and who wrote to explore what women "might become if and when the present restrictions on our lives vanish, or show us new problems and restrictions that might arise."[18] Moreover, in pointing out the roles and status hitherto assigned to women in SF, Sargent spelled out an important aspect of the genre that had not usually been mentioned in descriptions and definitions—that it had largely developed from the pulps as a particularly gender-specific escapist literature for men and boys:

Science fiction provided a world in which a male could experience high adventure and the interplay of scientific ideas and technological gadgets free from the interference of females. SF became the neighborhood clubhouse where the boys could get together away from the girls (or parents, or the short-sighted culture at large), who were a nuisance anyway. They got in the way in the clubhouse; they got in the way of the stories too, unless they stayed in their assigned domain. (xxxvii)

Notwithstanding Sargent's all-too-accurate description of early SF as a "boys club," it is important, as Brian Attebery reminds us, to note that "many SF stories in which women don't even appear turn out to be full of gender-linked imagery: the women are there but they have been disguised as planets, spaceships, robots, aliens, and the like."[19] Indeed, the affinity in SF between aliens and women and aliens and "monsters" has been noted so frequently as to have become something of a commonplace.[20]

Powerful stories in the *Women of Wonder* anthology by Sonya Dorman, Judith Merril, Katherine MacLean, Marion Zimmer Bradley, Anne McCaffery, Kit Reed, Kate Wilhelm, Carol Emshwiller, Ursula K. Le Guin, Chelsea Quinn Yarbro, Joanna Russ, and Vonda McIntyre alerted SF readers to the fact that women writers had not only achieved a significant critical mass in the genre, but also that they were now doing much of the genre's best and most exciting work. Sargent followed up this groundbreaking anthology in 1976 with *More Women of Wonder* and again in 1978 with *New Women of Wonder*. The indispensable stories in these anthologies, plus more-recent SF by women and feminist SF, have just been republished in the two volumes *Women of Wonder: The Classic Years: Science Fiction by Women from the 1940s to the 1970s* and *Women of Wonder: The Contemporary Years: Science Fiction by Women from the 1970s to the 1990s*.[21] Sargent's new introductions to these two volumes and the superb writing they contain form the starting point for any reader who wants to understand the huge importance of SF by women and feminist SF to twentieth-century science fiction. Other anthologies of SF by women include Vonda McIntyre's and Susan Janice Anderson's *Aurora: Beyond Equality* (1976), Alice Laurance's *Cassandra Rising* (1978), Virginia Kidd's *Millennial Women* (1978), and Shawna McCarthy's *Asimov's Space of Her Own* (1983).

Not only has feminist SF challenged and expanded theories about the nature of the genre but it has also been instrumental in moving discussions of SF ever closer to the discourses of critical theory. SF writers such as Joanna Russ, Ursula K. Le Guin, and Samuel R. Delany helped open the genre to theory and helped critical theorists such as Fredric Jameson, Jean Baudrillard, Donna Haraway, and Brian McHale see the potential of SF's metaphors for furthering cultural analysis. In particular, Haraway's well-known "A Manifesto for Cyborgs: Science, Technology, and Socialist Feminism in the 1980s" suggested the power of SF metaphors for feminist discourse.[22] Studies of feminist SF have produced some of the most rigorous and most productive investigations of the genre, including influential and energizing essays by the Canadian fan and critic Susan Wood, Marleen Barr's pioneering *Future Females: A Critical Anthology* (1981), Natalie M. Rosinsky's *Feminist Futures: Contemporary Women's Speculative Fiction* (1984), Barr's *Alien to Femininity: Speculative Fiction and Feminist Theory* (1987), Sarah Lefanu's *In the Chinks of the World Machine: Feminism & Science Fiction* (1988; 1989 American edition retitled *Feminism and Science Fiction*), Lucie Armitt's *Where No Man Has Gone Before: Women and Science Fiction* (1991), Barr's *Feminist Fabulation: Space/Postmodern Fiction* (1992) and her *Lost in Space: Probing Feminist Science Fiction and Beyond* (1993), and Jenny Wolmark's *Aliens and Others: Science Fiction, Feminism and Postmodernism* (1994). In addition, the March 1980 and July 1990 issues of *Science-Fiction Studies* were devoted to SF by women and to feminist SF. Of the above studies, Lefanu's *In the Chinks of the World Machine*, Barr's *Feminist Fabulation*, and Wolmark's *Aliens and Others* offer the best overviews of the importance of women and feminist writers to SF. Lefanu offers useful readings of major feminist SF works to support her contention that "science fiction is feminism-friendly," "ideally placed for interrogative functions" and for subverting "the unities of 'self.'"[23] Wolmark argues that feminist SF's construction of "expanded cognitive horizons" can best be explored within a framework informed by both feminist and postmodern theory, as she focuses on ways in which recent feminist texts move beyond new representations of women and female desire to deconstruct ideas both of gender and of genre.[24] And Barr's *Feminist Fabulation* rejects the notion of "feminist SF," arguing instead that feminist SF is not actually SF at all but is really metafiction about patriarchal fiction "to unmask the fictionality of patriarchy."[25] Apart from the larger theoretical propositions they advance, these three studies offer excellent readings of most of the important works of feminist SF written in the 1980s and 1990s.

Writing Like a Woman: Joanna Russ

The late 1960s and the 1970s were the years in which women codified their stake in the genre, showing ways in which SF was a most attractive vehicle for extending the considerations of the women's movement into fiction. SF's "elasticity as a genre allows women who are interested in gender issues (and those social, political, linguistic, and cultural issues that immediately arise from and attach themselves to gender issues) to invent alien worlds specifically tailored to highlight these issues," explains Larry McCaffery, who adds that SF also allows writers "to juxtapose alternate universes with our own for the purpose of examining contemporary gender roles—and their possible alternatives."[26] While the number of women writers who recognized and exploited SF's particular potential for combining gender with genre was quite large, much, if not most, of the work of acknowledging the genre's potential for feminist interrogations was accomplished by Joanna Russ, Ursula K. Le Guin, James Tiptree Jr. (Alice Sheldon), and Pamela Sargent.

Russ's was easily the most prominent critical voice calling in the 1960s and 1970s for an SF that would transcend its masculinist assumptions and become something more than a literature written primarily by men primarily for boys. In a series of incisive essays published in *Science-Fiction Studies* and other critical forums, Russ went far beyond a feminist critique of the genre to deconstruct some of its most basic assumptions.[27] In "Amor Vincit Foeminam: The Battle of the Sexes in Science Fiction," "Alien Monsters," "The Image of Women in Science Fiction," and "What Can a Heroine Do? Or Why Women Can't Write," Russ called attention to ways in which the genre had limited the roles of women in its semblances, while in essays such as "SF and Technology as Mystification" and "Towards an Aesthetic of Science

Fiction" she examined the genre's core epistemological and aesthetic assumptions. For example, "Alien Monsters" argues that the "real" monsters in SF are patriarchally drawn male protagonists, "He-Men" who are obviously unrealistic caricatures, but whose presence in a story precludes both significant roles for women and the interrogation of power. Even more critical of the underlying assumptions of the genre is her "SF and Technology as Mystification," which considers much of the genre's fascination with technology as an addiction, "a mystification for something else that ... becomes a kind of autonomous deity which can promise both salvation and damnation." In criticizing SF's technophilia/technophobia obsessions, Russ calls for a more realistic understanding in the genre of the practical role of politics and economics in understanding, much less solving, social problems. While not limited to, or even significantly focused on, SF, Russ's *How to Suppress Women's Writing* (1983) acerbically chronicles both the ways in which women's writing has been disparaged in SF and the mechanisms through which it may continue to be devalued in the future.

At roughly the same time as her essays were prompting debate within the SF community, in story collections such as *Alyx* (1976) and in novels such as *Picnic on Paradise* (1968), *And Chaos Died* (1970), *The Female Man* (1975), *We Who Are About To . . .* (1977), and *The Two of Them* (1978) Russ both expanded the boundaries of what female characters "could do" in SF and deconstructed the cultural assumptions about gender that had been incorporated into SF semblances. The best known and most influential of these works, *The Female Man*, presents frank dialogue among a Russ-like woman character with strong ties to what readers would think of as their referential reality and three of her alternate personae in other universes, one from the utopian Whileaway, a planet with no men, one from a dystopian patriarchal world, and one from a world in which men and women are in armed conflict. The feminist utopia of Whileaway, created after disease had killed all male settlers on the planet and women had learned how to give birth through parthenogenesis, had been introduced in "When It Changed," one of Russ's best known stories, originally published in *Again, Dangerous Visions* in 1972.

But the genius of *The Female Man* lies as much in its prose style and structure as in its imagination of Whileaway. Structurally experimental in its fragmented, collaged narrative, metafictional in its commentary on its own style and language, and groundbreaking within SF in its representation of female sexual desire and lesbian sex, Russ's novel collides the different worlds of Joanna, Janet, Jael, and Jeannine to decenter the value system and assumptions of each world. Describing the book's examination of the range of women's lives "from psychic servitude to fully matured freedom," the *Encyclopedia of Science Fiction* calls *The Female Man* "savage and cleansing in its anger" and judges it "one of the most significant uses of SF instruments to make arguments about our own world and condition" (1035).

But it is Russ's *We Who Are About To . . .* (1977) that may be her strongest challenge to the basic assumptions and values of genre SF, since its woman protagonist not only resists patriarchal cultural assumptions but also subverts a number of expectations about SF narratives.[28] *We Who Are About To . . .* chronicles the efforts of eight victims of a spaceliner accident (five women and three men) to survive on a barren, uncharted but completely unremarkable planet, a place that variously reminds Russ's narrator of the Australian outback and early-twentieth-century New Jersey. Actually, the book chronicles the efforts of only seven of the survivors: Russ's protagonist and narrator, a 42-year-old, worldly-wise woman, correctly realizes that survival will be impossible once they exhaust their six-month supply of emergency food, so she decides to meet death on her own terms and on her own schedule. "Do anything you please," she tells the others, "only leave me out of it" (24). She particularly refuses to become part of the group's grimly optimistic determination to "colonize" their new world, to breed a new generation who can preserve "civilization." "Civilization's doing fine," she observes. "We just don't happen to be where it is" (31).

Russ's survivors suspiciously resemble a somewhat curdled version of the characters in *Gilligan's Island*: an older, wealthy, married couple and their spoiled, 12-year-old adopted daughter, a "very minor intellectual" male professor; a simple, muscular young man waiting to regress; a fleshy blond earth mother; a secretive, resentful, dark young woman on her way to training as a government agent; and the narrator, a musicologist with a hazy but extensive multifaceted background. Their situation clearly evokes the classic robinsonade formula; the narrator even refers to the image of an "idyllic desert island," wondering by what etymological process the term "deserted island" evolved into desert. Having invoked the patterns of expectations associated with this formula, however, Russ quickly sets about thwarting them. Not only does our narrator summarily dismiss the men's plan for "running around cheerily into the Upper Paleolithic," but she also rejects the central appeal of the survival formula, sadly observing:

> I think everyone loves it here because their choices are all made for them; we were never very comfortable with our fate in our own hands, were we? Better to act on the modern religion: an incarnation of the immortal germ-plasm. Nostalgia for the mud. Simplicities. (We, 59–60)

Rightly perceiving that her refusal to subscribe to their myth of survival and colonization may be more threatening to her companions than her refusal to comply with their breeding schedule, the narrator slips away from them to practice what she refers to as the art of dying. When they follow and attempt to force her to return, she uses a small gas gun and a large rock to kill all but Cassandra, who commits suicide with drugs the narrator gives her. All of this occurs only slightly more than halfway through the novel. For its remainder, Russ's protagonist muses about her actions, experiences starvation-induced hallucinations concerning her past, preserves her story in a small recorder, and finally commits suicide.

What is remarkable about this novel is that Russ, while reversing a number of patterns in the literary formula, goes beyond reversal in her depiction of women. Ultimately her protagonist acts neither as a compliant victim nor as a superwoman, but as an individual unwilling to cede her independence to an abstraction. Neither Eve nor Bitch Goddess, Magna Mater nor Maiden Victim, Russ's protagonist is a new articulation of an unexpected literary myth—that of Melville's Bartleby the Scrivener—rather than a reinterpretation of expected cultural myths. Like Bartleby, who increasingly refuses to respond to the world around him, she is someone who "prefers not to," both in terms of the action of the story and the iconography of its formulas, and her characterization follows Russ's belief that "reversing sexual roles in fiction may make good burlesque or good fantasy, but it is ludicrous in terms of serious literature." Having defined myths as "dramatic embodiments of what a culture believes to be true—or what it would like to be true—or what it is mortally afraid may be true," Russ offers in this novel a work that so deconstructs both literary and cultural myths as to deprive her readers of all but the most enigmatic paradigms. Instead of filling a literary formula with compatible cultural images of female sexuality, Russ frustrates the literary formula by filling it with an antithetical, essentially genderless literary myth—that of Bartleby, though significantly changing the gender of the storyteller from male to female.

The Insistent Vision of Ursula K. Le Guin

Ursula K. Le Guin's fiction and criticism are much concerned with some of the same feminist issues to be found in Russ's writing, but almost always with less polemical power and without the uncompromising edge that made Russ so controversial. However, Le Guin has been a source of controversy in a different area, as her fiction often seems to cross the "line" into fantasy (a line she both recognizes and is not much concerned with), occasioning charges from SF gatekeepers that she is not a "real" SF writer. In this respect, oddly enough, Le Guin was doubly at the center of the genre in the 1970s, since that was the decade in which fantasy and feminism seemed its two major developments. While Russ seemed most interested in prompting debate within the genre, Le Guin's fiction and criticism during the 1960s and 1970s seemed aimed at a larger audience. Gathered in *The Language of the Night* (1979; edited and introduced by Susan Wood) and in *Dancing at the Edge of the World* (1989), Le Guin's essays reflect an engagement with a wide range of issues, having to do with social responsibility, literature, and, increasingly, with feminism. And, while her fiction, most notably *The Left Hand of Darkness* (1969) and *The Dispossessed: An Ambiguous Utopia* (1974) would at first seem to be singularly concerned with exploring issues of gender construction and sexuality, Le Guin has been criticized (by Joanna Russ, among others) for maintaining a kind of patriarchal focus in her writing, manifested in the fact that her significant characters tend to be male or to reflect male stereotypes. Even a cursory comparison of Le Guin's work with Russ's thus serves as a strong reminder that "feminist SF" is anything but a monolithic entity.

Le Guin's essays, particularly "American SF and the Other" (1975), "Science Fiction and Mrs. Brown" (1975), and "Is Gender Necessary Redux" (1976/88) suggest the degree to which character development rather than "ideas" or "issues" focuses her thinking about literature. These essays also remind us that Le Guin's critique of SF has never been limited to gender issues. "American SF and the Other" opens with the recognition of the low status of women in SF but quickly widens its scope to complain: "The people, in SF, are not people. They are masses, existing for one purpose: to be led by their superiors."[29] Le Guin charges that SF's galactic empires simply transpose the British Empire of 1880 into outer space, ignoring the real challenges of imagining the cultural and racial other, and settling for easy hatred or worship of aliens, with no interrogation of difference. "If you deny any affinity with another person or kind of person," warned Le Guin, "if you declare it to be wholly different from yourself—as men have done to women, and class has done to class, and nation has done to nation—you may hate it or deify it; but in either case you have denied its spiritual equality and its human reality" (LON, 95). Failure to investigate the nature of the other, she concludes, has led SF toward a simplistic emphasis on power relationships—a "brainless regressivism": "In general, American SF has assumed a permanent hierarchy of superiors and inferiors, with rich, ambitious, aggressive males at the top, then a great gap, and then at the bottom the poor, the uneducated, the faceless masses, and all the women" (LON, 95–96). From such critiques of genre practices by Le Guin and other SF writers and critics (not all of them women), the feminist countertradition significantly rethought and reshaped SF during the 1970s.

In "Science Fiction and Mrs. Brown," Le Guin extended Virginia Woolf's focus on character to SF to ask whether the genre can support the kind of character development called for by Woolf. Answering in the affirmative, Le Guin cites works by Zamyatin, Philip K. Dick, and Stanislaw Lem as evidence that "when science fiction uses its limitless range of symbol and metaphor novelistically, with the subject at the center, it can show us who we are, and where we are, and what choices face us, with unsurpassed clarity, and with a great and troubling beauty" (LON, 116). What is significant in her assessment of the genre is that she proposes that SF can and should be character-centered, exploring subjectivity rather than a "pseudo-objective listing of marvels and wonders and horrors," "a promise of continued life for the imagination, a good tool, an enlargement of consciousness," a chance to see "against a vast dark background, of the very frail, very heroic figure of Mrs. Brown" (117). In offering a view of SF not centered on some kind of novum, Le Guin both opened herself to criticism from SF traditionalists and opened the genre to new conceptions of its nature and purpose.

While Le Guin's essays helped shape a vision of an SF much closer to mainstream literature than was the pulp tradition, her fiction was even more influential in paving the way for new concerns. *Rocannon's World* (1966) combined anthropological interests with Norse mythology and codified the foundation for her Hainish stories—a future history of the parent species of humans and other races. Under the umbrella of the Hainish cycle, Le Guin has continued to imagine cultural and gender clashes occasioned by space travel—most effectively in *The Left Hand of Darkness* (1969) and *The Dispossessed: An Ambiguous Utopia* (1974). Set on a snow-covered planet called Winter, The *Left Hand of Darkness* explores the reactions of an observer from Earth, Genly Ai, to the Gethen, the planet's inhabitants. Androgynous except during "kemmer," the time in their sexual cycle when they become either male or female—with no control over which sex they will assume—Gethenians present fascinating and challenging prospect of a race that is not divided by permanent gender stereotypes and prejudices.

However radical Le Guin's "thought-experiment" about a nongendered society may at first seem, and despite its winning both Hugo and Nebula awards in 1970, it has nevertheless been criticized by feminist writers and critics for privileging male values and roles in its depictions of the supposedly genderless Gethenians and for ignoring the issue of sexual desire. Noting that *The Left Hand of Darkness* does shift its appeal from that of traditional masculinist SF by speaking "to liberal rather than misogynistic male readers, to readers who feel at ease with the kind of feminism that seeks to remove conflict and difference," Sarah Lefanu agrees with Joanna Russ that the problem with the novel is that it actually contains no women.[30] I cite this complaint in part to illustrate the working of SF's unique feedback loop, in which writers often engage in continuing dialogues with their readers, and in part as a reminder that Le Guin rarely uses the genre for a single purpose. For in 1976 Le Guin confronted criticisms of her novel with an essay titled "Is Gender Necessary?" and then further annotated her remarks in 1988, titling her marginal notations "Redux"(LON, 155–72).

Clearly somewhat defensive, Le Guin reminds her critics that she is a fiction writer rather than a theorist or activist and that *The Left Hand of Darkness* is not a polemic but the record of her consciousness. Claiming in the 1976 essay that "the real subject of the book is not feminism or sex or gender or anything of the sort" but "betrayal and fidelity," Le Guin admits in the 1988 notation: "I was feeling defensive and resentful that critics of the book insisted upon talking only about its 'gender problems,' as if it were an essay not a novel." Terming her specification of "the real subject of the book" bluster, she acknowledges "I had opened a can of worms and was trying hard to shut it." She does, however, continue to insist on "other aspects of the book, which are involved with its sex/gender aspects quite inextricably" (LON, 157). After imagining a world in which she hoped to eliminate gender "to find out what was left," Le Guin further created a world in which there has never been a war, a world free from ecological exploitation in the name of progress, and a world free from the pressures of sexuality as a continuous social factor. Notwithstanding her continuing pride in exploring these ideas, Le Guin ends her 1988 notations by remarkably agreeing with the women who wanted her to "explore androgyny from a woman's point of view as well as a man's," concluding: "I think women were justified in asking more courage of me and a more rigorous thinking-through of implications" (LON, 171). It's hard to imagine another popular genre in which the response to a highly successful and influential novel could generate such a discussion, much less one in which such a discussion would itself promote changes in the genre.[31]

SF's "Jill-in-the-Box": James Tiptree Jr.

Russ and Le Guin may have done much of the groundbreaking theoretical work for feminist SF in the 1970s, and they were responsible for several of the novels that codified feminism's hold on the genre, but in many ways the most remarkable of all feminist writers in the 1970s was James Tiptree Jr.—the pseudonym used (along with Raccoona Sheldon) by Alice Sheldon. Tiptree's SF stories began appearing in the late 1960s, and by the late 1970s were seen by many SF writers, critics, and fans as the most significant SF of the decade. While Tiptree's sensitive depictions of women were often remarked, "his" fiction was compared to that of Hemingway and praised by no less a stylist than Robert Silverberg, who found "something ineluctably masculine about Tiptree's writing."[32] Silverberg was hardly alone, and in 1975 Tiptree was asked by a panel of distinguished feminist SF writers (including Suzy McKee Charnas, Ursula Le Guin, and Joanna Russ) to withdraw from a written symposium on feminism and SF, because "the women found her male persona too irritating to deal with."[33] Accordingly, the SF community was both stunned and delighted to learn in 1977 that Tiptree was in fact Alice Sheldon, a 62-year-old behavioral psychologist who, after a childhood and early life swelled with exotic locations and occupations, lived with her husband outside Washington, D.C. Calling Tiptree a "beautiful Jill-in-the-box," Ursula K. Le Guin admitted: "She fooled us. She fooled us good and proper. And we can only thank her for it."[34]

While often displaying an almost swaggeringly masculinist point of view (most of Tiptree's narrators are men) and detailed knowledge of "masculine" concerns with hunting, fishing, flying, etc., Tiptree's stories usually undercut that swagger with a bleak fatalism that flies both in the face of SF's traditional "can do" attitude and in the face of the optimistic social meliorism (the confidence that power relations can be improved, social problems can be solved) at the heart of much feminist writing, most notably that of Ursula K. Le Guin. As Lillian Heldreth has so effectively documented, Tiptree's stories usually end in or lead toward death, conflict between the sexes or with aliens has no positive resolution, and ties between male aggression and sexuality seem incapable of being mediated.[35] It is important to note that Tip-

tree's view of human nature does not actually oppose essentialism, but substitutes a darkly essentialist view of human nature
for the optimistic view that characterized so much early SF. "Tiptree's postulation of humanity's inherently destructive nature,"
explains Veronica Hollinger, "results in an essentialist definition
of what it means to be human—'man does not change his behav-
iour'—and because of this, it becomes impossible to suggest any
practical solutions to the problems of human life."[36] In this
respect, Tiptree's stories doubly work against the grain of traditional SF, challenging both its patriarchal smugness and its positivism. These stories, most of which are collected in *Ten Thousand
Light-Years from Home* (1973), *Warm Worlds and Otherwise* (1975),
Star Songs of an Old Primate (1978), and *Out of the Everywhere and
Other Extraordinary Visions* (1981), not only exploded once and for
all assertions about innate differences between male and female
writing in SF but also brought to SF a relentlessly unsentimental
pragmatism and interrogation of human values and motivation.

A number of Tiptree's stories have been accorded high status
within SF, including "The Girl Who Was Plugged In," "Love Is
the Plan, the Plan Is Death," "Your Haploid Heart," "The Last
Flight of Dr. Ain," and "All the Kinds of Yes." However, two of
Tiptree's stories, "The Women Men Don't See" and "Houston,
Houston, Do You Read?" stand out even from this select company and are easily among the finest and most powerful in twentieth-century SF. "The Women Men Don't See" could almost
serve as a self-reflexive reminder of the role of women and
women writers in early SF, as it is narrated by a man who first
does not notice, then does not attempt to understand, and finally
cannot understand the mother and daughter marooned after a
plane crash with him and their Mayan pilot in the alien landscape of the Quintana Roo territory in the Yucatan.[37] Fenton and
the pilot seem quietly competent and knowledgeable, but as the
story unfolds it is they who more and more lose control of events
as the seemingly unremarkable Ruth Parsons and her equally
unremarkable-seeming daughter, Althea, reveal stranger and
stranger qualities of equanimity and independence. Ruth Parsons reveals just enough about her background to suggest that,
quite unlike Fenton's assumption that she is a faceless, dedicated
functionary in the federal bureaucracy, "the backbone of the system," she and her daughter have become at least psychic feminist

survivalists. Comparing themselves to opossums who manage to live even in New York City, Ruth cuts short Fenton's easy confidence in women's opportunities:

> Women have no rights, Don, except what men allow us. Men are more aggressive and powerful, and they run the world. When the next real crisis upsets them, our so-called rights will vanish like—like that smoke. We'll be back where we always were: property. And whatever has gone wrong will be blamed on our freedom, like the fall of Rome was. You'll see. (*Women*, 325)

When Fenton protests that women have great implicit power because they are so heavily depended upon, Parsons corrects him: "Women don't work that way. We're a—a toothless world." "What women do is survive," she quietly explains: "We live by ones and twos in the chinks of your world-machine" (326).

Fenton does not give a second thought to the wistful comment by Parsons that she sometimes dreams of going really far away, but her words come back to haunt him after she and her daughter choose—almost instantaneously—to leave Earth with aliens who have been conducting some sort of field trip to the Yucatan. (For that matter, Fenton does not really give a second thought to much of anything that the Parsonses say or do unless it is to be impatient with them for not validating his shallow stereotyping; in his blithe imperceptivity, Fenton is actually quite a humorous character, and the humor of this and other Tiptree stories is easy to overlook.) Inverting the pulp cliché of extraterrestrials who kidnap Earth women, these women practically force themselves on the bewildered aliens, choosing to exchange their situation on Earth for whatever they might find in the alien culture. To Fenton's panicky warning, "For Christ's sake, Ruth, they're aliens!" Parsons absently replies: "I'm used to it." In response to the eagerness of the two women to escape a world in which they feel completely alienated, Fenton can finally only wonder, "How could a woman choose to live among unknown monsters, to say good-bye to her home, her world?" Of course, the disturbing and uncompromising answer of Tiptree's story is "How could she not?"

Even more uncompromising is Tiptree's "Houston, Houston, Do You Read?" which not only subverts gender expectations but also stands as a grim parody of genre SF's first-contact formula.[38]

Here, the first contact is between NASA astronauts from the twentieth century and a future Earth clone culture in which there are no men. A solar flare transports the astronauts some 300 years into the future, where they gradually learn that a world epidemic has long since reduced the population of Earth to some two million women who can reproduce only through cloning. "Rescued" by a women-crewed spaceship, the three male astronauts can barely comprehend the women's nonhierarchical social organization, much less the relationships among clone "sisters." While "Doc" Lorimer, the least close-minded of the males, tries to understand this new world, Bud and Dave, the stereotypical alpha males, can think only of how they may reestablish patriarchal sexual and religious relations in the women's world. Bud, the most macho of the astronauts, cannot even believe that all men are gone, and desperately clings to his fantasy that there are still wild men hiding out in the hills of Earth, "some good old buckaroos," because there have to be men, "otherwise nothing counts" (*SFRA*, 469).

Realizing the disruptive threat these men pose to their culture, the women who have rescued them shield the men as long as possible from the discovery that no other males exist and that the women are all clones. When the women drug the men with a "disinhibitor" that serves as a kind of truth serum and emotional intensifier, Bud becomes a mysoginistic would-be rapist, Dave becomes a religious fanatic determined to restore "God's plan" for the subjection of women to men, and Lorimer helplessly tries to sort out his jumbled and contradictory attitudes toward his colleagues and his sex. The women easily subdue Bud and Dave—after having secured a sperm sample from the former—and regretfully tell Lorimer, "We can hardly turn you loose on Earth, and we simply have no facilities for people with your emotional problems." Speaking for his companions and for his sex, Lorimer offers the only defense he can think of:

> "They were good men," Lorimer repeats elegiacally. He knows he is speaking for it all, for Dave's Father, for Bud's manhood, for himself, for Cro-Magnon, for the dinosaurs too, maybe. "I'm a man. By god yes, I'm angry. I have a right. We gave you all this, we made it all. We built your precious civilisation and your knowledge and comfort and medicines and your dreams. All of it. We protected you, we worked our balls off keeping you and your kids. It was hard. It

was a fight, a bloody fight all the way. We're tough. We had to be, can't you understand? Can't you for Christ's sake understand that?" (*SFRA*, 473)

To which comes the deflating reply:

"We're trying," Lady Blue sighs. "We are trying, Doctor Lorimer. Of course we enjoy your inventions and we do appreciate your evolutionary role. But you must see there's a problem. As I understand it, what you protected people from was largely other males, wasn't it? We've just had an extraordinary demonstration. You have brought history to life for us." (*SFRA*, 473)

Accepting the unavoidable fact that there is no room in this world for even three men precisely because they do bring history to life, Lorimer acquiesces, almost eagerly, in his own euthenasia—part of a quite necessary gendercide.

The stark logic that makes the deaths of the three astronauts inevitable seems consonant with the separatist thrust of many of Tiptree's stories, but it would be a mistake for us to "read" "Houston, Houston, Do You Read?" as only the presentation of a feminist utopia. Nancy Steffen-Fleur, in an excellent and wide-ranging analysis of psychological patterns in Tiptree's writing, persuasively argues that Doc Lorimer is "one of Sheldon's metaphorically castrated pseudo-men who stand in for the gender-conflicted dimensions of her own personality."[39] Noting that Lorimer is a psychosexually displaced person almost equally alienated from his alpha male companions and the clone sisters, Steffen-Fleur specifies his tragedy as being "the wrong sex in the wrong place in the wrongest of all possible times." That the decision by the women that all three of the men must die includes the rationale that the sympathetic Lorimer must die "for his own good" should alert readers to Tiptree's deep ambivalence about the world of the sisters. "Sheldon makes it perfectly clear that the women's egalitarian, non-hierarchical, ecologically-minded culture is much preferable to the brutal, dominance/submission system which characterized the old patriarchy," concludes Steffen-Fleur, but she also identifies the women as unsettling big nurse figures who are not "inhumane" so much as they are "non-human" (207–8). In this as in her other narratives, Tiptree subverts not only the simple dichotomies of patriarchal genre SF but simple dichotomies of any sort, insisting instead on using SF to explore all of the facets of otherness.

Feminist SF Today: Gains, Losses, and Postfeminism

Tiptree, Sargent, Le Guin, and Russ supplied a canonical core for feminist SF, articulated the central concerns that shaped this countertradition, and made it impossible for anyone to deny the vital and necessary role played by women writers in the maturation of the genre as a whole. Of course, these central writers were by no means responsible for all of the important developments in feminist SF and SF by women, nor does their work alone adequately characterize the range of feminist concerns over the twentieth-century history of SF. Charlotte Perkins Gilman, for example, pioneered the utopian feminist novel in 1915 with *Herland*, Joan Slonczewski displayed the continuing viability of that form with her *A Door into Ocean* in 1986, and Katharine Burdekin's *Swastika Night* (1937) not only anticipated but may have influenced Orwell's *1984*. Gertrude Barrows Bennett (writing as Francis Stevens) brought the alternate history of *The Heads of Cerberus* to *The Thrill Book* in 1919, and Andre Norton, the first woman to be honored with the Grand Master Nebula Award, may have been as influential as Robert Heinlein in bringing younger readers to the genre in the 1950s and 1960s. Women editors of SF, particularly Judith Merril, Cele Goldsmith, Shawna McCarthy, Kristine Kathryn Rusch, and Ellen Datlow, have exercised strong influence on the genre, starting in the 1960s. Doris Lessing, Margaret Atwood, and Marge Piercy, feminist writers usually associated more with the mainstream than with SF, have produced some of the most powerful works of SF written in the 1980s and 1990s. Lessing's Canopus in Argos: Archives series of novels (1979–1983), Atwood's *The Handmaid's Tale* (1985), and Piercy's *He, She and It* (1991) have all enjoyed success both within and outside of the SF community. Within the genre, an older generation of important women writers such as Kate Wilhelm, Suzy McKee Charnas, Angela Carter, Tanith Lee, Phylis Gottlieb, Suzette Haden Elgin, Sheri S. Tepper, C. J. Cherryh, Vonda McIntyre, Joan Vinge, and Carol Emshwiller has been joined by a newer generation, with Octavia Butler, Pat Cadigan, Connie

Willis, Nancy Kress, Pat Murphy, Karen Joy Fowler, Lisa Goldstein, Sheila Finch, Lois McMaster Bujold, Emma Bull, Rebecca
Ore, Gwyneth Jones, and Maureen F. McHugh.

And the list could and should go on, making clear that in the
1990s SF cannot be defined, described, or understood without
prominent—if not primary—attention to women writers and
feminist fiction. As Pamela Sargent explains in her introduction
to *Women of Wonder: The Contemporary Years*, the interface
between SF and women writers has become a central feature of
the genre:

> It is no longer possible to discuss science fiction without mentioning
> the women who have contributed to it. Conversely, it is also impossi-
> ble to give an account of women science fiction writers and their
> work without discussing the genre as a whole. The topic of women
> and science fiction is not an ancillary topic anymore, one to be set
> aside from the history of the literature as a kind of sidebar or foot-
> note; to discuss women and science fiction is, of necessity, to discuss
> the entire field. Perhaps eventually, if sexism and racism diminish
> sufficiently, we may finally discuss only writers. (16)

But, as Sargent also acknowledges, the story of women and SF is
not without setbacks as well as victories.

One of the sad ironies widely remarked in discussions of SF in
the 1970s and 1980s is the fact that gains made in the representation of women and the interrogation of feminist issues within
written SF were not matched in television and film. *Star Trek* is
generally credited with attracting large numbers of women readers to SF in the late 1960s with its—for the times—sensitive
broaching of issues of gender and identity. The TV series is also
responsible for the rise of a fascinating subgenre of writing by
women fans, the K/S stories, in which Kirk and Spock are
depicted as lovers.[40] But SF film in the 1970s and 1980s, particularly in the Star Wars series, presented women almost exclusively
through limited stereotypes as crude as, if not cruder than, those
found in pulp SF of the 1930s. The decade of the 1970s, in which
SF film became hugely popular and in which feminist SF writing
soared to prominence in the field, was a disaster for representations of women and consideration of gender issues in SF film.

Reminders also abound of the strong ties of SF to the culture at
large, as the general retrenchment—if not loss of ground—by fem-

inists during the Reagan 1980s has been somewhat mirrored within discussions in the genre. Sargent reflects the concern of a number of feminist critics when she suggests in her introduction to *Women of Wonder: The Contemporary Years* that a backlash against the feminist writing of the 1970s has developed within discussions of SF. This backlash takes the form of grumbling that the great feminist works of the 1970s and early 1980s either were somehow not really SF or represented an ennervation of SF's traditional strengths. Gwyneth Jones has recently expressed her caustic view of this attempt to rewrite SF history:

> There seems to be a story going about at the moment, to the effect that feminist SF isn't real science fiction at all—it is a *raid* on the genre. These ruthless female bandits, post-holocaust amazons no doubt (many of them without so much as a single degree in astrophysics). They've never written SF before and they come along, smash open the science fiction shop front, and run off with all the high tech gear. They chuck away most of it after they've tried to eat it, found you can't use circuit boards as sanitary towels and so on. They keep a few of the little bitty glass bead things to wear in their nipple rings.[41]

Furthermore, the "boys' club" of pulp SF was seemingly at least partially resurrected in the cyberpunk movement of the mid-1980s, when Pat Cadigan was the only woman consistently identified with its concerns. And yet, Joan Gordon has persuasively argued that cyberpunk constituted a kind of covert feminist SF and may have offered feminist SF a way of reengaging cultural issues in a highly technologized and postmodern world.[42]

Following its first great wave in the 1970s, feminist SF has tended to move beyond what might be called the single-issue focus on the place of women, both in SF and in the culture at large. Perhaps more effectively than any other contemporary SF writer, Octavia Butler has combined feminist concerns with the investigation of racism and even of speciesism. In stories such as "Bloodchild" and in her Xenogenesis series—*Dawn* (1987), *Adulthood Rites* (1987), and *Imago* (1989)—Butler has challenged her readers to consider sexual and power relationships with aliens that transcend the kind of despair that haunts Tiptree's fiction. Her fiction consistently problematizes all manner of relationships between self and other, refusing to privilege any single value system, offering "solutions" to problems that are themselves always troubling. Another very important writer who resists easy classification is Connie Willis, whose stories such as "All My Darling Daughters," "Schwarzschild Radius," and "Even the Queen" (the best and funniest story ever written in any genre about menstruation) and novels such as *Lincoln's Dreams* (1987) and *Doomsday Book* (1992) are never limited to recognizable feminist issues but regularly probe human belief systems in ways described by Joan Gordon as "relegating the assumptions of feminism to the context of a story."[43] Grouping Willis with Sheri Tepper, Pat Cadigan, Pat Murphy, Elizabeth Ann Scarborough, and Karen Joy Fowler, Gordon suggests that their fiction submerges traditional feminist themes into the background of their novels in a manner that might be called postfeminist. Rather than neglecting feminist thought, explains Gordon, these postfeminist novels "assume, apply, and subsume it in their texts." The difference is that postfeminist writers, according to Gordon, present female characters who are "strong, active, given to non-gender-linked jobs, but although these characters may live as feminists have striven for women to be allowed to live, their right to live that way is not the central issue of the writing" (5).

While it seems likely to me that the attempt to devalue the feminist SF of the 1970s should be considered as part of a larger conservative holding action against what I will discuss in chapter 5 as "soft agenda SF," it also seems clear to me that the first wave of overtly feminist writers like Sargent, Russ, Tiptree, and Le Guin and the newer wave of feminist and postfeminist writers such as Butler, Willis, Jones, Cadigan, Murphy, Kress, and Fowler continue to offer to SF a conceptual vitality and intellectual toughness that will insure the gains of this countertradition will never be lost, its significance never denied.

Chapter Five

New and Newer Waves

"But this was, well, the literature of the future."
"Their future, our past—what of it?"

Gregory Benford, "Centigrade 233"

"I feel I am no part of the New Wave, I was here before 'em, and by God I mean to be here after they've gone (still writing bloody science fiction)!"

Brian Aldiss, letter to Judith Merril

"The best SF being fashioned today . . . is like a squabble of shrews in a Mesozoic midden: it will eat anything."

John Clute, *Nebula Awards 28*

The vaguely entropic future of Gregory Benford's "Centigrade 233" proposes a specifically nightmarish future for SF.[1] Print has been supplanted by the technology of interactive, hyper-texted 3-D movies, and the genre of SF is dead, as is linear text in general. In Benford's play on *Fahrenheit 451*, fossil fuels are so depleted in the twenty-first century that it is against the law to burn firewood or even old furniture, but no one had thought to outlaw the burning of books in a postliterate society. So, when

Alex, Benford's protagonist, finds that no one is interested in buying his late uncle's magnificent collection of SF books and magazines, he hits upon the perversely brilliant idea of staged burnings at fashionable parties, a kind of heady excess in which the burning of SF classics not only appeals atavistically but also involves a symbolic revenge against a past that imagined such wonders for the future but could only produce one that was mean and bleak. As Alex ceremonially ignites ancient copies of pulps such as *Amazing* and *Thrilling Wonder Stories* and novels such as *Odd John*, he realizes that his rapt audience is celebrating the death of an indulgent past in which SF epitomized "easy optimism and unconscious swank," actually betraying the future it so longed for.

William Gibson's "The Gernsback Continuum" similarly targets the grandiose ideas of an SF that promoted visions of flying-wing liners the size of cruise ships, of privately owned flying cars, dream cities, and perfected humans—"a stage set, a series of elaborate props for playing at living in the future."[2] With its catalogue of streamlined 1930s architecture and its reminders of a "World of Tomorrow" that was almost taken for granted, Gibson's story at once reminds us of the naively optimistic hold that science-fictional ideas once had over our vision of the future and grimly reminds us how far that vision missed the actual mark. When "semiotic ghosts" from SF's notion of the future start invading the reality of Gibson's protagonist, only immersion in sordid popular culture can banish these dead dreams of a perfect future. In dramatizing two "deaths" of science fiction, "Centigrade 233" and "The Gernsback Continuum" join a long line of critical and fictional considerations of the genre's passing. Some of these considerations are laments, some are warnings, and some are celebrations, but all posit some form of end to SF, or at least to SF as commonly recognized. These predictions of the death of science fiction variously see the genre "dying" into mainstream literature, into film, TV, electronic culture, fantasy, publishing formulae, etc. At the most "positive" end of these speculations is a view of SF triumphant—a literature that disappears into a culture that has so internalized its assumptions about change and technology that any literary invocation of this world must inevitably invoke the worldview of SF. Or the "death of SF" may turn out to mean a birth of a new form of SF, as happened with the New Wave in the 1960s and with cyberpunk in the

1980s. And, for all their pronouncements about the death of the old, these new forms tend to expand the genre, eventually taking their place along with the older forms they claimed to kill. At the "negative" end of these speculations are views of SF so moribund that it disappears into nostalgia or so driven by publishing decisions that it disappears into predictable "blockbusters" or unrigorous blends with fantasy. Or SF may disappear into the inverted millenarianism of postmodern culture, yielding to the resignation that the "future is used up." And, oddly straddling these antithetical views is the fear suggested in "Centigrade 233" that the very technologies SF has so long envisioned might themselves spell the end of print culture and linear narrative—a triumph that proves grimly Pyrrhic.

So common have these concerns with the end of SF become that Roger Luckhurst has proposed an explanation tying SF's preoccupation with its own death to the genre's longstanding ambivalent and ambiguous struggle for legitimation. The way Luckhurst sees it in his award-winning essay, "The Many Deaths of Science Fiction: A Polemic," almost all histories of SF bog down at some point in trying to erect or to erase borders that mark a distinction between high and low literature, between mainstream and genre, or—within the genre—between "proper " and "improper" articulations (pulp and "literary" SF, hard and soft SF, cyberpunk and not-cyberpunk, golden age and New Wave, etc.).[3] Moreover, Luckhurst argues, in trying to erect or erase these borders, commentators on SF return again and again to the rhetoric of death of one phase, aspect, stage, or movement—if only to prepare the way for the rebirth of another. As he puts it, "for the genre as a whole to become legitimate paradoxically involves the very destruction of the genre" (Luckhurst, 38). Histories and theories of SF, he explains, no matter how divergent their surfaces may seem, tend to be united by some form of desire to return to the mainstream, whether to the mainstream of literature or to the mainstream of some Platonic form of SF. In this view

> The history of SF is a history of ambivalent deaths. The many movements within the genre—the New Wave, feminist SF, cyberpunk—are marked as both transcendent death-as-births, finally demolishing the "ghetto" walls, and as degenerescent birth-as-deaths, perverting

the specificity of the genre. To be elevated above the genre is transcendent death and the birth of Literature, but as these movements
harden, coalesce, are *named*, they fall back as subgeneric moments of
SF. They become detours on the road to the proper death of SF.
(Luckhurst, 43)

J. G. Ballard's fiction, Luckhurst suggests, emblematically performs this longing within SF criticism for some form of generic
death as a prelude to transcendent resurrection, while Freud the-
orizes the process of the death instinct as a desire to restore an
earlier stage of life or affairs.

What Luckhurst would have us do is to link these and other
views of borders between SF and everything else to a longstanding critical tendency to view the genre apocalyptically—either
mourning its imminent demise or celebrating its death into new
life beyond the confining or protective borders of the genre
ghetto. Luckhurst's essay, then, is ultimately concerned not with
the death or the survival of SF but with the ways in which SF criticism (and I would add self-reflexive SF stories such as "Centigrade 233" and "The Gernsback Continuum") repeatedly invokes
the rhetoric of death in its efforts to retard, to celebrate, or just to
recognize changes within the "literature of change" itself. More
controversially, Luckhurst calls attention to the ways in which
manically disparate and frequently opposed critical efforts to valorize SF rest on the shared assumption that for SF to be recognized as a significant and valuable literature it must first die—or
be killed—as a popular genre and/or publishing category. "That
death is so central to the history of SF, that death *propels* the
genre is," Luckhurst insists, "the effect of the structure of legitimation: SF is a genre seeking to bury the generic, attempting to
transcend itself so as to destroy itself as the degraded 'low.'" And
even in those histories that valorize SF for its scientific rather
than literary import another kind of death always lurks, as fact
threatens to overtake fiction, as science fiction disappears or dies
into scientific progress. Accordingly, Luckhurst concludes that
"SF is produced from crisis, from its intensive self-reflexive anxi-
ety over its status as literature," rather than being threatened
from without.

I give such prominence to Luckhurst's argument because I
believe it does point to one of the genre's central preoccupa-

tions—what we might call the quest for legitimation on its own terms. This final chapter will start from one of SF's most significant crises of legitimation—the proclaimed death and rebirth of the genre occasioned by the New Wave in the late 1960s—and will look at another proclaimed cycle of death and rebirth in the 1980s occasioned by cyberpunk. While it is too early to predict the nature of SF at the beginning of the next millennium, too early to claim whether or not the genre can survive in an increasingly electronic culture, it is possible to sample its diversity and vitality in the 1990s. Toward this end, I will look at the 23 stories collected by Gardner Dozois in his *The Year's Best Science Fiction: Twelfth Annual Collection*, taking these stories from 1994 not necessarily as the best of contemporary SF but as the best single cross section of the genre's current state.

While this chapter will move from considering SF in the 1960s to SF in the 1980s and then the 1990s, I must stress that it does not offer any kind of history, nor does it imply any clear lines of development. Any focus on the New Wave and cyberpunk will almost inevitably shortchange developments in SF in the 1950s and the 1970s, obscuring important relationships such as that between the great explosion of feminist SF in the 1970s and a cyberpunk that, at first glance, is almost parodically masculinist. Accordingly, it is crucial to remember that this chapter is organized around moments in the evolution of SF when the cycle of proclaimed death and rebirth charted by Luckhurst has been most dramatic.

The New Wave

Pamela Zoline's "The Heat Death of the Universe," discussed at some length in chapter one, was first published in *New Worlds* Magazine in 1967. With its emphasis on entropy, its concern with the "inner space" of the housewife Sarah Boyle's disintegrating worldview, and with its mosaic structure of 54 numbered paragraphs, Zoline's story illustrates some of the most distinctive features of New Wave writing, the movement or convergence of interests tightly associated with the British SF magazine *New Worlds* under the editorship of Michael Moorcock. While "New Wave" is a widely accepted term for describing the changes in SF during the 1960s, the term has specific application only for a small group of writers in England—most notably Moorcock, J. G. Ballard, Brian Aldiss, John Brunner, Pamela Zoline, John Sladek, Christopher Priest, Thomas Disch, and Samuel R. Delany. Somewhat complicating this listing, however, is the fact that Delany, Disch, and Aldiss have all disavowed their inclusion in this "movement," underscoring the point that it was more an attitude toward SF and toward literature, an attitude sharing many of the values and interests of 1960s counterculture. The term "New Wave" has also been applied to a number of American writers of the 1960s, including Harlan Ellison, Philip K. Dick, Robert Silverberg, Roger Zelazny, Disch, Delany, and enough others to lead Brian Aldiss to grumble that in the United States "any writer with a freaky style became an honorable member of the New Wave."[4] The American editor and critic Judith Merril was largely responsible for such an enthusiastic application of the term in the United States, particularly with her 1968 anthology *England Swings SF*. While the "American New Wave" was indeed responsible for significant changes in the nature of SF, it was even less a codified movement than its British progenitor and had a much more comfortable relationship with the pulp tradition of genre SF. In fact, Delany specifies that by the mid-1960s there were not two but three different "islands" of innovative SF: the New Wave in England, one organized around Damon Knight's hardcover anthology series *Orbit*, and one broadly organized around Harlan Ellison's *Dangerous Visions* anthologies (with which Delany does associate himself), and I'll briefly return to these latter two "islands" after considering the British New Wave.[5]

Such distinctions should not cloud the fact that the changed values and focus of writing loosely referred to as New Wave resulted in huge changes in the relationship of SF to mainstream writing, its engagement with cultural issues, its attitude toward science and technology, its treatment of sex, and its growing concern with the "soft" sciences of psychology, sociology, and anthropology. SF reflected the cultural turbulence and controversy of the 1960s, and what certainly felt like a revolution then still seems to mark a sea change in the genre. While the New Wave did not spell the end of older SF traditions, it relegated many of them to the genre's nostalgic hard core while extending to SF the literary techniques and standards of the mainstream.

Under the editorship of John Carnell, *New Worlds* had become England's leading SF magazine and in the early 1960s was already more open to experimentation than were its American counterparts. In 1963 Carnell published a guest editorial by Moorcock in which that young writer declared that "science fiction has gone to hell," suffering from boy authors "writing boys' stories got up to look like grown-ups stories," and listed its shortcomings:

> Let's have a quick look at what a lot of science fiction lacks. Briefly, these are some of the qualities I miss on the whole—passion, subtlety, irony, original characterization, original and good style, a sense of involvement in human affairs, colour, density, depth and, on the whole, real feeling from the writer. . . .[6]

Moorcock's complaint added to J. G. Ballard's call in a 1962 *New Worlds* editorial for an SF that would escape the influence of H. G. Wells and "turn its back on space, on interstellar travel, extra-terrestrial life forms, galactic wars," as well as its "present narrative forms and plots."[7] "The biggest developments of the immediate future will take place, not on the Moon or Mars, but on Earth," insisted Ballard, "and it is inner space, not outer, that needs to be explored. The only truly alien planet is Earth." Later, in his well-known preface to the 1974 French edition of *Crash*, Ballard detailed his belief—shared by many, if not all, of his New Wave colleagues—that the world had so outpaced SF that it had become a casualty of the very future it had helped to shape:

> The future envisaged by the science fiction of the 1940s and 1950s is already our past. Its dominant images, not merely of the first Moon flights and interplanetary voyages, but of our changing social and political relationships in a world governed by technology, now resemble huge pieces of discarded stage scenery. For me, this could be seen most touchingly in the film *2001: A Space Odyssey*, which signified the end of the heroic period of modern science fiction—its lovingly imagined panoramas and costumes, its huge set pieces, reminded me of *Gone With the Wind*, a scientific pageant that became a kind of historical romance in reverse, a sealed world into which the hard light of contemporary reality was never allowed to penetrate.[8]

When Moorcock assumed the editorship of *New Worlds* in 1964, he identified William Burroughs as the producer of "the SF we've all been waiting for," championing the highly subjective, nonlinear, intensely metaphoric and metonymic experiments of a writer then still considered on the extreme fringe of mainstream fiction. Soon, Moorcock would add Ballard as another primary model. What Burroughs (and Ballard) refused to subscribe to was any sense of objective reality, and this seemed to Moorcock and other New Wave writers a change sorely needed in SF. As Edward James sums up the New Wave view:

> SF should no longer be an exploration of the possibilities for humanity and science in the future or an educational introduction to aspects of science wrapped in the sugar coating of plot and adventure. SF should not be an exploration of a hypothetical external reality, because objective reality is, in the post-Heisenberg world (and in the world of Timothy Leary and mind-altering drugs), a dubious concept. . . . SF should be a means to explore our own subjective perceptions of the universe and our fellow human beings.[9]

And, while it was important to the New Wave to put SF to new uses, give it new purposes, it was also extremely important to invigorate its prose style, to create a new kind of SF that would be taken seriously as literature. Not all older SF writers, however, were willing to take New Wave writing seriously as SF, objecting to what they saw as its valorization of subjectivity over science, feelings over thinking, and pessimism over positivism. In a most restrained, but also obviously sympathetic recounting of the case made against the New Wave ethos, James Gunn records: "Some readers have objected to what they considered the inconclusiveness, the willful obscurity, the pointlessness, and the aping of mainstream experimental technique at the expense of content."[10] In the contrasting accounts of the New Wave offered by Gunn in his *Alternate Worlds* (1975) and by Norman Spinrad in his *Modern Science Fiction* (1974) can be found some of the conflict created by this overt challenge to the way SF had been written and what it had become.[11] By any standards, however, the challenge of the New Wave was successful—not in ending the practices of traditional SF, but in expanding the genre's sense of its territory to include radically new perspectives and values.

What resulted were stories like Zoline's "The Heat Death of the Universe" and even more experimental pieces such as Ballard's *The Atrocity Exhibition* (1970), a collection of 15 chapters, most consisting of between 20 and 30 titled sections.[12] Some of these chapters—or chapter titles—such as "Why I Want to Fuck Ronald Reagan," "The Assassination of John Fitzgerald Kennedy ˙Considered as a Downhill Motor Race," and "Plan for the Assassination of Jacqueline Kennedy," so disturbed Ballard's American publisher, Doubleday, that it decided to pulp the already printed edition, leaving it to Grove Press to first publish an American edition, under the title *Love and Napalm: Export U. S. A.*, in 1972. No single section or even chapter can capture the disjunctive variability of *The Atrocity Exhibition*, but the following sections may suggest some of its strangeness:

> **But isn't Kennedy already dead?** Captain Webster studied the documents laid out on Dr Nathan's demonstration table. These were (1) a spectroheliogram of the sun; (2) tarmac and takeoff checks for the B-29 Superfortress *Enola Gay*; (3) electroencephalogram of Albert Einstein; (4) transverse section through a pre-Cambrian trilobite; (5) photograph taken at noon, August 7th, 1945, of the sand-sea, Qattara Depression; (6) Max Ernst's "Garden Airplane Traps." He turned to Dr Nathan. "You say these constitute an assassination weapon?" (34)

> **The Exploding Madonna.** For Travis, the ascension of his wife's body above the target area, exploding madonna of the weapons range, was a celebration of the rectilinear intervals through which he perceived the surrounding continuum of time and space. Here she became one with the madonnas of the billboards and the opthalmic films, the Venus of the magazine cuttings whose postures celebrated his own search through the suburbs of Hell. (16)

Developing the themes and settings that Ballard has pursued throughout his career in works such as the short story collections *The Terminal Beach* (1964), *Myths of the Near Future* (1982), and *War Fever* (1990) and novels such as *Crash* (1973), *Concrete Island* (1974), *Empire of the Sun* (1984), *The Kindness of Women* (1991), and *Rushing to Paradise* (1995), *The Atrocity Exhibition* may be his most important and most difficult work, one that emblemizes the revolutionary attitudes and style of the New Wave.

This collection of what Ballard has called "condensed novels" is only loosely unified by any recognizable plot progression but is compellingly structured by its obsessive themes and images of a technologically fallen world. Norman Spinrad does a fine job of explaining the design behind these condensed novels in a review of Ballard's career that uses his case to epitomize the difference between American and British SF:

> Scenes are rendered as sequences of rapid-fire images, each of which is redolent with multiple and ambiguous meaning. The scenes in turn succeed each other other in rapidly cut montage, the structure arises out of their successive and sometimes repetitive juxtapositions, the psyches of the characters are seen to mutate in a series of isolated cuts rather than linearly, and the resolutions, such as they are, are imagistic, rather than climactic.
>
> It is as if Ballard took whole novels and edited out all the transitions, all the build-ups to situations, all the personal interactions, most of the dialogue, all extraneous description, and condensed them to a series of freeze-frames, extracted moments of epiphany, a kind of flipbook version in which the essence of a whole novel is conveyed in a perfectly selected series of still-shots.[13]

A protagonist variously named Travis, Talbot, Traven, Tallis, Trabert, Talbert, and Travers wanders through the chapters of *The Atrocity Exhibition*, absorbing and meditating on the "media landscape" of a surrealistic culture—the vast "toxic" pool of advertising, political, sexual, and medical images that surround us in daily life. This media landscape is for Ballard the invisible technology of the twentieth century, "the stuff of which our dreams are made," as opposed to the ruined artifacts and abandoned sites of industrial technology that surround his characters. Traven/Travis/Talbot interacts with a series of women—Catherine Austin, Margaret Travis, Karen Novotny, Coma—who share in being victims of violence and in being sexual objects and who are at least metonymically connected to the media-constructed phenomena of Marilyn Monroe, Elizabeth Taylor, and Jackie Kennedy. Media "events" such as the deaths of John F. Kennedy and Marilyn Monroe, the space program, the political ascendancy of Ronald Reagan, James Bond Movies, the Vietnam War, car crashes—all strike Ballard as "pieces of geometry interlocking in a series of mysterious equations." For Ballard, the human body also becomes a landscape of geometries, particularly those having to do with sex and/or traumatic wounds, leading to hauntingly abstract and affectless descriptions: "The young woman was a geometric equation, the demonstration model of a landscape. Her breasts and buttocks illustrated Enneper's surface of negative constant curve, the differential coefficient of the pseudo-sphere" (40).

Clinically scrutinized death and media fascination with death permeate *The Atrocity Exhibition*, as Traven in his various selves both imagines and stages "alternate deaths" for public figures and unknowns alike, perhaps justifying Luckhurst's claim that Ballard's fiction performs the desire of SF to "die into" mainstream literature (Luckhurst, 37) but certainly offering a kind of fiction not previously seen in the genre. For Ballard's protagonist (and one must suspect for Ballard himself) "science is the ultimate pornography, analytic activity whose main aim is to isolate objects or events from their contexts in time and space," a view that completely inverts SF's use of science for imaginary worldbuilding, recasting science as a means of deconstructing humanity and reality alike. In a rhetoric saturated with "modules," "units," "planes," "conjunctions," "equivalencies," "geometries," "equations," Ballard uses the sound of, if not the sense of, science to theorize radically new associations and connections that blur the notion of the interior and exterior of the body, leading to claims such as "all junctions, whether of our own soft biologies or the hard geometries of these walls and ceilings, are equivalent to one another" (56). Unlike William Burroughs, who employs radical disruptions such as his cut-up method to break the "control system" of the mediascape's image tracks, Ballard paratactically collides images and rhetorics of medicine, surrealist art, psychology, pathology, desire, to begin to break down the media landscape into its manifest and latent content. As a character "explains":

> "Any great human tragedy—Vietnam, let us say—can be considered experimentally as a larger model of a mental crisis mimetized in faulty stair angles or skin junctions, breakdowns in the perception of environment and consciousness. In terms of television and the news magazines the war in Vietnam has a latent significance very different from its manifest content. Far from repelling us, it *appeals* to us by virtue of its complex of polyperverse acts." (77)

Trying to "build bridges between things," Ballard looks for "hidden agendas" in contemporary culture, the "hidden logic" of the detritus of technology, the pornography of science, the life of media images that constitute "a map in search of a territory." And particularly in suggesting the sexual allure of car crashes, a theme he would fully develop in *Crash* (1973), Ballard deconstructs sexuality, exploring its nonsexual roots and technological imbrication in chillingly precise terms.

"*Crash* is the first great novel of the universe of simulation," says the cultural theorist Jean Baudrillard, "the world that we will be dealing with from now on: a non-symbolic universe, but one which, by a kind of its reversal of its mass-mediated substance (neon, concrete, cars, mechanical eroticism), seems truly saturated with an intense initiatory power." Echoing Ballard's 1971 claim that "everything is becoming science fiction," Baudrillard notes of *Crash* that it is a new kind of SF which is no longer SF, explaining that "SF of this sort is no longer an elsewhere, it is an everywhere."[14] Whether or not readers follow Baudrillard's theoretical argument, however, *Crash*—like *The Atrocity Exhibition* before it—is now very widely accepted as SF, an acceptance based in part on Ballard's other, more traditional SF writing and in part on our growing sense of the previously unexamined implications of technology and science, but also a dramatic acknowledgment of the reshaping impact of the New Wave.

While Ballard quickly became the model for *New World*'s SF, his writing quickly found admirers in U.S. publishing circles as well. Although it did not win, his "The Cloud-Sculptors of Coral D" was nominated for a Nebula in 1967 and was reprinted both in *Nebula Award Stories Three*, edited by Roger Zelazny, and in Judith Merril's *SF 12*, along with stories by the New Wave or New Wave-like authors Thomas Disch, Brian Aldiss, and Samuel R. Delany. In fact, Ballard and other writers now rightly or wrongly associated with the New Wave began to dominate the Nebula Awards in the late 1960s and began appearing in influential American anthologies such as *Dangerous Visions* and Damon Knight's *Orbit* series, begun in 1966 and running through 1980. Judith Merril's, Knight's and Ellison's anthologies became sites for the publishing of American SF inspired by or converging with that of the *New Worlds* writers. Knight, for example, obviously liked the poetic writing of James Sallis, one of the American New Worlds writers, and he enthusiastically published fiction by R. A.

Lafferty, Kate Wilhelm, and Gene Wolfe that certainly resembled New Wave more than traditional SF. But it was Ellison's *Dangerous Visions* (1967) and its sequel, *Again, Dangerous Visions* (1972), that formed the centerpiece of American New Wave.

Dangerous Visions was innovative and influential before it had any readers simply because it was the first big original anthology of SF, offering prices to its writers that were competitive with the magazines. The readers soon followed, however, attracted by 33 stories by SF writers both well-established and relatively unheard of. These writers responded to editor Harlan Ellison's call for stories they could not publish elsewhere or had never written in the face of almost certain censorship by SF editors. Among the stories Ellison received were the almost Joycean "Riders of the Purple Wage," by Philip Jose Farmer, "Carcinoma Angels," by Norman Spinrad, and "Aye and Gomorrah," by Samuel R. Delany, as well as pieces by Brian Aldiss, Philip K. Dick, J. G. Ballard, John Brunner, John Sladek, Roger Zelazny, David R. Bunch, Theodore Sturgeon, Carol Emshwiller, and Sonya Dorman. Arguments still rage over the true originality and quality of most of these stories, and SF writers and critics frequently claim that Ellison's anthology was more bluster than revolution, but to SF readers, particularly in the United States, *Dangerous Visions* certainly felt like a revolution, and most of its stories seemed incredibly new, different, and exciting. Nearly 30 years after their publication, many of those stories still do, and *Dangerous Visions* marks an emblematic turning point for American SF.

In what now seems an unlikely and somewhat awkward foreword to the anthology, Isaac Asimov, the perfect exemplar of Cambellian SF, suggests that a second revolution in SF (Cambell's was the first) may be inevitable and that it may be all right for readers to enjoy it. Reasoning that changes in both "real science" and "real story" had robbed SF of some of its former sense of wonder, Asimov seems almost to be giving Ellison's readers permission to embrace the changes in *Dangerous Visions* SF, even though he himself had not felt able to contribute a story that responded to Ellison's charge and even though he mourns the past golden age ethos of the 1940s that seems to be slipping away.

Ellison's introduction offers a stark contrast to Asimov's elegiac tone, as it proclaims *Dangerous Visions* to be a revolution, a "new thing" unlike those of either Michael Moorcock or Judith Merril and more controversial than either.[15] Announcing that his anthology "was intended to shake things up," Ellison explained that it was "conceived out of a need for new horizons, new forms, new styles, new challenges in the literature of our times." Insistently referring to this new literature as "speculative fiction" rather than as "science fiction," Ellison observed that the mainstream, in the guise of writers such as Anthony Burgess, Kurt Vonnegut, and John Hersey, had already discovered its techniques and possibilities and that speculative fiction had "arrived" everywhere but in the cloistered world of traditional SF fans, writers, and editors. Employing a phrase that would again become a rallying cry for cyberpunk writers some 20 years later, Ellison cited Charles Fort's theory about "steam engine time"—when it's time for the steam engine to be invented, it will be invented, if not by James Watt, then by someone else. "It is 'steam engine time' for the writers of speculative fiction," proclaimed Ellison: "We are what's happening" (Ellison, 22).

Although he claimed that *Dangerous Visions* was "intended as a canvas for new writing styles, bold departures, unpopular thoughts," Ellison remained vague about the nature of those styles, departures, and thoughts, insisting on the novelty and controversial nature of the stories he had collected, but not attempting to mold them to any particular stylistic or political agendas. Indeed, at times Ellison seems to be saying simply that the older writers and editors of SF are no longer up to the task and that his "thirty-two soothsayers" (several of whom clearly belonged to the old guard) were. Accordingly, some detractors of the American New Wave criticize it for lacking the unifying themes and vision of the *New Worlds* writers, but Ellison's reticence to force a manifesto from his collection now seems incredibly savvy, as its eclecticism foreshadowed the future of SF much better than did the British New Wave. Ellison's second anthology in this series, *Again, Dangerous Visions* (1972), continued the innovative success of the first, using only writers who had not appeared in it, and with Joanna Russ's "When It Changed" and Ursula K. Le Guin's *The Word for the World Is Forest* struck the note that was to dominate SF in the 1970s and early 1980s.

Cyberpunk

Discussions of "waves" in SF can hardly fail to note similarities between the oppositional rhetoric of the New Wave and that of a group of young writers in the mid-1980s who proclaimed once again that the old science fiction was dead. The 1984 publication of William Gibson's *Neuromancer* effectively marks the beginning of SF's newest New Wave—cyberpunk. To borrow Carl Malmgren's view of SF as structured by oscillations between "extrapolative" and "speculative" semblances or world building (extrapolative semblances closely tied to the real world, speculative semblances much more disjunctive and visionary), cyberpunk can be thought of as a sharply extrapolative swing, while the New Wave was sharply speculative.[16] And discussion of waves or swings must remind us of the futility of attempting a static description of science fiction in the twentieth century. Cyberpunk once again marked the appearance of a movement—or at least a powerful impulse—to respond to an obvious and growing divergence between SF's traditional visions of the future and an increasingly uncooperative future that consistently fell far short of that vision. In this sense, cyberpunk was itself a site of resistance to the metanarrative of SF, a corrective attempt to bring its positivist and optimistic epistemology more into line with reality. For some, this new emphasis on recognizing the complexities of cultural and technological change seemed pessimistic and "antihumanist," a betrayal of SF values; for others, it seemed sophisticated and rigorous, in keeping with the traditions of hard SF.

Like their predecessors in the New Wave, cyberpunks—most notably Bruce Sterling, who assumed the role of spokesperson and polemicist for the movement—proclaimed that the old SF of galactic empires and big science was dead. "Technology itself has changed," wrote Sterling in the preface to his *Mirrorshades: The Cyberpunk Anthology* (1986). "Not for us the giant steam-snorting wonders of the past: the Hoover Dam, the Empire State Building, the nuclear power plant. Eighties tech sticks to the skin, responds to the touch: the personal computer, the Sony Walkman, the portable telephone, the soft contact lens."[17] Gibson's "Gernsback Continuum" made the same point less polemically, and stories in the *Mirrorshades* anthology by Lewis Shiner, John Shirley, Pat

Cadigan, Rudy Rucker, Tom Maddox, and Marc Laidlaw began to stake out the new territory Sterling had so confidently claimed. Critical attention organized by Larry McCaffery quickly followed in a special cyberpunk issue of *Mississippi Review* that in turn formed the backbone of *Storming the Reality Studio*.[18]

These and a few other writers constituted what was for a short while called a movement, loosely unified by overlapping, if not shared, assumptions about postmodern culture, the future, and SF itself. (Despite Sterling's bravura pronouncements, most of the writers initially identified as cyberpunks were always uneasy with the label, all too aware, as Lewis Shiner has explained, of the shifting nature of their associations and varying agendas.[19]) The "cyber" part of this movement's name recognized its commitment to exploring the implications of a cybernetic world in which computer-generated and -manipulated information becomes the new foundation of reality. The "punk" part recognized its alienated and often cynical attitude toward authority and establishment of all kinds—SF's specific embodiment of the general tendency of postmodern culture to "resist metanarratives." Indeed, the fascinatingly reciprocal relationship between cyberpunk and postmodernism has been widely studied, perhaps most thoroughly by Brian McHale in his *Constructing Postmodernism*.[20]

Unlike their New Wave predecessors, however, the cyberpunks did find some earlier SF writers worthy models, including Philip K. Dick, Alfred Bester, John Brunner, John Varley, Samuel R. Delany, Norman Spinrad, and Harlan Ellison. Apart from these routinely named "fathers," Samuel Delany reminds us that cyberpunk might actually owe more to its "mothers," the truly oppositional feminist writers of the 1970s and early 1980s such as Joanna Russ, Ursula K. Le Guin, Vonda McIntyre, and Joan Vinge (*Silent Interviews*, 176–77). Moreover, whereas the New Wave desired to bring mainstream literary values to SF, the cyberpunks shared with William Burroughs, Philip K. Dick, and Thomas Pynchon a pronounced dissatisfaction with mainstream narrative techniques. And unlike the New Wave writers who tended to be disinterested in technology, if not technophobic, cyberpunk writers were intensely interested in new technological frontiers—but wary of the implications of these new technologies. As spelled out by Sterling, their thematic concerns tended to be:

The theme of body invasion: prosthetic limbs, implanted circuitry, cosmetic surgery, genetic alteration. The even more powerful theme of mind invasion: brain-computer interfaces, artificial intelligence, neurochemistry—techniques radically redefining the nature of humanity, the nature of the self. (*Mirrorshades*, xiii)

Cyberpunk hit SF with a wallop, occasioning heated arguments about what SF should and should not be, as well as numerous arguments about what cyberpunk actually was. There was even talk of a "humanist" SF movement that would counter cyberpunk's perceived postmodern nihilism. Perhaps because it found a such a powerful spokesperson in Bruce Sterling and such a successful writer in William Gibson, cyberpunk actually attracts a disproportionate amount of attention in studies of SF of the 1980s, offering an appealing but chimerical sense of unity in the face of equally or even more talented and innovative writers who resisted categorization. Octavia Butler, Connie Willis, Karen Joy Fowler, Pat Murphy, Kim Stanley Robinson, John Kessel, Nancy Kress, Lucius Shepard, Howard Waldrop, Greg Bear, Orson Scott Card—to name but a few of the most prominent younger writers—all invigorated and shaped 1980s SF as much as did cyberpunk, but presented such a many-faceted face to the genre as to defy all but the most undiscriminating generalizations.

Within five years of its burst into prominence, however, cyberpunk had evolved from loose movement to a widely shared sensibility. Writers who seemed most influenced by, but not necessarily limited by, this sensibility included Walter Jon Williams, Richard Kadrey, K. W. Jeter, Elizabeth Hand, Michael Swanwick, Jack Womack, Tom Maddox, George Alec Effinger, Emma Bull, Charles Platt, Lucius Shepard, Neal Stephenson, and Jeff Noon. Stephenson's *Snow Crash* (1992) and Noon's *Vurt* (1995) wear their cyberpunk ancestry proudly, even while turning the aesthetic in engaging new directions. Cyberpunk's influence on SF and on the culture at large, however, extends far beyond any list of writers, no matter how large. For the cyberpunk view of the future as vaguely posthuman and of future culture as darkly postmodern has inexorably permeated the SF megatext, leaving traces in the work of even the writers who most vociferously denounced the cyberpunk aesthetic.

Cyberpunk was always more than *Neuromancer*, but that book remains the best single entry to the cyberpunk aesthetic. Gibson's 1984 classic confronts us with a fast-forward near future so culturally complicated and technologically determined that no individual can do much more than survive, relatively powerless but able to carve out small zones of possibility. High-tech but dingy, *Neuromancer's* future is a time of electronic and medical marvels, a time of vicious multinational, Japanese-dominated corporate competition and of vaguely postapocalyptic decay. High culture—the arts—seems pretty much dead and pop culture has taken over. Reflection, surface, simulation become the operating reality in the novel, as electronic images, holographs, clones, cyborgs, and hallucinations intermingle in a world where copies are often better than originals and where almost everything reflects, replicates, or imitates something else. Interest in outer space has waned and the inner spaces of computers and the human body have become the new frontiers and the new battlegrounds.

Parodying both capitalism and consumerism, *Neuromancer* equally divides its future economy between the smothering corporate power of the multinationals and a thriving black market in almost everything. Key to both economies is the manipulation or theft of information, the primary occupation of a cynically resigned counterculture of drug-dependent mercenaries and computer-hacking "cowboys"—protagonists such as Gibson's Molly and Case, pawns in an ambiguous conspiracy to unite two powerful artificial intelligences.

More important, in cultural terms, *Neuromancer* showed readers cyberspace, "a consensual hallucination" built of graphically represented data—an artificial or virtual reality—and sold them on the need to get there, both in fiction and in reality. More than any other novel in recent memory, *Neuromancer* went beyond creating a compelling fictional world to compelling us to shape our world to its fiction; rather than predict the future, *Neuromancer* proclaimed it.

In the cyberspace of Gibson's matrix the world of electronic information becomes a field of striking images, a visually metaphoric world anticipated by the movie *Tron* and later illustrated by the TV show "Max Headroom." Of course, Gibson's cyberspace had also been preceded by virtual reality pioneers such as Ivan Sutherland, Myron Krueger, and Jaron Lanier, as well as by supercomputer scientific visualization and other computer animations. But when Gibson called his virtual construct of data "cyberspace" the name stuck and cyberspace became a powerful metaphor for researchers and theorists of virtual reality. Accordingly, *Neuromancer*, probably more than any other novel in the history of SF, is a bridge to and from other media, in particular to the technologies of electronic culture. And it is precisely the electronic technology *Neuromancer* foregrounds that may supply a narrative experience which so overshadows that of print fiction as to lead to the postliterate world envisioned in Benford's "Centigrade 233."

Without directly addressing the issue, Gibson made us realize the incredible implications computers pose for human memory—and thereby for history, for our sense of reality itself. Without having mastered the current technology of human-computer interface, Gibson managed to imagine and make real the next generation of computer interface, in which the user moves "into" the screen, into cyberspace, where the user has the sense of being inside a simulated three-dimensional world. Without specific reference to the postmodern concern with the "denaturing" of the body, Gibson recast the body as "meat," information that can be "edited" by drugs and surgery and prosthetics into new forms, or even escaped from entirely into the disembodied experience of cyberspace, an escape that ultimately challenges our understanding of what it means to be human. And, without having polemical designs for the future of SF, Gibson wrote a novel that has inexorably altered SF's future.

Apart from its necessary associations with ideas and movements larger than itself—cyberpunk, postmodernism, virtual reality—*Neuromancer* must finally be considered for precisely what it is: a powerfully affective reading experience. From its famous tone-setting opening sentence—"The sky above the port was the color of television, tuned to a dead channel"—through its lushly evocative descriptions of urban decay and the dance of data in cyberspace, *Neuromancer* offers its readers the persuasive feel of a future so informationally hyper that language itself must be speeded up. The key to the novel's affective power is the sensory texture of Gibson's prose—a kind of verbal density in which every scene is a fractal of the larger semblance. What seems to guide Gibson's prose is a desire to parallel the information overload of electronic culture with a sensory overload of embedded images. His plot actually turns out to be equal parts of pretense and sense, itself a simulacrum of suspense and action in which not much really happens (two artificial intelligences merge and the resulting supersentience proclaims: "Things aren't different. Things are things.")

Finally, what is so remarkable about this novel is that any description of it will almost certainly sound familiar to many who have never read *Neuromancer* simply because the contours of its semblance have become a kind of generic standard in SF film, music videos, and now interactive computer games. If you have seen *Blade Runner*, you have seen much of Gibson's future, and if you have seen *Tron, Lawnmower Man, Johnny Mnemonic*, or *Virtuosity*, you have also seen the inner landscape of *Neuromancer*'s cyberspace. In this sense, the megatext of cyberpunk clearly derives from more than print, suggesting that SF in this mode at least has already blurred into a multimedia metagenre that makes strict references to science fiction as a literary genre somewhat misleading.

Certainly, *Neuromancer* well illustrates the uniquely reciprocal relationship between cyberpunk and other media. Cyberpunk is probably the first SF to take the cultural implications of technology completely seriously, to realize that Velcro and video games have changed our world much more than has spaceflight, and to remind us that drugs and rock music are as much a part of high tech as are computers. "The cyberpunks," points out Bruce Sterling, "are perhaps the first SF generation to grow up not only within the literary tradition of science fiction but in a truly science fictional world" (xi). More than anyone else writing today in any form or genre, the cyberpunks realize that electronic and medical technology now surrounds us, not as tools or toys, but as a new environment, an ecosystem that influences almost every aspect of our existence. Arguably the first movement in SF history with roots in traditions of SF film, TV, and other media, cyberpunk writing has more in common with contemporaneous film, TV, video, and computers than has ever been true of relations between print and visual SF. Furthermore, cyberpunk was a literary movement in many ways more concerned with extrapolating the future of electronic media than with anything else; what cyberpunk may have imagined most compellingly was nothing less than the future of the image, and the future relationship between words and images in artificial realities.[21]

And yet, cyberpunk may also represent two significant disappointments—possibly even a crippling failure in science fiction. The first disappointment is that the cyperpunk semblance has become a far too predictable formula, a prefab world into which too many writers have moved without much thought or originality. The second disappointment is that this intensely self-reflexive critique of earlier SF never explored the implications of technology for writing SF; this first SF to take technology seriously finally settled for the kind of narrative conservativism that has so long characterized SF.

If Gibson's *Neuromancer* did not launch cyberpunk, it certainly was the movement's flagship literary work, a novel so popular and powerful that its near-future semblance became almost the universal background world for the cyberpunk sensibility. What *Neuromancer* offered cyberpunk and its commentators was not a formula to be followed but a conveniently emblematic semblance, something that was easy to point to and say "Cyberpunk is like that." The only problem with this arrangement was that Gibson's example was so powerful that it spawned succeeding generations of cyberclone writers who replicated *Neuromancer*'s semblance without tapping its genius or interrogating the issues that shaped the original cyberpunk movement. Accordingly, Ed Bryant may be justified in his sardonic dismissal of a spate of NOGS—Novels of Gibsonian Sensibility—and it's easy to understand why Bruce Sterling and Lewis Shiner react so strongly to what they call "scifiberpunk," the formulaic frenzy of some writers to catch all they can of *Neuromancer*'s reflected heat.

More important, because the genre represents a wavering in the determination to look unblinkingly at the implications of technology, cyberpunk writers have proved oddly wedded to older models of writing. In failing to imagine that the computers that so radically reshaped the cyberpunk semblance could also radically reformulate narrative structure itself, cyberpunk may eventually prove to be no more than a last gasp of print fiction as it slips under the steamroller of electronic culture. Unwilling to tolerate the "tired furniture of galactic empire" in their stories, cyberpunk writers have proved all too willing to continue to employ the tired furniture of linear narrative, leaving the exploration of hypertext narrative to writers who remember that writing is itself a technology and who take seriously the implications of computers for narrative itself.

A little over 10 years after the publication of *Neuromancer*, cyberpunk may better describe elements of culture outside of SF than any other body of writing. The energy that made early cyberpunk writing so dense and fast, an energy that seemed theory driven and concerned with interrogating technology as it had never before been examined in either SF or culture, seemed to dissipate before cyberpunk explored the implications of its own beliefs. William Gibson toyed briefly with computer narrative in his non-fictional and self-consuming performance piece *Agrippa*, Bruce Sterling has become one of the world's experts on computer and hacker culture, and Rudy Rucker remains at the forefront of experimentation with small artificial computer "lifeforms"—cellular automata—but cyberpunk writers in general have been content to limit their narratives to fixed print, championing the future idea of cyberspace human/computer interfaces but reluctant to consider the nonlinear, hypertexted narratives that computer technology makes possible today. Oddly enough, the implications of computer technology for narrative are being explored mainly outside of SF, suggesting that changes in the technology of writing, the technology that should stick most closely to the skin of SF writers in general and cyberpunks in particular, is of little interest to the "literature of change." The movement's manifestos have given way to retrospectives, and the considerable talents of its small cadre of original members have turned in new directions. A wild and rollicking ride while it lasted, cyberpunk came, saw, conquered, and then abandoned ship. Born in controversy and hype, cyberpunk mutated into respectability and influence, becoming both more and less than anyone could have imagined: more as an emblem of a cultural convergence that quickly outstripped the traditional boundaries of SF and of literature itself, less as a wave within SF that rocked a lot of boats and wrecked its share of coastline but which finally was just a wave, and not, as some expected and others claimed, a whole new kind of ocean. If such a new kind of writing is to appear once again in SF, it will almost certainly be based on a tide of interactive nonlinear narratives made possible by the computers that SF has so long loved to write about but has been so slow to apply to science fiction thinking.

SF Approaching the Millennium

In his "Summation: 1994," the preface to *The Year's Best Science Fiction: Twelfth Annual Collection*, veteran editor Gardner Dozois notes that *HotWired*, the online World Wide Web version of *Wired* magazine, plans to serialize Alexander Besher's novel *RIM: A Novel of Virtual Reality*, "with added hypertext links and multimedia enhancements."[22] While this on-line publication of a hypertext SF novel may represent precisely the kind of narrative experimentation SF needs to explore, it is also the case that Besher is neither an established SF writer nor, to my knowledge, previously associated with SF, a point that is of interest only insofar as technological innovations in writing itself seem to be coming primarily from outside the genre. Also having noted that *Omni* magazine was ceasing publication of its regular monthly edition in favor of converting to "interactive online information services" supplemented by quarterly "super" editions, Dozois concluded: "People keep telling me that Electronic Publishing in any significant form is decades away, if it ever comes at all—but I dunno. Seemed to me you could see the seeds of it everywhere this year, if you looked around" (xxxiv).

Whether or not electronic publishing will prove to be the next big wave for SF, it is clear that such a wave remains, at least for now, offshore, leaving us in the 1990s with a genre that cannot be characterized by any single feature, movement, concern, or form. As evidence of the continuing diversity of SF in the twentieth century and as a sign of the vitality of the genre as the millennium approaches, I want to close this study with a brief look at the 23 stories Dozois selected for his *Year's Best* anthology for 1995. These stories, all published in 1994, may not form a rigorous inductive sample, but they are the best single cross section I know of, chosen by one of SF's most respected editors for the series that has firmly established itself over its 12-year history as the best in the genre.

John Huntington, whose *Rationalizing Genius: Ideological Strategies in the Classic American Science Fiction Story* has figured prominently in my understanding of SF, has offered the definitive discussion of the problem of the sample in popular literature scholarship, and my choice of the Dozois anthology does not meet most of the tests met by Huntington's choice of *The Science*

Fiction Hall of Fame anthology for his study. However, since my goal in this final section is to give a snapshot of the genre as it now is, rather than an overview of its formative 30-year period, the Dozois collection, generally recognized as the best recurring SF anthology, seems to me a reasonable, if not inevitable, choice. All but four of the twenty-two authors included in this collection are covered by entries in either *The Encyclopedia of Science Fiction*, *The Anatomy of Wonder*, or Pringle's *The Ultimate Guide to Science Fiction*. Seven of the writers are women; fifteen are men. While the anthology has no commitment to representing international SF, it contains stories by writers from the United States, Canada, England, and Australia. Roughly a third of the authors here have won Hugo and/or Nebula Awards (and the editor has repeatedly won awards both for his writing and for his editing), and many more have been award nominees. Eight of the stories (in the categories short story, novella, and novelette) in this collection were nominated for 1995 Hugo Awards, and one of those nominated had already won a 1994 Nebula. And yet there is nothing too established about this list of writers, since it includes a number who have come to prominence only quite recently and several who will be unknown to all but the most comprehensive of SF readers. All of the stories in the anthology first appeared in recognized SF magazines or SF or fantasy anthologies, so while several of these stories might conceivably be published in the mainstream, they were ostensibly written for genre audiences.

What most emerges from any attempt to offer an overview of these 23 stories is their dissimilarity, reminding me of John Clute's reference to the "almost lubricious heterogeneity" of the SF he surveyed for 1992. The opening story, Ursula K. Le Guin's "Forgiveness Day," continues the future anthropology of her Hainish worlds of *The Left Hand of Darkness* and *The Dispossessed*, in the interstellar community of the Ekumen. Le Guin's story focuses on clashing cultural and political values on a planet striving to join the Ekumen, dramatized in male and female characters from different planets who are thrown together as victims of a political kidnapping. "Forgiveness Day" suggests that extreme differences in gender and power assumptions can be rationally bridged by individuals and then by their cultures in a kind of inexorable move toward perfectible relationships. "The Matter of

Seggri," Le Guin's second story in this collection, consists of a mosaic of Ekumen reports over hundreds of years about the evolution of the matriarchal culture on the planet Seggri. These reports chronicle the slowly equalizing gender inversion of Seggri, offering a kind of utopian process story in which constructed gender disparities slowly disappear. Brian Stableford's "*Les Fleurs du Mal*," which closes the anthology, offers a highly allusive future detective story in which Holmesian ratiocination must be supplemented by the artistry of an Oscar Wilde figure in order to solve a series of murders by a "designer plant." Containing self-reflexive nods to great nineteenth-century proto–science fiction such as "Rappaccini's Daughter," and *The Island of Dr. Moreau*, Stableford's detectives finally unravel an intricate revenge and protest by a scientist denied the near, but often empty, immortality of his onetime colleagues.

Le Guin's and Stableford's stories are set in futures where conflict resolution has markedly improved and where gender equality seems within reach. Stableford's story is closely pegged to biomedical technological advances, but its plot has exclusively to do with discovering the human motivation behind a series of ingenious and theatrical murders, and its thematic focus is on the psychological implications of extreme longevity and body rejuvenation. Science and technology are so far in the background of Le Guin's future as to have little or no impact on her stories, which have to do primarily with the discovery of individual identity once artificial cultural constructions are stripped away.

Apart from their mutual investment in a distant future, Le Guin's and Stableford's stories are driven by different purposes, manifest very different relationships to science and technology, and also have very different relationships to literary megatexts, with Stableford's story self-consciously metaliterary. Both "Forgiveness Day" and "*Les Fleurs du Mal*," however, are clearly SF by any definition or standard I can think of. The same cannot be said of several other stories in the Dozois anthology, most notably "Going After Old Man Alabama," by William Sanders; "The Sawing Boys," by Howard Waldrop; and "Split Light," by Lisa Goldstein. Two other stories—"Red Elvis," by Walter Jon Williams, and "The Hole in the Hole," by Terry Bisson—fit well-established SF categories, but with twists that complicate our notion of the genre.

"Going After Old Man Alabama" and "The Sawing Boys" will remind most readers of magic realism or fantasy more than of the protocols of SF. Old Man Alabama turns out to be a Cherokee witch in current-day Oklahoma who develops medicine that will allow him to travel back in time. His goal is to intercept Columbus before he reaches the New World, then turn him and his crew into birds so that the white man's invasion of America will never take place. When two other medicine men follow him back in time, they discover that Old Man Alabama's history and timing left something to be desired, as he had confused the *Mayflower* with Columbus's expedition and had actually managed to return to and depopulate not even the *Mayflower*, but the *Mary Celeste*. This hilariously deadpan story might be thought of as a kind of failed alternate history, but its style has the flavor of the tall tale more than of SF. However, in presenting Native American magic as an internally consistent and effective belief system, Sanders constructs magic very much like SF usually constructs science. Waldrop's "The Sawing Boys" also feels more like a tall tale, but one that collides the registers of European fairy tale, frontier and backwoods humor, and Runyonesque gangster patois. For both of these stories, the prose surfaces of sentences and the vernacular dialogue contribute far more to their appeal than does any single novum or SF concept. And yet both stories probably fall into the general category of metaliterary SF covered in the *Encyclopedia of Science Fiction* by the broad term "fabulation."

Defined as "any story which challenges the two main assumptions of genre SF: that the world can be seen; and that it can be told" (ESF, 400), fabulation "articulates the fableness of things," shifting attention from the SF world of the story to its prose surface. While such stories can be read as SF, they also can be read through a number of other narrative protocols, and if read as SF will probably be done so more for contextual reasons or the private purposes of the reader than for any aspects of content or purpose. Terry Bisson's "The Hole in the Hole" displays some of the characteristics of fabulation but is more of a technological tall tale. An absurdist story about a fold in space that lets small-time entrepeneurs step directly from a car junkyard in New York onto the surface of the Moon, "The Hole in the Hole" abounds in what might be called mock-scientific explanations of its Earth/Moon "adjacentcy," delivered by a contemporary parody of the edison-ade hero. Introduced by editor Dozois as a work in the tradition of R. A. Lafferty, Bisson's story reminds us of the way in which SF formulas or categories spring up around individual authors. Indeed, Bisson, author of the uniquely strange and absurd "Bears Discover Fire," and Waldrop, author of three collections of incredibly offbeat short stories, have already become just such a name locus for a kind of distinctive twist on SF concerns. Bisson's, Sanders's, and Waldrop's stories also remind us of the prominence and importance of humor in SF, a characteristic that often escapes mention in studies of the genre.

Both Lisa Goldstein's "Split Light" and Walter Jon Williams's "Red Elvis" offer alternate worlds in which history took quite different turns. Goldstein's story presents the ruminations of Shabbetai Zevi, a seventeenth-century messianic leader of Sabbatarianism, a Jewish movement that in this story might have swept the world and led to nuclear apocalypse had not its leader chosen to convert to Islam. In "Red Elvis," Williams considers a world in which Elvis died at birth and his twin brother Jessie goes on to have the singing career we associate with Elvis—with the small exception that Jessie also becomes a fervent Marxist-Leninist dedicated to the people's struggle. The alternate world story has become an SF staple, but these stories tighten the formula's focus, examining what changed history might mean to the individual more than what it might mean to society. A frenetic mixture of alternate world–parallel world elements and time travel elements, Eliot Fintushel's "Ylem" presents a collapse of identity and reality that may be the protagonist-writer's nervous breakdown or may tell the story of a return in time to before the Big Bang to change the composition of the universe for corporate profit. Although its prose surface is the most experimental in the collection, with disruptions in time and character identity, those disruptions are all "rational" consequences of the story's time-travel novum—or of the alternate explanation that the narrator is having a breakdown.

The time distortion abstracted in "Ylem" becomes intensely personal and concrete in "Melodies of the Heart," by Michael F. Flynn. This story takes a long tour through American cultural history in unravelling the past of a woman in a nursing home whose jumbled memories span a lifetime of nearly 200 years. In discovering the pattern in her memories and the aberrant DNA that is the secret of her longevity, a young doctor whose daughter is dying from progeria—premature aging—also finds his own humanity. Recognizably dystopian futures appear in Katharine Kerr's "Asylum" and Maureen F. McHugh's "Nekropolis," and Geoff Ryman's "Dead Space for the Unexpected" presents a specifically corporate dystopia, reminiscent of Eileen Gunn's gleefully rapacious "Stable Strategies for Middle Management." The apocalyptic Big One, the great and devastating California earthquake, sets up Mary Rosenblum's "California Dreamer," but her story quickly shifts focus from the power of nature to the power of human need and concentrates on the effects of the disaster only on a woman who has lost her partner and a young girl who has lost her mother. "Paris in June," by Pat Cadigan, has ties to the paranoid tradition in SF in which humans are the puppets of alien forces. In this case, the puppet seems to be an alien construct, an information-gathering mechanism, that vampirically "records" human memories and then yields them to unseen aliens.

Several of the stories Dozois selected display clear ties to more than one SF theme or formula. For example, both "Flowering Mandrake," by George Turner, and "Cilia-of-Gold," by Stephen Baxter, are first-contact stories, the former exploring the idea of plant-based intelligent life with cross-galactic hatred of red-blood life-forms, the latter positing intelligent life-forms in pockets of water beneath the surface of Mercury. Evolutionary extrapolation, an SF mainstay since Wells, also undergirds both stories (as it also undergirds Robert Reed's "The Remoras" and Mike Resnick's "Seven Views of Olduvai Gorge"), but "Cilia-of-Gold" is also a veritable hard-science festival, with information and speculation about astronomy and physics on nearly every page. Moreover, in presenting one-time space travellers who, after five billion years of devolution, retain only the blind and hopeless urge to fight up through Mercury's ice toward the stars, "Cilia-of-Gold" pays homage to James Blish's classic "Surface Tension."

Joe Haldeman's "None So Blind" can only be a descendent of Wells's "In the Country of the Blind," with the twist that its motto would be "In the country of the sighted, the properly surgically blinded is king." Cletus, Haldeman's nerdy protagonist, is also squarely in the edisonade tradition of the boy genius, and Cletus's discovery that bypassing the visual cortex allows the brain to vastly improve its partitioning, and thus to become five or six times faster and more powerful, continues the fascination with genius in classic American SF so well charted by John Huntington. What Haldeman brings to this long-standing fascination, however, is a kind of resignation to the inexorable spread of even the most troubling deals with the devil of medical technology. In many ways the most old-fashioned-seeming of the stories in *The Year's Best Science Fiction*, Haldeman's "None So Blind" displays a wariness and sadness both at the price of genius and at the number willing to pay that price. A similar poignancy pervades Robert Reed's "The Remoras," whose title refers to a class of workers on the exterior of a larger-than-Earth-sized spaceship. Over millions of years, these workers have learned to control the cancerous mutations of their bodies caused by radiation exposure, and have gained the ability to mutate their bodies at will—at the cost of never being able to see entire or touch those bodies, which must be permanently encased in self-sustaining space suits. Named after the small parasitical fish that attach themselves to sharks, the Remoras have evolved a culture of body modification that makes them either gods or prisoners within their space suits.

If Haldeman's story suggests a way in which evolution can be technologically accelerated (genius begetting genius), and if "The Remoras" suggests one kind of evolutionary endtime when evolutionary change has become virtually instantaneous, Resnick's "Seven Views of Olduvai Gorge" offers the "inverted nostalgia" of another kind of evolutionary endtime "when mankind's day is done and we must pass on our legacy to the inheritors of Earth (or of the Universe)" (ESF, 396). Briefly connected to the future history of Kenya developed in "Kirinyaga" and other stories, "Seven Views of Olduvai Gorge" seems to be an elegy for the extinct human race—right up to the point where what has seemed to be evidence of humanity's aggressive and self-destructive folly is also revealed to be evidence of an indomitable toughness and resiliency.

Body modification, although at the level of microscopic nanotechnology, also plays a prominent role in Nancy Kress's "Margin of Error," in which a woman researcher whose work and husband have been pirated by her sister exacts a terrible revenge.

Kress's story imagines a kind of perfected cyborg body, kept eternally youthful by cellular nanotechnology, but choosing this technology means accepting sterility, a sacrifice Kress's protagonist would not make. Maneuvered out of the nanotechnology research project and out of her marriage by an unscrupulously ambitious sister who became the celebrated first human test case for the nanotechnology, Kress's protagonist did manage to engineer a sister-specific cellular time bomb in which the nanoassemblers run wild, creating a kind of cyborg cancer. The story reveals all of this in a conversation between the harried but satisfied ex-researcher mother and the glamorous but desperate and doomed ruthless sister, ultimately offering an ideologically ambivalent view of science but a very traditional smugness in genius. While Kress's story questions not science but the temptations and trade-offs made possible by scientific progress, it does share some of the resignation of Haldeman's "None So Blind." "Margin of Error," "The Remoras," "Melodies of the Heart," "None So Blind," and Greg Egan's "Cocoon" all continue the cyberpunk and postmodern obsession with the easy edit, the assumption that any aspect of reality, including the body, can be edited, modified, reengineered, redesigned, although in a distinctly somber rather than celebratory vein.

A New Agenda?

Finally, what do the 23 stories in *The Year's Best Science Fiction: Twelfth Annual Collection* suggest about the overall state of the genre—as a fixed-print phenomenon—as the twentieth century comes to an end? Certainly the diversity and imaginative appeal of these stories do not suggest a genre that has become moribund. The stories may, however, suggest a genre whose agenda or purpose continues to change. Early in the century, and through at least the golden age of the pulps, SF pursued an agenda of paving the way for the future, primarily by encouraging its readers to think about scientific and technological change. While this did not necessarily mean that SF was "pro" science or technology, it generally meant that SF encouraged the thinking that would make scientific or technological change acceptable, if not desirable. More frequently, of course, the message of SF was that change was progress and that progress was good—if not the most exciting prospect in human existence. Clearly, the stories in the Dozois anthology do not support that kind of an agenda.

Nor does the anthology support the pessimism of John Clute, expressed in an essay he wrote for *Nebula Awards 28*, an anthology presenting some of the nominees and winners of Nebulas for 1992. There Clute added his influential voice to "the many deaths of science fiction" tradition:

> Though sales remain high, the genre is clearly in crisis. I, among others, have tended to think that over the past decade or so the old "agenda" SF has aged—prematurely, and at a savage rate—into a purveyor of nostalgic pabulum for consumers, and that the form of SF that Jack Williamson helped invent has become something like a poison fossil. Science fiction, born to advocate and enthuse and teach, has come by century's end, it seems, to lay a mummy's curse upon the new. Despite occasional fresh words from those who continue to write as though SF were a Door in the Wall, most of what is published is now industrial-base frozen food, portion-controlled, Sanisealed, and sharecropped, spilling like plastic hot-dogs from a million identical slots in a million vending machines.[23]

Clute's concerns with publishing pressures on the genre echo those of many SF writers and critics, and have recently been elaborated by Christina Sedgwick and Samuel R. Delany.[24] These economic and publishing pressures are beyond the scope of this study, but Clute's warning about the "death" of "old 'agenda' SF" seems to me to be answered, at least in part, by signs in the Dozois anthology of what might be called "new" or "soft" agenda SF. Soft agenda SF takes scientific and technological advance as an inexorable given, ascribes neither positive nor negative value to scientific change, and, rather than focusing on the impact of science and technology on humanity, seems most concerned with improving the human condition. The social meliorism that has been a traditional mainstay of mainstream literature has long been a feature of SF, but soft agenda SF tends to set this social meliorism in an assumed technosphere where scientific and technological change is no longer of much interest in its own right. Attention that once centered on the novum of a science fiction narrative seems more and more displaced in soft agenda SF to the ideological, political, and social issues that dominate mainstream and academic discourse. The difference is subtle, but instead of emphasizing dynamics of social and psychological change driven by scientific and technological "progress," soft agenda SF emphasizes problems and conditions already clearly recognized in contemporary society, suggesting either that these problems will continue despite "old agenda" changes or will be intensified and foregrounded by those changes. In this respect, soft agenda SF clearly continues programs associated with the New Wave and with the eco-feminist writing of the 1970s and 1980s.

Soft agenda SF responds to the world theorized by Jean Baudrillard and Donna Haraway, a world in which distinctions between the imaginary and the real have been blurred by science and technology to the point where old agenda SF now describes our lives more than it does the future—because the world itself has become science fictional. It is this change that Larry McCaffery acknowledges when he suggests: "One of the greatest strengths of SF, then, is its capacity to defamiliarize our science fictional lives and thereby force us to temporarily inhabit worlds whose cognitive distortions and poetic figurations of our own social relations—as these are constructed and altered by new technologies—make us suddenly see our own world in sharper relief."[25] And the writers interviewed by McCaffery in *Across the Wounded Galaxies*—Gregory Benford, William S. Burroughs, Octavia Butler, Samuel R. Delany, Thomas Disch, William Gibson, Ursula K. Le Guin, Joanna Russ, Bruce Sterling, and Gene Wolfe—can all be thought of as pursuing soft agenda concerns in their fiction.

McCaffery's observation that it is "now possible for people physically to inhabit their lives without imaginatively or ethically inhabiting them" precisely points to the need for a new SF agenda that will help us to understand the "startling transformations and reconsiderations" in "the basic paradigms and oppositions that we've relied upon to understand ourselves and our relationship to the universe—the categorical oppositions, for example, of organic/inorganic, male/female, originality/duplication (image/reality, artifice/nature), human/nonhuman." And it is in these terms that what I'm so unimaginatively referring to as the soft agenda owes more to the deconstructive investigation of control mechanisms by William Burroughs (with an eye toward his use of the term "soft machine") than to soft science SF or to the "soft science fiction" unfairly associated by Charles Platt with women writers and shortsightedly judged by him to be an erosion of SF's great strength.[26] Soft agenda SF should not be confused with sentimental SF, nor necessarily limited to "soft science" SF, as the writers selected by McCaffery for his *Across the Wounded Galaxies* interviews should remind us.

When Donna Haraway functionally describes SF as "generically concerned with the interpenetration of boundaries between problematic selves and unexpected others and with the exploration of possible worlds in a context structured by transnational technoscience," her definition reflects soft agenda SF.[27] When Istvan Csicsery-Ronay observes that "SF embeds scientific-technological concepts in the sphere of human interests and actions, explaining them and explicitly attributing social value to them," and argues that SF is not a formal genre but a "mode of awareness, characterized by two linked forms of hesitation, a pair of gaps," he helps locate the shift from old to soft agenda.[28] What Csicsery-Ronay identifies as hesitations or gaps are concerns with the plausibility of the SF novum, the first gap focused on the plausibility of novum, the second on its ethical implications and resonances. Both hesitations are present in most SF, but old agenda SF tends to privilege the first concern while soft agenda SF tends to privilege the second.

Evidence of the shifting focus of soft agenda SF can be found in a number of stories in the Dozois anthology. Ursula Le Guin, who might be considered the patron saint of soft agenda SF and whose *Norton Book of Science Fiction*, coedited with Brian Attebery, may be this new agenda's emblematic text, illustrates its commitment to social meliorism with both of her stories, each of which assumes a kind of utopian social evolution in which cultural differences and gender and power inequalities within cultures gradually disappear or at least cease to be points of contention. For all of their medical and technological backgrounds, both Michael Bishop's "*Cri de Coeur*" and Michael F. Flynn's "Melodies of the Heart" are essentially family dramas, driven by the challenges of a child with Downs' syndrome and another suffering from progeria—premature aging. In the Flynn story, a father's love for his congenitally afflicted and dying daughter is balanced against his intolerance for an aged female patient; as his understanding and compassion for his aged patient grows, he also realizes that she is a kind of genetic inverse of his daughter and may hold the key to a cure for his daughter's condition. While science-fictional ideas are interwoven throughout both of these stories, neither is as concerned with an attitude toward a technologized environment or with change itself as with human compassion and understanding.

"Nekropolis" features as characters a woman who has agreed to sell herself into a kind of institutionalized psychological abuse and an artificially constructed male AI, but the story has to do with the birth of freedom, not freedom from technology or freedom that depends in any way on the manipulation of technology. Both "Asylum" and "Cocoon" caution against intolerance, the former against what Kerr terms "Christian fascism," the latter against homophobia. Nominally a postapocalyptic story set in the aftermath of the great California earthquake, "California Dreamer" has everything to do with the psychological mechanisms of compensation and denial and nothing to do with medical or technological mediations or interventions in those processes. And the heavy irony of an alternate world in which Graceland is called The People's Palace of Labor and the alternate Elvis dies saving Martin Luther King from assassination derives entirely from issues that have nothing to do with SF's old agenda.

Indeed, even the stories in the Dozois anthology that seem to retain the strongest ties to what Clute calls "old agenda SF" reveal new epistemological sympathies. Discovery of the life-forms on Mercury in the patently hard science "Cilia-of-Gold" automatically means that the commercial use of the planet will stop; the life-forms will be studied, but they will apparently not be harmed or exploited. Humans flunk the test of first-contact protocols in "Flowering Mandrake," as the green-blooded alien plant form commits suicide, taking hundreds of his red-blood enemies with him. And the Charles Fortean resonance ("We are property") of "Paris in June" is mediated by small steps toward independence taken by the alien-designed but human-seeming "information gathering mechanism." Moreover, "Paris in June" is told in such a way that its narrator may simply be crazy, rather than an alien pawn.

Of course, what I'm calling "soft agenda" has always existed to some extent in twentieth-century SF, and as many as a third of the stories collected in *The Science Fiction Hall of Fame* might fit this very loose description. Certainly Zelazny's "A Rose for Ecclesiastes," Merril's "Only a Mother," Padgett's "Mimsy Were the Borogroves," and Keyes's "Flowers for Algernon"—to name only the most obvious—display characteristics very similar to those I find in the Dozois anthology, sharing a preoccupation with subjectivity, identity, and difference. And almost all of the stories in *The Norton Book of Science Fiction* foreground these qualities. Soft agenda SF, then, is nothing new, but marks an intensification and spread of tendencies long found; rather than a wave, it is a ripple running throughout the history of the genre. But it is precisely this ripple and many others that can be retroactively recognized that innoculate SF from any single "death," almost certainly ensuring that science fiction will continue to be born anew in the future where it has already so brashly lived.

Notes and References

Preface

1. Robert A. Heinlein, in *Requiem: New Collected Works by Robert A. Heinlein and Tributes to the Grand Master*, ed. Yoji Kondo (New York: TOR, 1992), 157.

2. Rosemary Herbert, "Science Fiction Today: The Now and Future Marketplace," *Publisher's Weekly* 229 (May 23, 1996): 59.

3. Octavia E. Butler, *Parable of the Sower* (New York: Four Walls Eight Windows, 1993), 3.

4. Hugo Gernsback, pioneering editor of *Amazing Stories*—the first true SF magazine in English—did not originate "science fiction" as a term, but his criticism, as Gary Westfahl has persuasively argued, and as I will discuss in chapter two, was instrumental in codifying SF as a genre.

5. William Sims Bainbridge, *Dimensions of Science Fiction* (Cambridge, Mass.: Harvard University Press, 1986), 4.

6. Eric S. Rabkin and Robert E. Scholes, *Science Fiction: History, Science, Vision* (New York: Oxford University Press, 1977), vii. The discussion of "Science Fiction in Other Media" (100–109) in this excellent work is particularly insightful.

7. John Clute and Peter Nicholls, *The Encyclopedia of Science Fiction* (New York: St. Martin's Press, 1993), xi–xii; hereafter cited in text as ESF.

8. Editor Neil Barron's indispensable annotated bibliography *Anatomy of Wonder 4: A Critical Guide to Science Fiction* (New Providence, New Jersey: R. R. Bowker, 1995) significantly updates, but does not replace, the *Third Edition* (1987). Both editions are essential sources of information about SF.

9. R. A. Lafferty, "Nine Hundred Grandmothers," in *The Norton Book of Science Fiction*, eds. Ursula K. Le Guin and Brian Attebery (New York: W. W. Norton, 1993). Lafferty's protagonist, Ceran Swicegood, proves to be a rapacious and selfish scholar who is hilariously frustrated by ancient and wise aliens when he tries to unravel all of their secrets.

10. J. G. Ballard's claim that SF is "the main literary tradition of the twentieth century" appears in his influential and prescient "Introduction to the French Edition" of *Crash* (New York: Vintage, 1985; originally published 1974). Istvan Csicsery-Ronay's argument that SF is an attitude toward the world appears in his award-winning essay "The SF of Theory: Baudrillard and Haraway," *Science-Fiction Studies* 18 (November 1991): 387–404.

11. Paul K. Alkon, *Science Fiction before 1900: Imagination Discovers Technology* (New York: Twayne Publishers, 1994), xii; hereafter cited in text.

12. Marleen S. Barr, *Feminist Fabulation: Space/Postmodern Fiction* (Iowa City: University of Iowa Press, 1992).

13. Jean Baudrillard, "Simulacra and Science Fiction," in "Two Essays," *Science Fiction Studies* 18 (November 1991): 312.

14. Gardner Dozois, ed., *The Year's Best Science Fiction: Twelfth Annual Collection* (New York: St. Martin's Press, 1995).

Chapter One

1. Theodore Sturgeon, *Venture Science Fiction* 2 (March 1958): 66–67; quoted from Bainbridge, 12.

2. James Gunn, *Alternate Worlds: The Illustrated History of Science Fiction* (New York: Prentice Hall, 1975), 13; hereafter cited in text. J. G. Ballard, *Crash* (New York: Vintage Books, 1985), 1–6. Earlier, in 1971, Ballard had simply stated: "Everything is

becoming science fiction. From the margins of an almost invisible literature has sprung the intact reality of the 20th century" (REsearch 98).

3. Bruce Sterling, ed., *Mirrorshades: The Cyberpunk Anthology* (New York: Ace Books, 1988), ix.

4. Brian Aldiss with David Wingrove, *Trillion Year Spree: The History of Science Fiction* (New York: Atheneum, 1986), 407.

5. H. Bruce Franklin, *Robert Heinlein: America as Science Fiction* (New York: Oxford University Press, 1981), 3.

6. In *War Stars: The Superweapon and the American Imagination,* Franklin has charted the conflation of science fiction and American weapons policy. In his *Science-Fiction Studies* essay "The Vietnam War as American SF and Fantasy," Franklin developed the thesis that "America's war in Indochina cannot be dissociated from American SF, which shaped and was reshaped by the nation's encounter with Vietnam" (341). And in a paper first delivered at the Eaton Conference "America as Science Fiction: 1939," Franklin terms the New York World's Fair "the principal form of science fiction in 1939," explaining: "A fair billing itself as the World of Tomorrow may be considered just as much a work of science fiction as a short story or a novel, a comic book or a movie" (119).

7. Joanna Russ, "The Image of Women in Science Fiction," *Vertex* 1 (February 1974): 32.

8. Frederik Pohl, "Two-Way Look at the Literature of Change," *New Scientist* (22 May 1993), 48.

9. Samuel R. Delany, *Starboard Wine: More Notes on the Language of Science Fiction* (Pleasantville, New York: Dragon Press, 1984), 34; hereafter cited in text.

10. Brian M. Stableford, *The Sociology of Science Fiction* (San Bernardino, California: Borgo Press, 1987), 68; hereafter cited in text.

11. SF's two best-known awards are the Hugo and the Nebula. Hugos are determined by SF fans, while Nebulas are determined by SF writers.

12. Samuel R. Delany, *The Jewel-Hinged Jaw: Notes on the Language of Science Fiction* (New York: Berkley Windhover Books, 1977), 21–37; hereafter cited in text.

13. Ursula K. Le Guin, Introduction to *The Norton Book of Science Fiction: North American Science Fiction, 1960–1990*, eds. Ursula K. Le Guin and Brian Attebery (New York: W. W. Norton & Co., 1993), 30–31; hereafter cited in text as NBSF.

14. Brian Attebery, *Strategies of Fantasy* (Bloomington: Indiana University Press, 1992), 107–8. Damien Broderick also discusses the concept of the megatext in "Reading SF as a Mega-Text," *New York Review of Science Fiction* 47 (July 1992): 1, 8–11.

15. Mark Rose, *Alien Encounters: Anatomy of Science Fiction* (Cambridge, Massachusetts: Harvard University Press, 1981), 5; hereafter cited in text.

16. E. M. Forster, "The Machine Stops," in *The Road to Science Fiction #2: From Wells to Heinlein*, ed. James Gunn (New York: Mentor, 1979), 36; hereafter cited in text as MS.

17. Wilfred Stone, *The Cave and the Mountain* (Palo Alto, California: Stanford University Press, 1966), 152–54.

18. Two important recent studies of the scientific romance are Brian Stableford's *Scientific Romance in Britain 1890–1950* (London: Fourth Estate, 1985) and Darko Suvin's *Victorian Science Fiction in the UK: The Discourses of Knowledge and of Power* (Boston: G. K. Hall & Co., 1983).

19. Since the novellas included in the *Science Fiction Hall of Fame* volume were selected by polling the members of the Science Fiction Writers of America, "The Machine Stops" has been published in one of science fiction's most authoritative series, a series of anthologies whose contents were selected by the primary organization of science fiction writers. Here, as is frequently the case, science fiction considered as a publishing phenomenon also reflects the phenomenon of SF's being constructed as an expectation of readers, since it was as readers that the SFWA members made their choices. I mention this not to invoke the SFWA poll as any kind of ultimate arbiter of what is or is not science fiction in theoretical terms, but to suggest how this particular story has become a more or less "official" part of the literary history of science fiction.

20. John Clute and Peter Nicholls, "Genre SF," *The Encyclopedia of Science Fiction* (New York, St. Martin's Press, 1993), 483–85; hereafter cited in text as ESF.

21. Gary K. Wolfe, *The Known and the Unknown: The Iconography of Science Fiction* (Kent, Ohio: Kent State University Press, 1979); hereafter cited in text.

22. Carl D. Malmgren, *Worlds Apart: Narratology of Science Fiction* (Bloomington, Indiana: Indiana University Press, 1991), 10.

23. Suvin's *Metamorphoses of Science Fiction: On the Poetics and History of a Literary Genre* (New Haven: Yale University Press, 1979) supplies what is probably the most widely cited definition of SF as "a literary genre whose necessary and sufficient conditions are the presence and interaction of estrangement and cognition and whose main formal device is an imaginative framework alternative to the author's empirical environment" (7–8). While this definition is in many ways compelling, Suvin uses it to exclude almost all genre SF and indeed to exclude many, if not most, of the works I will discuss in this book. Like many SF critics, I choose to respect this definition but to apply it quite differently from Suvin.

24. Joanna Russ, "Towards an Aesthetic of Science Fiction," reprinted in *Science-Fiction Studies: Selected Articles on Science Fiction 1973–1975*, eds R. D. Mullen and Darko Suvin (Boston: Gregg Press, 1976), 9–10. Le Guin's comment comes from her introduction to the *Norton Book of Science Fiction*, 23.

25. David Hartwell, *Age of Wonders: Exploring the World of Science Fiction* (New York, Walker and Company, 1984), 42; hereafter cited in text.

26. Alexei Panshin and Cory Panshin, *The World Beyond the Hill: Science Fiction and the Quest for Transcendence* (Los Angeles: Jeremy P. Tarcher, 1989).

27. Drawing from Edmund Burke, Immanuel Kant, and other philosophers, Cornel Robu offers a fascinating and rigorous argument that science fiction is an art of the sublime in his "A Key to Science Fiction: The Sublime," *Foundation* 42 (Spring 1988): 21–37.

28. Brian Attebery, *Teacher's Guide to Accompany the Norton Book of Science Fiction* (New York: W. W. Norton, 1993), 21.

29. John Campbell (writing as Don A. Stuart), "Twilight," *The Science Fiction Hall of Fame, Volume I: The Greatest Science Fiction Stories of All Time* (New York: Avon Books, 1971), 40–61; hereafter cited in text as TWI.

30. John Huntington, *Rationalizing Genius: Ideological Strategies in the Classic American Science Fiction Short Story* (New Brunswick: Rutgers University Press, 1989); hereafter cited in text.

31. Cited in Alexei and Cory Panshin's *The World Beyond the Hill*, 249.

32. Cited in Paul Carter, *The Creation of Tomorrow: Fifty Years of Magazine Science Fiction* (New York: Columbia University Press, 1977), 213.

33. Albert I. Berger, *The Magic That Works: John W. Campbell and the American Response to Technology* (San Bernardino, California: Borgo Press, 1993), 27.

34. Tom Godwin, "The Cold Equations," *The Science Fiction Hall of Fame, Vol I: The Greatest Science Fiction Stories of All Time*, ed. Robert Silverberg (New York: Avon Books, 1971), 543–69.

35. Pamela Zoline, "The Heat Death of the Universe," *The Heat Death of the Universe and Other Stories* (Kingston, New York: McPherson & Co., 1988), 13–28; hereafter cited in text as HD.

36. Sarah Lefanu, *Feminism and Science Fiction* (Bloomington: Indiana University Press, 1989), 98. Lefanu offers an excellent discussion of this story in support of her larger thesis that "science fiction is feminism-friendly."

37. James Gunn, *The Road to Science Fiction #2: From Wells to Heinlein* (New York: Mentor Books, 1979), 1. A well respected SF writer and editor, Gunn has also been one of the pioneers of SF scholarship, and I give some prominence to his definition because it attempts to offer a broadly inclusive introduction to the genre. The very length of Gunn's definition reveals his desire to avoid some of the definitional battles that attend the discussion of SF, and his use of qualifiers such as "often" and "usually" is further sign of his desire to advance a "reasonable" and broad-ranging understanding of the genre.

38. While science fiction has been largely associated with the valorization and promotion of science, it is important to note that in one sense science fiction stories are born from a dissatisfaction with science. For all its scientific trappings, science fiction is more properly "fictional science," its rhetoric of plausibility masking an impatience with what science has not yet done or cannot seem to do. And some of this dissatisfaction with the status quo of science must surely spill over into

a dissatisfaction with the status quo of formula. Or, to put this in Brian Aldiss's words, science fiction is "both formulaic and something more than a genre. It is a mode which easily falls back into genre. The model is flexible, changing with the times. New designs are forever produced" (1986). When the designs get too familiar, SF devolves from being an interrogating (dissatisfied) attitude toward the world (a mode) into being a formal genre (satisfied with formula) that contains recognizable SF "machinery," but the machine has stopped.

39. William J. Schafer, "On Being Read by Science Fiction," *New England Review & Bread Loaf Quarterly* 12 (Summer 1990): 389; hereafter cited in text.

Chapter Two

1. Larry Niven, "The Return of William Proxmire," *Requiem: New Collected Works by Robert A. Heinlein and Tributes to the Grand Master*, ed. Yoji Kondo (New York: TOR, 1992), 275–85; hereafter cited in text.

2. For an extended discussion of the relationship between SF film and SF literature, see Brooks Landon, *The Aesthetics of Ambivalence: Rethinking Science Fiction Film in the Age of Electronic (Re)Production* (Westport, Connecticut: Greenwood Press, 1993).

3. See Thomas D. Clareson, *Some Kind of Paradise: The Emergence of American Science Fiction* (Westport, Connecticut: Greenwood Press, 1985).

4. H. Bruce Franklin, *Future Perfect: American Science Fiction of the Nineteenth Century* (New York: Oxford University Press, 1978), ix. Franklin's invaluable study was republished in a revised and expanded edition by Rutgers University Press in 1995.

5. See Sam Moskowitz, *Science Fiction by Gaslight: A History and Anthology of Science Fiction in the Popular Magazines, 1891–1911* (Cleveland: The World Publishing Company, 1968).

6. Paul Alkon has detailed the importance of the robinsonade to SF in his *Science Fiction Before 1900: Imagination Discovers Technology* (New York: Twayne Publishers, 1994), 17, 23–24; hereafter cited in text.

7. ESF, 368.

8. Andrew Ross, "Getting Out of the Gernsback Continuum," *Strange Weather: Culture, Science and Technology in the Age of Limits* (New York: Verso, 1991), 124–25.

9. See Alkon, 115–38, for a more detailed discussion of this novel's contributions to SF. See H. Bruce Franklin's *War Stars: The Superweapon and the American Imagination* (New York: Oxford, 1988), 54–77, for a complete discussion of Edison's contribution to the myth of the superweapon.

10. See Alkon, 84–89, for a detailed discussion of *L'Eve future*.

11. Cecelia Tichi, *Shifting Gears: Technology, Literature, Culture in Modernist America* (Chapel Hill: University of North Carolina Press, 1987).

12. E. F. Bleiler traces the evolution from the Newark Steam Man through the dime novels to the Tom Swift books in "From the Newark Steam Man to Tom Swift," *Extrapolation* 30.2 (1989): 101–16.

13. Reprinted in E. F. Bleiler, *Eight Dime Novels* (New York, Dover Publications, 1974), 107–21.

14. Sam Moskowitz, "Ghosts of Prophecies Past, or, Frank Reade, Jr., and 'Forgotten Chapters in American History,'" *Explorers of the Infinite: Shapers of Science Fiction* (Cleveland: The World Publishing Co., 1963), 115–17; hereafter cited in text.

15. Francis J. Molson, "Great Marvel: The First American Hardcover Science Fiction Series," *Extrapolation* 34 (Summer 1993): 101–22; quoted from 120–21.

16. Sam Moskowitz, "Teen-Agers: Tom Swift and the Syndicate," *Strange Horizons: The Spectrum of Science Fiction* (New York: Charles Scribner's Sons, 1976), 180.

17. Eric S. Rabkin, *Science Fiction: A Historical Anthology* (New York: Oxford University Press, 1983), 234.

18. Smith's original work was coauthored with a neighbor, Mrs. Lee Hawkins Garby, enlisted to help him draw his female characters and shape their dialogue. *The Skylark of Space* was first published as a novel in 1946 as a Buffalo Book, with Mrs. Garby continuing to receive credit. When the novel was

revised for the second time in 1958, she was not listed as a coauthor. My references are to that 1958 Pyramid edition.

19. Joe Sanders, E. E. *"Doc" Smith* (San Bernardino, California: Borgo Press, 1986), 21–24.

20. Ross, "Getting Out of the Gernsback Continuum," (New York: Verso, 1991), 107; hereafter cited in text.

21. Westfahl's championing of Gernsback's importance to the genre flies in the face of the received truth (explicitly advanced by Brian Aldiss) that Gernsback's approach to SF was so crude and heavy-handed that it actually initiated most of the negative stereotypes that have been advanced to disparage science fiction. In rigorously reasoned and well-documented essays, Westfahl has established that Gernsback established the critical foundation so effectively built upon by John W. Campbell, editor of *Astounding*, who exercised strong influence on SF during its "golden years" of 1939–1945 and into the 1950s. Anyone seriously interested in the emergence of genre SF should read Westfahl's Gernsback essays, including "On the True History of Science Fiction," *Foundation* 47 (Winter 1989/90): 5–27; "'An Idea of Significant Import': Hugo Gernsback's Theory of Science Fiction," *Foundation* 48 (Spring 1990): 26–50; "'The Jules Verne, H. G. Wells, and Edgar Allan Poe Type of Story': Hugo Gernsback's History of Science Fiction," *Science-Fiction Studies* 19 (November 1992): 340–53; and "'This Unique Document': Hugo Gernsback's Ralph 124C 41+ and the Genres of Science Fiction," *Extrapolation* 35 (Summer 1994): 95–119.

22. James Gunn, *Alternate Worlds: The Illustrated History of Science Fiction* (Englewood Cliffs, N.J.: Prentice-Hall, 1975), 128.

23. Theodore Sturgeon, introduction to *Roadside Picnic and Tale of the Troika*, Arkady Strugatsky and Boris Strugatsky (New York: Macmillan, 1977), viii.

24. Albert I. Berger, *The Magic That Works: John W. Campbell and the American Response to Technology* (San Bernardino, California: The Borgo Press, 1993).

25. Edward James, *Science Fiction in the 20th Century* (New York: Oxford University Press, 1994).

26. John Campbell, introduction to *Prologue to Analog*, ed. John W. Campbell (Garden City, New York: Doubleday, 1962), 12–13.

27. John Campbell, "The Science of Science Fiction Writing," *Of Worlds Beyond: The Science of Science Fiction Writing*, ed. Lloyd Arthur Eshbach (Chicago: Advent, 1964), 92; hereafter cited in text.

28. Isaac Asimov, "Social Science Fiction," in *Turning Points: Essays on the Art of Science Fiction*, ed. Damon Knight (New York: Harper & Row, 1977), 41–42.

29. H. Bruce Franklin, *Robert A. Heinlein: America as Science Fiction* (New York: Oxford University Press, 1980), 68. Franklin's fine ideological critique of Heinlein is starkly contrasted by Leon Stover's lionizing *Robert A. Heinlein* (Boston: Twayne, 1987). More useful than Stover's reverential approach is that found in Alexei Panshin's *Heinlein in Dimension: A Critical Analysis* (Chicago: Advent, 1968) and George Slusser's two insightful meditations on Heinlein's writing: *Robert A. Heinlein: Stranger in His Own Land* (San Bernardino: Borgo Press, 1976) and *The Classic Years of Robert A. Heinlein* (San Bernardino: Borgo Press, 1977).

30. Robert A. Heinlein, "On the Writing of Speculative Fiction," in *Of Worlds Beyond: The Science of Science Fiction Writing*, ed. Lloyd Arthur Eshbach (Chicago: Advent, 1964), 13–15; hereafter cited in text.

31. Robert A. Heinlein, "The Discovery of the Future" in *Requiem: New Collected Works by Robert A. Heinlein and Tributes to the Grand Master*, ed. Yoji Kondo (New York: TOR, 1992), 157.

32. From a January 4, 1942, letter from Heinlein to Campbell, in *Robert A. Heinlein: Grumbles from the Grave*, ed. Virginia Heinlein (New York: Ballantine, 1989), 33; hereafter cited in text as *Grumbles*.

33. Robert A. Heinlein, *Starship Troopers* (New York: G. P. Putnam's Sons, 1959). Page references are to the 1987 Ace Books edition.

34. Samuel R. Delany, *The Motion of Light in Water: East Village Sex and Science Fiction Writing: 1960–1965* (London: Paladin Grafton Books, 1990), 171.

35. Brian Aldiss with David Wingrove, *Trillion Year Spree: The History of Science Fiction* (New York: Atheneum, 1986), 388.

36. Joe Haldeman, *The Forever War* (New York: Avon, 1991), 226–27.

37. Lewis Shiner, ed., *When the Music's Over: A Benefit Anthology* (New York: Bantam Spectra, 1991), 2.

38. Farah Mendlesohn, review of *There Won't Be War* and *When the Music's Over: A Benefit Anthology*. *Foundation* 56 (Autumn 1992): 114–17.

Chapter Three

1. Murray Leinster, "First Contact," *The Science Fiction Hall of Fame, Vol I*, ed. Robert Silverberg (New York: Avon, 1971), 310–43.

2. Ivan Yefremov, "The Heart of the Serpent," *The Heart of the Serpent*, ed. Ivan Yefremov (Moscow: Foreign Languages Publishing House, 1959), 64.

3. Franz Rottensteiner, ed. *View from Another Shore: European Science Fiction* (New York: Seabury Press, 1973), xiv.

4. Brian Aldiss with David Wingrove, *Trillion Year Spree: The History of Science Fiction* (New York: Atheneum, 1986), 175–205.

5. Sam J. Lundwall, *Science Fiction: An Illustrated History* (New York: Grosset & Dunlap, 1977), 201.

6. Franz Rottensteiner, "European Science Fiction," *Science Fiction: A Critical Guide*, ed. Patrick Parrinder (New York: Longman, 1979), 203. As Stanislaw Lem's literary agent and champion, Rottensteiner's view of European SF is not free from obvious bias, but he has written several useful overviews of the European tradition, including the introduction to his anthology *View from Another Shore: European Science Fiction* (New York: Seabury Press, 1973) and his *The Science Fiction Book: An Illustrated History* (New York: Seabury Press, 1975.

7. Edward James, *Science Fiction in the 20th Century* (New York: Oxford, 1994), 72.

8. Christopher Priest, "British Science Fiction," *Science Fiction: A Critical Guide*, ed. Patrick Parrinder (New York: Longman, 1979), 187.

9. Brian Stableford, "Science Fiction Between the Wars: 1916–1939," *Anatomy of Wonder 4: A Critical Guide to Science*

Fiction, ed. Neil Barron (New Providence, New Jersey: R. R. Bowker, 1995), 62–78; hereafter cited in text.

10. Andrew Ross, "Getting Out of the Gernsback Continuum," *Strange Weather: Culture, Science and Technology in the Age of Limits* (New York: Verso, 1991), 104–5; hereafter cited in text.

11. Gary Westfahl, "On The True History of Science Fiction," *Foundation* 47 (Winter 1989–1990), 24.

12. Brian Stableford offers a very useful summary of these origins and of the treatment of aliens in SF in his *The Sociology of Science Fiction* (San Bernardino, California: Borgo Press, 1987), 111–20.

13. Curiously, however, only two book-length studies of Lem's writing have been published in English: Richard E. Ziegfeld's *Stanislaw Lem* (New York: Frederick Ungar, 1985) and J. Madison Davis's *Stanislaw Lem* (San Bernardino, California: Borgo Press, 1990). The latter book was written as number 32 in the Starmont Reader's Guide series. Both studies are very introductory.

14. Rottensteiner, *View from Another Shore*, xiv.

15. Darko Suvin, Preface to *Other Worlds, Other Seas: Science-Fiction Stories from Socialist Countries* (New York: Random House, 1970), xxvi.

16. This troubling and fascinating episode can be partially reconstructed through accounts given in "On the Ouster of Stanislaw Lem from the SFWA," *Science-Fiction Studies* 4.2 (July 1977): 126–43. While resentment toward Lem clearly played a major role in the retraction of his honorary SFWA membership, it would not be accurate to say that the SFWA as a whole ever acted in this matter, and a number of SFWA members such as Ursula K. Le Guin, Pamela Sargent, and George Zebrowski publicly deplored the SFWA handling of the controversy.

17. Stanislaw Lem, "Science Fiction: A Hopeless Case—With Exceptions," *Microworlds* (New York: Harcourt Brace Jovanovich, 1984), 69.

18. Subsequent page references will be to Stanislaw Lem, *His Master's Voice*, trans. Michael Kandel (New York: Harcourt Brace Jovanovich, 1983).

19. Stanislaw Lem, *Microworlds: Writings on Science Fiction and Fantasy* (New York: Harcourt Brace Jovanovich, 1984), 243–78.

20. Alla Bossart, "Interview with the Strugatskys," trans. Mary Meyer, *Foundation* 50 (Autumn 1990): 73.

21. Vladimir Gopman, "Science Fiction Teaches the Civic Virtues: An Interview with Arkadii Strugatsky," trans. Mark Knighton, ed. Darko Suvin, *Science-Fiction Studies* 18.1 (March 1991): 7; hereafter cited in text as Gopman.

22. Darko Suvin, *Metamorphoses of Science Fiction: On the Poetics and History of a Literary Genre* (New Haven: Yale University Press, 1979), 243; hereafter cited in text.

23. Patrick L. McGuire, "Russian SF," *Anatomy of Wonder: A Critical Guide to Science Fiction*, third edition, ed. Neil Barron (New York: R. R. Bowker, 1987), 441–73; hereafter cited in text. McGuire is also the author of *Red Stars: Political Aspects of Soviet Science Fiction* (Ann Arbor: UMI Research Press, 1985).

24. Istvan Csicsery-Ronay Jr., "Zamyatin and the Strugatskys: The Representation of Freedom in *We* and *The Snail on the Slope*" in *Zamyatin's We: A Collection of Critical Essays*, ed. Gary Kern (Ann Arbor: Ardis, 1988), 236–37; hereafter cited in text.

25. Istvan Csicsery-Ronay Jr., "Towards the Last Fairy Tale: On the Fairy-Tale Paradigm in the Strugatskys' Science Fiction, 1963–72," *Science-Fiction Studies* 13 (1986): 21. Csicsery-Ronay's brilliant reading of this novel is its definitive critical treatment, although perceptive readings can also be found in Stanislaw Lem's *Microworlds*, Carl Malmgren's *Worlds Apart*, and Stephen W. Potts's *The Second Marxian Invasion: The Fiction of the Strugatsky Brothers*. I am greatly indebted to Csiscery-Ronay both for his specific reading of *Roadside Picnic* and for his discussions of the political factors surrounding the writing of this book and of the importance of the fairy tale to Russian literature.

26. Arkady and Boris Strugatsky, *Roadside Picnic/Tale of the Troika* (New York: Macmillan Publishing Co, 1977), 102. Subsequent page references in the text are to this edition.

Chapter Four

1. Jenny Wolmark, *Aliens and Others: Science Fiction, Feminism and Postmodernism* (Iowa City: University of Iowa Press, 1994), 47.

2. Sarah Lefanu, *In the Chinks of the World Machine: Feminism and Science Fiction* (London: The Women's Press, 1988), 3–4. (This book was reprinted in 1989 by Indiana University Press, under the title *Feminism and Science Fiction.*)

3. Fredric Jameson, "Futurist Visions That Tell Us about Right Now," *In These Times* 6:23 (May 5–11, 1982): 17.

4. Dick was painfully aware of the literary prejudice against science fiction. In "Now Wait for This Year" he recalled the derision directed against SF writers early in his career: "To select SF writing as a career was an act of self-destruction; in fact, most *writers*, let alone other people, could not even conceive of someone considering it. . . ."

5. Kim Stanley Robinson, *The Novels of Philip K. Dick* (Ann Arbor, Michigan: UMI Research Press, 1984), xi.

6. Lem's "Philip K. Dick: A Visionary Among the Charlatans," originally published in the 1975 *Science-Fiction Studies* special issue on Dick, is republished in *Microworlds: Writings on Science Fiction and Fantasy*, ed. Franz Rottensteiner (New York: Harcourt, 1985). Disch's best known blasts against the genre are "The Embarrassments of Science Fiction" in *Science Fiction at Large*, ed. Peter Nicholls (New York: Harper, 1977), and a 1993 denunciation in *Harpers*. His comments about Dick come from his introduction to Dick's *Solar Lottery* (Boston: Gregg Press, 1976).

7. The number of studies of Dick's work is large and growing. I have found most helpful *The Novels of Philip K. Dick*, by Kim Stanley Robinson (Ann Arbor: UMI Research Press, 1984); *Philip K. Dick*, ed. Joseph D. Olander and Martin Harry Greenberg (New York: 1983); two special issues of *Science-Fiction Studies* devoted to Dick—those of March 1975 and July 1988; *Philip K. Dick*, by Douglas A. Mackey (Boston: Twayne, 1988); and *Only Apparently Real: The World of Philip K. Dick*, Paul Williams (New York: Arbor House, 1986). My understanding of Dick has also been influenced by Aaron Barlow's unpub-

lished dissertation, "Reality, Religion, and Politics in Philip K. Dick's Fiction," University of Iowa, 1988. Two very useful readings of *The Man in the High Castle* appear in Clareson's *Understanding Contemporary American Science Fiction* (Columbia: University of South Carolina Press, 1990), 155–65, and in Mark Rose's *Alien Encounters* (Cambridge: Harvard University Press, 1981), 119–27, and fine tribute to Dick appears in Norman Spinrad's *Science Fiction in the Real World*, cited below.

8. Ursula K. Le Guin, "Science Fiction as Prophecy: Philip K. Dick," *The New Republic* (30 October 1976): 34; hereafter cited in text.

9. Carl Freedman, "Editorial Introduction: Philip K. Dick and Criticism," *Science-Fiction Studies* 15 (July 1988): 123. Freedman refers in this introduction to his earlier article "Towards a Theory of Paranoia: The Science Fiction of Philip K. Dick," *Science Fiction Studies* 11 (1984): 15–24. This article has been republished in *Philip K. Dick: Contemporary Critical Interpretations*, ed. Samuel J. Umland (Westport, Connecticut: Greenwood Press, 1995).

10. Peter Fitting, "*Ubik*: The Deconstruction of Bourgeois SF," in *Philip K. Dick*, ed. Joseph D. Olander and Martin Harry Greenberg (New York: Taplinger, 1983), 150.

11. Norman Spinrad, "The Transmogrification of Philip K. Dick," *Science Fiction in the Real World* (Carbondale: Southern Illinois University Press, 1990), 214.

12. John Huntington, "Philip K. Dick: Authenticity and Insincerity," *Science-Fiction Studies* 15.45 (July 1988): 155; hereafter cited in text.

13. Michael Bishop, "In Pursuit of *Ubik*," in *Philip K. Dick*, ed. Martin Harry Greenberg and Joseph D. Olander (New York: Taplinger Publishing Co, 1983), 139; hereafter cited in text. Bishop's 1987 novel *Philip K. Dick Is Dead, Alas* offers one of the most fascinating homages to Dick's life and work.

14. Rose, 119–20.

15. Philip K. Dick, *Ubik* (New York: Vintage Books, 1991), 215. Page references are to this edition.

16. Cited in Lefanu's *In the Chinks of the World Machine*, 18.

17. Eric S. Rabkin, "Science Fiction Women before Liberation," in *Future Females: A Critical Anthology*, ed. Marleen S. Barr (Bowling Green, Ohio: Bowling Green State University Popular Press, 1981), 25.

18. Pamela Sargent, "Introduction: Women and Science Fiction," *Women of Wonder: Science Fiction Stories by Women about Women*, Pamela Sargent, ed. (New York: Vintage, 1975), lx.

19. Brian Attebery, writing in the "Gender" section of his *Teacher's Guide to The Norton Book of Science Fiction* (New York: W. W. Norton, 1993), 42. Attebery's brief discussion of gender is very useful, as are his discussions of gender-focused stories within the very "feminist-friendly" *Norton Book*. Foremost among those stories are: Sonya Dorman Hess's "When I Was Miss Dow," James Tiptree's "The Women Men Don't See," Carol Emshwiller's "The Start of the End of the World," Octavia Butler's "Speech Sounds," Pat Cadigan's "After the Days of Dead-Eye 'Dee,'" Pat Murphy's "His Vegetable Wife," Connie Willis's "Schwarzschild Radius" (not specifically gender-related, but a powerful deconstruction of war fantasies), Candace Jane Dorsey's "(Learning About) Machine Sex," Margaret Atwood's "Homelanding," Kate Wilhelm's "And the Angels Sing," Lisa Goldstein's "Midnight News," and Nancy Kress's "Out of All Them Bright Stars." While not as overtly feminist or gender-intensive as many of the stories in *Women of Wonder*, stories in the *Norton Book* by men and women alike tend to offer or imply sophisticated critiques of gendered assumptions in SF.

20. Veronica Hollinger has used this affinity between women and "hopeful monsters" in SF to challenge feminist critics to continue and extend the work of feminist SF writers. "Introduction: Women in Science Fiction and Other Hopeful Monsters," *Science-Fiction Studies* 17.2 (July 1990): 133.

21. Pamela Sargent, ed., *Women of Wonder: The Classic Years: Science Fiction by Women from the 1940s to the 1970s* (New York: Harcourt Brace, 1995), and *Women of Wonder: The Contemporary Years: Science Fiction by Women from the 1970s to the 1990s* (New York: Harcourt Brace, 1995).

22. Donna Haraway, "A Manifesto for Cyborgs: Science, Technology, and Socialist Feminism in the 1980s," *Socialist Review* 15 (1985): 65–107.

23. Lefanu, *In the Chinks of the World Machine*, 95.

24. Wolmark, *Aliens and Others*.

25. Marleen S. Barr, *Feminist Fabulation: Space/Postmodern Fiction* (Iowa City: University of Iowa Press, 1992).

26. Larry McCaffery, ed. Introduction to "An Interview with Joanna Russ," *Across the Wounded Galaxies: Interviews with Contemporary American Science Fiction Writers* (Urbana: University of Illinois Press, 1990), 176. McCaffery's interviews with Russ, Ursula K. Le Guin, and Octavia Butler offer many insights into the appeal held by SF for women writers and readers.

27. Russ's "Amor Vincit Foeminam" appeared in *Science-Fiction Studies* 7 (March 1980): 2–15; "Towards an Aesthetic of Science Fiction" appeared in SFS 2 (July 1975): 112–19; "SF and Technology as Mystification" appeared in SFS 5 (1978): 250–60; "Alien Monsters" appeared in Damon Knight's *Turning Points: Essays on the Art of Science Fiction* (New York: Harper & Row, 1977), 132–43; "Recent Feminist Utopias" appeared in Marleen S. Barr's *Future Females: A Critical Anthology* (Bowling Green, Ohio: Bowling Green University Popular Press, 1981), 71–85. "What Can a Heroine Do? Or Why Women Can't Write" appeared in *Images of Women in Fiction: Feminist Perspectives*, Susan K. Cornillon, ed. (Bowling Green, Ohio: Bowling Green University Popular Press, 1972), 3–20. Russ's *How to Suppress Women's Writing* was published by the University of Texas Press in 1983. Many of Russ's most important essays are now collected in her *To Write Like a Woman: Essays in Feminism and Science Fiction* (Bloomington: Indiana University Press, 1995).

28. Joanna Russ, *We Who Are About To . . .* (London: The Women's Press, 1977). Page reference are to this edition.

29. Ursula K. Le Guin, "American SF and the Other," *The Language of the Night: Essays on Fantasy and Science Fiction* (New York: HarperCollins, 1989), 94. Hereafter, LON in the text.

30. Lefanu, *In the Chinks of the World Machine*, 137–40.

31. Pamela Sargent cites in her introduction to *Women of Wonder* another interesting exchange in the pages of SF commentary about *The Left Hand of Darkness* between Le Guin and Stanislaw Lem, who faulted Le Guin for failing to understand the

psychological cruelty to the individual inherent in her concept of the Gethenian sexual cycle. Le Guin answers Lem with some exasperation.

32. Silverberg's comment appeared in 1975 in a generally perceptive introduction to Tiptree's second collection of stories, *Warm Worlds and Otherwise* (New York: Del Rey, 1979), xii. After Tiptree's real identity was learned, Silverberg graciously admitted in a postscript to the 1979 second edition of this collection: "She fooled me beautifully, along with everyone else, and called into question the entire notion of what is 'masculine' or 'feminine' in fiction."

33. Lefanu details this incident in her useful discussion of Tiptree in *In the Chinks of the World Machine* (a title Lefanu derived from a line in Tiptree's "The Women Men Don't See"), 105–6.

34. Le Guin's comment comes from her introduction to Tiptree's *Star Songs of an Old Primate* and is cited in LeFanu, 106.

35. Lillian Heldreth, "'Love Is the Plan, the Plan Is Death': The Feminism and Fatalism of James Tiptree Jr." *Extrapolation* 23.1 (Spring 1982): 22–30.

36. Veronica Hollinger, "'The Most Grisly Truth': Responses to the Human Condition in the Works of James Tiptree, Jr." *Extrapolation* 30.2 (1989): 117–32.

37. James Tiptree Jr., "The Women Men Don't See," *Women of Wonder: The Classic Years*, ed. Pamela Sargent (New York: Harcourt Brace, 1995), 308–34. Page references in text are to this collection. This story can also be found in *The Norton Book of Science Fiction*.

38. James Tiptree Jr., "Houston, Houston, Do You Read?" in *Science Fiction: The Science Fiction Research Association Anthology*, Patricia S. Warrick, Charles G. Waugh, and Martin H. Greenberg, eds. (New York: Harper & Row, 1988), 434–75. Hereafter cited in text as *SFRA*.

39. Nancy Steffen-Fluhr, "The Case of the Haploid Heart: Psychological Patterns in the Science Fiction of Alice Sheldon ('James Tiptree, Jr.')," *Science-Fiction Studies* 17.2 (July 1990): 188–220.

40. The phenomenon of K/S stories has been studied by Joanna Russ in her *Magic Mommas, Trembling Sisters, Puritans and Per-*

verts (Trumansburg, New York: The Crossing Press, 1985). For further discussion of K/S stories, see Henry Jenkins, *Textual Poachers: Television Fans and Participatory Culture* (New York: Routledge, 1992), and Patricia Frazer Lamb and Diana L. Veith, "Romantic Myth, Transcendence, and Star Trek Zines," in *Erotic Universe: Sexuality and Fantastic Literature*, ed. Donald Palumbo (Westport, Connecticut: Greenwood Press, 1986), 235–55.

41. Gwyneth Jones, "Riddles in the Dark," in *The Profession of Science Fiction: Writers on Their Craft and Ideas*, eds. Maxim Jakubowski and Edward James (Houndmills, Basingstoke, Hampshire: Macmillan, 1992), 173.

42. Joan Gordon, "Yin and Yang Duke It Out," *Storming the Reality Studio: A Casebook of Cyberpunk and Postmodern Science Fiction*, ed. Larry McCaffery (Durham: Duke University Press, 1992).

43. Joan Gordon, "Connie Willis's Doomsday for Feminism: *Doomsday Book* by Connie Willis," *New York Review of Science Fiction* 58 (June 1993): 5.

Chapter Five

1. Gregory Benford, "Centigrade 233," *Matter's End* (New York: Bantam Spectra, 1995), 24–38.

2. William Gibson, "The Gernsback Continuum," *Mirrorshades: The Cyberpunk Anthology*, ed. Bruce Sterling (New York: Ace, 1986), 3.

3. Roger Luckhurst, "The Many Deaths of Science Fiction: A Polemic," *Science-Fiction Studies* 21.1 (March 1994): 35–50; hereafter cited in text.

4. Brian W. Aldiss with David Wingrove, *Trillion Year Spree: The History of Science Fiction* (New York: Atheneum, 1986), 307.

5. Samuel R. Delany, *Silent Interviews: On Language, Race, Sex, Science Fiction, and Some Comics* (Hanover, Connecticut: Wesleyan University Press, 1994), 69; hereafter cited in text.

6. Michael Moorcock quoted in Edward James's *Science Fiction in the 20th Century* (New York: Oxford University Press, 1994), 168.

7. J. G. Ballard, quoted in James, 169–70.

8. J. G. Ballard, "Introduction to the French Edition," *Crash* (New York: Vintage, 1985), 4.

9. James, *Science Fiction in the 20th Century*, 170.

10. James Gunn, *Alternate Worlds: The Illustrated History of Science Fiction* (New York: Prentice-Hall, 1975), 236.

11. Norman Spinrad, ed., *Modern Science Fiction* (Garden City, N.Y.: Doubleday, 1974). Spinrad's introductions to stories by Ballard, Moorcock, Ellison, Zelazny, Disch, and others reveal his sense of the vitality and importance of the New Wave sensibility, and he offers a brief overview of the movement on pages 271–74 and 327–28. Spinrad also offers an interestingly inverted view of New Wave writers, suggesting that "the commercial and subcultural influences of science fiction began to mold the work of the new writers towards the traditional norms of the genre" (272).

12. J. G. Ballard, *The Atrocity Exhibition* (San Francisco: REsearch, 1990). This revised edition containing Ballard's annotations and commentary on the original 1970 text adds the feel of hypertext to Ballard's already radical narrative form, becoming more a new text and new reading experience than just a new edition. Page references are to this edition.

13. Norman Spinrad, "The Strange Case of J. G. Ballard," *Science Fiction in the Real World* (Carbondale: Southern Illinois University Press), 187–88.

14. Jean Baudrillard, "Simulacra and Science Fiction," *Science-Fiction Studies* 18.3 (November 1991): 312.

15. Harlan Ellison, "Introduction: Thirty-Two Soothsayers," *Dangerous Visions* (New York: Berkley Medallion Books, 1972), 19–29.

16. Carl Malmgren, *Worlds Apart: Narratology of Science Fiction* (Bloomington: Indiana University Press, 1991), 11–15.

17. Bruce Sterling, ed., *Mirrorshades: The Cyberpunk Anthology* (New York: Ace, 1988), xiii; hereafter cited in text.

18. Larry McCaffery, *Storming the Reality Studio: A Casebook of Cyberpunk and Postmodern Fiction* (Durham: Duke University Press, 1991).

19. Lewis Shiner, "Inside the Movement: Past, Present, and Future," *Fiction 2000: Cyberpunk and the Future of Narrative*, ed. George Slusser and Tom Shippey (Athens: University of Georgia Press, 1992), 17–25. This excellent collection of essays offers both an appreciation of and an elegy for cyberpunk.

20. Brian McHale, *Constructing Postmodernism* (New York: Routledge, 1992). Chapter 10, "POSTcyberMODERNpunkISM" and chapter 11, "Towards a poetics of cyberpunk," are particularly useful.

21. I have examined the relationship between SF and media in general and between cyberpunk and media in particular much more thoroughly in my *The Aesthetics of Ambivalence: Rethinking Science Fiction Film in the Age of Electronic (Re)Production* (Westport, Connecticut: Greenwood Press, 1992).

22. Gardner Dozois, ed., *The Year's Best Science Fiction: Twelfth Annual Collection* (New York: St. Martin's Press, 1995).

23. John Clute, "Is Science Fiction Out to Lunch? Some Thoughts on the Year 1992," *Nebula Awards 28: SFWA's Choices for the Best Science Fiction and Fantasy of the Year*, ed. James Morrow (New York: Harcourt Brace, 1994), 2.

24. Christina Sedgwick, "The Fork in the Road: Can Science Fiction Survive in Postmodern, Megacorporate America?" *Science-Fiction Studies* 18 (March 1991): 11–52; Delany, *Silent Interviews*, 257–59.

25. Larry McCaffery, *Across the Wounded Galaxies: Interviews with Contemporary American Science Fiction Writers* (Urbana: University of Illinois Press, 1990), 3–4.

26. Charles Platt, "The RAPE of Science Fiction," *Science Fiction Eye* 1.5 (July 1989): 44.

27. Donna Haraway, "The Promises of Monsters: A Regenerative Politics for Inappropriate/d Others," in Lawrence Grossberg, Cary Nelson, and Paula Treichler, eds., *Cultural Studies* (New York: Routledge, 1992), 300.

28. Istvan Csicsery-Ronay Jr., "The SF of Theory: Baudrillard and Haraway," *Science-Fiction Studies* 18.3 (November 1991): 387.

Bibliographic Essay

Reference Works

The Encyclopedia of Science Fiction, ed. John Clute and Peter Nicholls (New York: St. Martin's Press, 1993), offers new science fiction readers and experienced SF scholars alike a magnificently comprehensive and critically astute view of science fiction literature, film, TV, comics, and related media. This indispensable work contains entries by more than 100 well-respected and well-credentialed authorities on SF; however, the fact that roughly 85 percent of its entries are by John Clute, Peter Nicholls, and Brian Stableford gives the work a coherence that suggests a finely crafted critical study more than an encyclopedia. This sense of coherence is further intensified by an elaborate system of "links," or cross-references among related entries, making it almost impossible to stop reading without following a string of associations through SF themes, writers, and history. Indeed, this delightful work invites and rewards cover-to-cover reading just as surely as it serves as a reference work that seems to have anticipated almost every question about the world of science fiction.

Perhaps the greatest value of *The Encyclopedia of Science Fiction* is that its Borgesian sweep mirrors and invokes the sweep and complex interrelationships of SF itself. In 1,370 pages the *Encyclopedia* offers critically incisive entries on some 2,900 authors, over 300 of whom are from 27 countries other than the United States and Great Britain. Pocket essays illuminate over 200 themes, such as boys' papers, conceptual breakthroughs, definitions of SF, dime-novel SF, edisonade, eschatology, genre SF, graphic novel, linguistics, lost worlds, postmodernism and SF, space opera, steampunk, and women SF writers. Somewhat briefer terminological entries cover literary categories such as oulipo, magic realism, and slipstream, as well as SF-specific terms such as shared world and pocket universe. SF film and TV and comics are well covered in this volume, as are topics inextricably involved with the history of SF—topics ranging from Plato's philosophy to Von Däniken's *Chariots of the Gods*.

While the description and explanation of genre SF is the heart of this encyclopedia, it also recognizes the extent to which SF has long since transcended the printed page, and, equally important, the extent to which SF has become part of a cultural feedback loop in which non- and extratextual SF phenomena also lead back to fixed-print embodiments. The editors cite "game worlds, film and TV spin-offs, shared worlds, graphic novels, franchises, young-adult fiction, choose-your-own-plot tales, technothrillers, survivalist fiction, SF horror novels, fantasy novels with SF centres," as examples of SF that cannot be accounted for by traditional literary production models, noting that many of these phenomena were not significant in 1978 when they published the first edition of *The Science Fiction Encyclopedia*. Indeed, in calling attention to the vast changes in SF between 1978 and 1992, the editors indicate not only the extent to which contemporary SF has been marked by change but also the extent to which the critical response to SF has itself undergone tremendous changes. If science fiction scholars are justified in their despair at the size and complexity of their critical task, and I believe they are, they can find more than a little solace in the fact that no other popular literature or, for that matter, few if any forms of literature whatsoever benefit from a central reference work so comprehensive and authoritative as is *The Encyclopedia of Science Fiction*.

An equally indispensable reference work is Neil Barron's *Anatomy of Wonder: A Critical Guide to Science Fiction*, both the third edition (New York: R. R. Bowker Co., 1987) and *Anatomy of Wonder 4* (New York: R. R. Bowker Co., 1995). The 1995 fourth edition significantly updates and expands the 1987 third edition, but the new edition drops coverage of foreign-language SF. For this reason, the fourth edition should be considered an important supplement to, rather than replacement for, the third. While the *Encyclopedia of Science Fiction* discusses or at least mentions most significant individual books of science fiction, it contains no entries for book titles, which must be pursued through author and theme entries. Accordingly, *Anatomy of Wonder* is the most authoritative, most comprehensive, and most useful source of information about works of and works about science fiction. The third edition (1987) of *Anatomy of Wonder* English-language SF is organized by author within three sections: The Emergence of Science Fiction: The Beginnings to the 1920s, Science Fiction Between the Wars: 1918–1938, and The Modern Period: 1964–1986. There is also a section Children's and Young Adult Science Fiction. The section Foreign-Language Science Fiction is organized by country of origin, with German, French, Russian, Japanese, Italian, Danish, Swedish, Norwegian, Dutch, Belgian, Romanian, Yugloslav, and Hebrew sub-sections. *Anatomy of Wonder* also contains an extensive survey of research aids, including essays and bibliographies on general reference works, history and criticism, author studies, science fiction on film and television, science fiction illustration, teaching materials, science fiction magazines, library and private collections of science fiction and fantasy, and Barron's core collection checklist of most significant and award-winning SF.

The annotated bibliographies in *Anatomy of Wonder* can be depended upon both for accurate thumbnail sketches of a book's subject matter and primary themes and for dependable critical evaluation. Works are cross-referenced to similar or contrasting works, a feature that is particularly helpful for readers new to the field. Essays introducing individual sections of the bibliography are uniformly excellent, making *Anatomy* not only a powerful research tool but also a fine introduction to the central concerns of SF. The third edition greatly expands and updates the second edition of 1981 but does not include all entries from that edition, so the historical researcher may find it useful to consult the earlier edition for titles that have been deleted or superseded.

Anatomy of Wonder 4 maintains this pattern, significantly updating and expanding but not entirely supplanting the third edition. Major changes include the dropping of coverage of SF not translated into English, the addition of more than 100 new annotations for works of fiction, sections on poetry and comics, a theme index, and biocritical cross references to other reference works such as *The Encyclopedia of Science Fiction*. Science fiction is legendary for its disagreements about the worth of particular books and particular authors, but *Anatomy of Wonder* is as close to a completely authoritative bibliographic overview of the field as is likely ever to exist; it is an essential work for fan and scholar alike, and studies such as this one would be lost without it.

While *The Encyclopedia of Science Fiction* and *Anatomy of Wonder* are the most comprehensive and most authoritative reference works in the field, several other books can be quite useful. *The New Encyclopedia of Science Fiction*, ed. James Gunn (New York: Viking, 1988), lacks the scope and the rigor of the Clute and Nicholls encyclopedia but contains a number of useful essays by well-respected SF writers and scholars. David Pringle's *The Ultimate Guide to Science Fiction* (New York: Pharos Books, 1990) contains this very knowledgeable British SF expert's descriptions and capsule evaluations of some 3,000 SF titles, making this a very useful tool for the SF reader. This work has been updated by a second edition (Aldershot, England: Scolar Press, 1995), which includes entries on some 3,500 works, including for the first time novelizations of SF films and tie-in works, spun off from print and media successes. The addition by Pringle of novelizations and spin-offs marks a significant recognition of the fact that SF has truly become a multimedia genre, with strong lines of influence *from* as well as *to* film, TV, comics, etc. Robert Reginald's two-volume work, *Science Fiction and Fantasy Literature: A Checklist, 1700–1974* and *Contemporary Science Fiction Authors II* (Detroit: Gale Research, 1979), offers in the second volume interesting information about SF authors, often including a brief statement from the writer. H. W. Hall's *Science Fiction and Fantasy Book Review Index, 1878–1985: An International Author and Subject Index to History and Criticism*, (Detroit: Gale Research, 1985) collects book reviews from SF magazines and reviewing publications such as *Library Journal* and *Publisher's Weekly*. Hall's *Science Fiction and Fantasy Reference Index, 1878–1985* comes in two volumes, the first listing pieces about SF by author, the second offering subject entries such as "Fanzines," "First Contact," and "Sociology of SF." This edition has been supplemented by *Science Fiction and Fantasy Reference Index, 1985–1991: An International Author and Subject Index to History and Criticism*, ed. Hal W. Hall (Englewood, Colorado: Libraries Unlimited, 1993). A number of other useful indices to SF works and works about SF are described in The "General Reference Works" chapter of Barron's *Anatomy of Wonder*.

One of the banes of the SF scholar's existence is the fact that SF is published at such a rate that it is almost impossible to keep up with. Four very helpful partial solutions to this problem are *The New York Review of Science Fiction*, with an editorial staff anchored by David G. Hartwell; *Science Fiction & Fantasy Book Review Annual, 1991*, eds. Robert A. Collins and Robert Latham (Westport, Connecticut: Greenwood Press, 1994); *Locus: The Newspaper of the Science Fiction Field*, ed. Charles N. Brown; and *Science Fiction Chronicle*, ed. Andrew J. Porter. *The New York Review of Science Fiction* offers reviews and review essays of recent SF, as well as broader essays about the field. The Collins and Latham *Book Review Annual* is the fourth volume in a series that draws reviews from the membership of the International Association of the Fantastic in the Arts and the Science Fiction Research Association. These volumes also contain excellent year-in-review articles, survey articles suggesting recent trends in SF and fantasy, and review articles addressing themes and issues in recent works, as well as author profiles, making this series the most complete source for critical commentary on contemporary SF. Considerable disparity in rigor and tone exists among the individual reviews, but the reviewers are generally quite knowledgeable. *Locus* is simply the one source of information about SF and fantasy publishing that approaches comprehensive coverage of the field, including announcements of contracts, forthcoming books, awards, and author profiles, as well as excellent reviews.

Reference Works Devoted to Science Fiction Magazines

Since the history of genre SF depends heavily on an understanding of the pivotal role played by SF magazines, reference works focused on these magazines are particularly important. An excellent introduction to SF magazines is Paul A. Carter's *The Creation of Tomorrow: Fifty Years of Magazine Science Fiction* (New York: Columbia, 1977), a thematically organized study. While not limited only to magazine stories, Everett F. Bleiler's *Science-Fiction: The Early Years* (Kent, Ohio: Kent State University Press, 1990) provides descriptions of more than 3,000 SF stories written before

1930, many of which are now extremely difficult to locate. Sam Moskowitz provides commentary on and samples of very early magazine SF in his *Science Fiction by Gaslight: A History and Anthology of Science Fiction in the Popular Magazines, 1891–1911* (Chicago: World, 1968) and *Under the Moons of Mars: A History and Anthology of "The Scientific Romance" in the Munsey Magazines, 1912–1920* (New York: Holt, 1970). *The History of the Science Fiction Magazines*, by Mike Ashley (Chicago: Henry Regnery, 1976) is a four-volume work containing introductory essays, samples from, and thorough bibliographic information about science fiction magazines, starting with the appearance of SF stories in nonspecialty magazines before 1926 and continuing through SF magazines in 1965. Mike Ashley's and Marshall B. Tymn's *Science Fiction, Fantasy, and Weird Fiction Magazines* (Westport, Connecticut: Greenwood Press, 1985) updates Ashley's *History of the Science Fiction Magazine* through 1983 and includes detailed essays on major SF magazines.

Science Fiction Journals

The three primary scholarly journals devoted to science fiction are *Science-Fiction Studies*, *Extrapolation*, and *Foundation: The Review of Science Fiction*. While generalizations about these journals are risky at best, *Science-Fiction Studies* has a traditional interest in theoretical and ideological issues in SF, *Extrapolation* has focused more on single-author studies and on historical concerns, and *Foundation*, published in England, offers more non-American and non-Canadian criticism and tends to publish more essays by science fiction writers. SF scholars and SF writers also contribute important essays and interviews to *Science Fiction Eye*, ed. Stephen P. Brown, and to *The New York Review of Science Fiction*.

Historical Studies

Histories of science fiction abound, each implying its own definition, critical values, and consequent canon. Two very useful general histories are Brian Aldiss's and David Wingrove's *Trillion Year Spree: The History of Science Fiction* (London: Victor Gollancz, 1986) and James Gunn's *Alternate Worlds: The Illustrated History of*

Science Fiction (Englewood Cliffs, N.J.: Prentice-Hall, 1975). Both of these histories contain excellent information about and insight into SF's rise in the twentieth century, but both offer a much less thorough and critical overview of SF after its "golden age." Aldiss's work, like its predecessor, *Billion Year Spree: The True History of Science Fiction* (1973) (which it largely supersedes) is the more lively and occasionally idiosyncratic history, distinguished by Aldiss's literary judgments. *Alternate Worlds* contains many useful illustrations and photographs and a more concise view of the stages of SF's development, but its history—heavily slanted toward Campbellian values—is writer and intentionally centered, what Neil Barron has called a "consensus history," valuing SF writers' claims about SF over critical analysis. One other history, Alexei and Corey Panshin's mammoth *World Beyond the Hill* (Los Angeles: Jeremy P. Tarcher, 1989), offers fascinating details and anecdotes about the development of SF through 1945, with particular attention to American genre SF and particular enthusiasm for Campbellian ideals, but is weakened by the authors' polemical preoccupation with science fiction's vaguely defined "transcendent" qualities. At precisely the point where many histories note that SF became markedly less technophilic and darker, but also more mature and challenging, *The World Beyond the Hill* ends with the claim that after 1945 SF ceased "to be about transcendent science." One of the most useful introductory "histories" of science fiction is Eric S. Rabkin's and Robert Scholes's *Science Fiction: History-Science-Vision* (New York: Oxford University Press, 1977), in which the succinct history is complemented by discussions contextualizing SF, explaining key scientific concepts, central themes, and ten important SF novels.

Samuel Moskowitz is the dean of SF historians, having devoted numerous volumes to preserving SF's prehistory and early years. Moskowitz's approach to SF is primarily anecdotal, his attribution of sources is frequently sketchy, and he is well known for his preoccupation with SF "firsts" (first time the term "science fiction" was used, first time a sentient robot appeared in an SF story, etc) but, in works such as *The Immortal Storm: A History of Science Fiction Fandom* (1951), *Explorers of the Infinite* (1963), *Seekers of Tomorrow* (1966), and *Strange Horizons* (1976), Moskowitz codified much of the oral history, received values, and ephemera of early-twentieth-century SF. All of his works are important and instructive—as documents of the culture of SF, if not as rigorous works of scholarship.

Another pioneer of SF history and of SF scholarship is Thomas D. Clareson, a founder of the Modern Language Association Seminar on Science Fiction and the subsequent Science Fiction Research Association and the first editor of *Extrapolation*. Clareson's *Some Kind of Paradise: The Emergence of American Science Fiction* (Westport, Connecticut: Greenwood Press, 1985) details the cultural and literary context that gave rise to American SF, focusing on the late nineteenth century to the birth in the mid-1920s of genre SF. Together with H. Bruce Franklin's *Future Perfect: American Science Fiction of the Nineteenth Century* (New York: Oxford University Press, 1978), Clareson's *Some Kind of Paradise* offers an invaluable analysis of early American SF's culture-specific aspects. A companion work featuring brief descriptions of 838 early SF works is Clareson's *Science Fiction in America, 1870s–1930s: An Annotated Bibliography of Primary Sources* (Westport, Connecticut: Greenwood Press, 1984). Clareson's *Understanding Contemporary American Science Fiction: The Formative Period (1926–1970)* (Columbia, South Carolina: University of South Carolina Press, 1990) offers a brief introduction to American genre SF through the New Wave, containing more plot summary than analysis. Of Clareson's several other important contributions to SF scholarship, probably the most widely cited work is his edited collection *SF: The Other Side of Realism, Essays on Modern Fantasy and Science Fiction* (Bowling Green, Ohio: Bowling Green University Popular Press, 1971).

Theoretical Studies

Somewhere between a theory of SF and a history lies *New Maps of Hell: A Survey of Science Fiction* by Kingsley Amis (New York: Harcourt Brace, 1960). Amis's pioneering study grew from a series of lectures delivered at Princeton in 1959, and this work represents the first sustained "academic" analysis of SF, even if, as Amis proudly notes, he is not an intellectual slumming in unfamiliar popular culture. While his "survey" is heavily slanted by his belief that SF should primarily be a vehicle for social satire, his perceptive overview notes much that was good and bad in SF up to the time of his writing, and some of his criticisms call for precisely the kind of fiction produced in the British New Wave. *New Maps of Hell* remains an important early attempt to explain SF as a genre, the first written by someone truly knowledgeable about SF but not so immersed in its culture as to subscribe to all of its received ideas.

In *Science Fiction Before 1900: Imagination Discovers Technology*, the fine companion to this volume and the best study of the origins of SF, Paul Alkon has justly praised Darko Suvin's *Metamorphoses of Science Fiction: On the Poetics and History of a Literary Genre* (New Haven: Yale University Press, 1979) as "the best introduction to the genre's theoretical issues," but it should be noted that Suvin's pioneering study dismisses most genre SF—and thereby most SF written since 1900—as unworthy paraliterature. A work that clearly reflects Suvin's influence but that takes a broader view of science fiction is Carl D. Malmgren's *Worlds Apart: Narratology of Science Fiction* (Bloomington: Indiana University Press, 1991), which, apart from its structural theory of SF based on the "worlds" in which SF stories unfold, offers a number of excellent readings of paradigmatic texts and a fine discussion of science fantasy, an increasingly problematic interface combining characteristics of the two ostensibly antithetical worldviews of SF and fantasy.

One of the most influential and most insightful approaches to understanding science fiction is Gary K. Wolfe's *The Known and the Unknown: The Iconography of Science Fiction* (Kent, Ohio: Kent State University Press, 1979. Wolfe's delightfully engaging discussions of SF images or icons such as those of the barrier, the spaceship, the city, and the robot offer a perceptive and thought-provoking analysis of the conceptual appeals of SF, making this one of the indispensable works of SF scholarship. Mark Rose's *Alien Encounters: Anatomy of Science Fiction* (Cambridge, Mass.: Harvard University Press, 1981) offers a somewhat similar but much less thorough and less textually specific discussion of SF organized around the paradigms of space, time, machine, and monster. More limited in scope, but extremely provocative and insightful, is John Huntington's *Rationalizing Genius: Ideological Strategies in the Classic American Science Fiction Short Story* (New Brunswick: Rutgers University Press, 1989). Specifically pegged to the canonical short stories gathered in the *Science Fiction Hall of Fame*, Huntington's analysis persuasively establishes the myth of genius as an underlying preoccupation of genre SF.

Two works that are particularly useful for understanding the larger culture of science fiction are Brian Stableford's excellent *The Sociology of Science Fiction* (San Bernardino, California: Borgo Press, 1987) and David Hartwell's disarmingly informal but very well-informed *Age of Wonders: Exploring the World of Science Fiction* (New York: Walker, 1984). By far the best available general introduction to the culture of science fiction, however, is *Science Fiction in the 20th Century*, by Edward James (New York: Oxford University Press/Opus, 1994). James, the editor of *Foundation*, offers a brief overview of the history of the development of SF since 1895, emphasizing the twin evolutions of science fiction into a cultural product and the inexorable identification of that product with the United States. His chapters "Reading Science Fiction" and "The SF Community" build on works such as those by Stableford and Hartwell, but always with an eye more toward cultural study than toward genre analysis, exploring at once the culture of SF and the ways in which SF has "become part of the modern idiom, infusing our language, our media culture, and our children's world of play with its images and its concepts." "The main underlying thesis of the book," states James, "is that sf is a major cultural phenomenon, an understanding of which is essential if one wants to comprehend the ways in which Western societies have come to terms with the rapid change and uncertainty which have characterized our century." *Science Fiction in the 20th Century* makes a clear, insightful, and compelling case for that thesis.

In *Dimensions of Science Fiction* (Cambridge, Mass.: Harvard University Press, 1986), William S. Bainbridge offers a knowledgeable analysis of SF culture broken down into the ideological appeals of hard science, New Wave, and fantasy writing. Bainbridge's analysis is statistically based on questionnaires given to registrants at the 1978 world SF convention, and, while his quantitative approach is no doubt rigorous in terms of sociological research, it raises many questions—some quite troubling—when applied to reader response.

Cyberpunk was correctly perceived by a number of critics as one of the responses of science fiction to the conditions of postmodern culture, and several theoretical works explore this new interface. *Storming the Reality Studio: A Casebook of Cyberpunk and Postmodern Fiction*, ed. Larry McCaffery (Durham, N.C.: Duke University Press, 1991), offers the most extended consideration of the cultural implications of cyberpunk, using that term in a broad sense not limited to the brief literary movement. Of postmodern literary critics, Brian McHale has devoted the most attention to SF, identifying science fiction as a good example of the ontological orientation of postmodern literature. In *Postmodernist Fiction* (New York: Methuen, 1987) and in *Constructing Postmodernism*, McHale offers a fascinating brief for SF not as genre or marginal literature but as an integral part of a new cultural dominant. The most original and in many ways the most significant theoretical approach to SF in recent years has been that of Scott Bukatman in *Terminal Identity: The Virtual Subject in Postmodern Science Fiction* (Durham: Duke University Press, 1993). Bukatman's brilliant cultural study, also described below for its contribution to film and electronic media scholarship, offers a theory of SF that embraces the cultural condition of a world that has itself become science fictional.

Other valuable works offering distinctive theories of science fiction are David Ketterer's *New Worlds for Old: The Apocalyptic Imagination, Science Fiction, and American Literature* (Bloomington: Indiana University Press, 1974), Ketterer's *Canadian Science Fiction and Fantasy* (Bloomington: Indiana University Press, 1992), and Colin Manlove's *Science Fiction: Ten Explorations* (Kent, Ohio: Kent State University Press, 1986). And no discussion of SF theory can afford to ignore the key contributions of Samuel R. Delany in essays collected in *The Jewel-Hinged Jaw: Notes on the Language of Science Fiction* (New York: Berkley Windhover, 1977) and in *Starboard Wine: More Notes on the Language of Science Fiction* (Pleasantville, New York: Dragon Press, 1984). Stanislaw Lem, who, like Delany, is one of contemporary SF's most brilliant writers, presents his often highly critical views of the field in *Microworlds: Writings on Science Fiction and Fantasy*, ed. Franz Rottensteiner (New York: Harcourt, 1985).

Feminist approaches to both the writing and the study of science fiction have been one of the most exciting and productive developments in the field, particularly since the mid-1970s. One of the first volumes devoted exclusively to feminist criticism was *Future Females: A Critical Anthology*, ed. Marleen S. Barr (Bowling Green, Ohio: Bowling Green State University Popular Press, 1981). Barr's powerful commitment to bringing feminist perspectives to the study of science fiction has continued through her *Feminist*

Fabulation: Space/Postmodern Fiction (Iowa City: University of Iowa Press, 1992) and *Lost in Space: Probing Feminist Science Fiction and Beyond* (Chapel Hill: University of North Carolina Press, 1993). *Feminist Fabulation* advances the radical but persuasive thesis that "feminist science fiction" is not science fiction at all but part of a broader transgeneric writing—feminist fabulation—that gives primacy to the criticism of patriarchal thinking. Two other excellent feminist studies that construct SF as "feminist-friendly" discourse are Sarah Lefanu's *In the Chinks of the World Machine: Feminism and Science Fiction* (London: The Women's Press, 1988) and Jenny Wolmark's *Aliens and Others: Science Fiction, Feminism and Postmodernism* (Iowa City: University of Iowa Press, 1994). In a number of influential articles in *Science-Fiction Studies*, *Extrapolation*, and critical anthologies; in her *How to Suppress Women's Writing* (Austin: University of Texas, 1983); and somewhat more obliquely in her *On Strike Against God* (Trumansburg, New York: The Crossing Press, 1980), Joanna Russ has been a most uncompromising and effective champion of women's concerns in science fiction. And, of course, Ursula K. Le Guin has consistently advanced a feminist critique of science fiction, most recently in her introduction to *The Norton Book of Science Fiction*, as well as in her *The Language of the Night: Essays on Fantasy and Science Fiction*, ed. Susan Wood, revised edition ed. Ursula K. Le Guin (New York: HarperCollins, 1992), and in her *Dancing at the Edge of the World: Thoughts on Words, Women, Places* (New York: Perennial, 1990).

Excellent proceedings volumes from the J. Lloyd Eaton Conference and from the Conference on the Fantastic in the Arts should be consulted for essays on specific topics within SF. The Greenwood Press series Contributions to the Study of Science Fiction, established by Marshall B. Tymn, contains many valuable works on a broad range of topics.

Anthologies

The two anthologies that seem likely to occupy center stage in SF discussions in years to come are Ursula K. Le Guin and Brian Attebery's *The Norton Book of Science Fiction* (New York: W. W. Norton, 1993) and David G. Hartwell and Kathryn Cramer's *Ascent of Wonder: The Evolution of Hard SF* (New York: TOR, 1994). *The Norton Book* contains North American short fiction published between 1960 and 1990, selected by Le Guin, Attebery, and Karen

Joy Fowler. While their selections have been criticized for not accurately representing the contour of SF during that period, with hard SF, in particular, underrepresented, this volume contains stories that brilliantly suggest the range and diversity of modern SF and that may in fact represent the future of SF more than its past. This anthology will undoubtedly shape the teaching of SF (Attebery's excellent teacher's manual will make it a popular choice for SF courses), and it may well prove to be one of the most influential of all SF anthologies. Hartwell and Cramer's *Ascent of Wonder* offers an obvious corrective for those who feel that hard SF has been slighted in the *Norton Book*. Since its selections range from the nineteenth century through the 1980s, *The Ascent of Wonder* offers a more comprehensive overview of what many see as the conceptual core of SF, but its selections are by no means rigid, including a number of works that stretch or defy usual notions of what constitutes hard SF. When combined, these two anthologies offer a most useful window on the diversity and complexity of modern SF. *The Oxford Book of Science Fiction*, ed. Tom Shippey (New York: Oxford University Press, 1992), will no doubt benefit both from its prominent publisher and from Shippey's reputation as an SF scholar, but its selection has been criticized as idiosyncratic both in terms of the writers it contains and in terms of the stories selected from those writers.

Science Fiction: A Historical Anthology, ed. Eric S. Rabkin (New York: Oxford University Press, 1983), remains one of the best introductions to the historical sweep of science fiction. James Gunn's four-volume series *The Road to Science Fiction* offers a superior range of fiction and more detailed commentary, making it one of the most comprehensive and most useful of all SF anthologies. Judged by many teachers and scholars as the best historical anthology of SF, *The Road to Science Fiction* series is being reprinted in updated and revised form by White Wolf Publishing (Clarkston, Calif.). The volumes in the *Science Fiction Hall of Fame* contain what might be thought of as the canonical core of genre SF, and the first volume of short stories is essential reading for anyone with any interest in the history of SF. *Science Fiction: The SFRA Anthology*, eds. Patricia S. Warrick, Charles G. Waugh, and Martin H. Greenberg (New York: Harper & Row, 1988), offers a productive blend of old and relatively recent SF short fiction. Harlan Ellison gave American New Wave SF one of its most influential venues in *Dangerous Visions* (Garden City, N.Y.: Doubleday, 1967) and *Again, Dangerous Visions*

(Garden City, N.Y.: Doubleday, 1972). Norman Spinrad complemented a powerful selection of golden age and New Wave SF in *Modern Science Fiction* (Garden City, N.Y.: Anchor/Doubleday, 1974) with even-handed and insightful commentary. Few anthologies of any era have had the impact of Pamela Sargent's *Women of Wonder* (New York: Vintage, 1975) and its sequels—collections that supported and energized feminist SF. The works in those Sargent collections have now been republished in two indispensable anthologies: *Women of Wonder: The Classic Years: Science Fiction by Women from the 1940s to the 1970s* (New York: Harcourt Brace, 1995) and *Women of Wonder: The Contemporary Years: Science Fiction by Women from the 1970s to the 1990s* (New York: Harcourt Brace, 1995). Likewise, *Mirrorshades: The Cyberpunk Anthology*, ed. Bruce Sterling (New York: Arbor House, 1986), codified the initial impact of William Gibson's *Neuromancer* and with Sterling's polemical introduction became a central document for cyberpunk writing.

Author Studies

The number of studies of individual SF writers has grown so large that it would be impossible to do justice to them here. Readers interested in individual authors should consult the chapter "Author Studies" in Barron's *Anatomy of Wonder*. Three series of author studies should be noted: Twayne, Starmont House, and Borgo Press have published a number of generally brief, but very useful introductory studies of SF authors. There also now exist more sources of author interviews than can be surveyed here. However, two excellent sources of interviews are Charles Platt's *Dream Makers: Science Fiction and Fantasy Writers at Work* (New York: Ungar, 1987), which features interviews with writers who came to prominence mainly in or before the 1970s, and Larry McCaffery's *Across the Wounded Galaxies* (Urbana: University of Illinois Press, 1990), which primarily features writers who came to prominence in the 1980s.

CD-ROM and World Wide Web Resources

More and more useful information about SF is starting to appear on CD-ROM and on the internet. A CD-ROM based on the *Encyclopedia of Science Fiction* has been published by Grolier as *Science Fiction: The Multimedia Encyclopedia of Science Fiction* (Danbury,

Conn.: Grolier Electronic Publishing, 1995). Containing illustrations, photographs, movie clips, author soundbites, and video interviews not to be found in the original *Encyclopedia*, this CD-ROM provides easy navigational tools, search engines, and numerous hypertext links. While not as useful or as thorough for systematic research as is the print *Encyclopedia*, the *Multimedia Encyclopedia of Science Fiction* offers a fascinating environment of information to be browsed or toured.

Science fiction–related material can be found at a growing number of sites on the World Wide Web, and it is certain that the Web will become an increasingly significant source of SF information. For example, current online information includes addenda to *The Encyclopedia of Science Fiction*, a large number of reviews of recent SF books, archived fanzines such as *Cheap Truth*, several newsletters from SF publishers (including sample chapters of recent books), and information about a number of SF writers. While Web addresses (URLs) remain too transitory for listings here, subject or author searches will produce good starting points for further research.

Science Fiction Film and Electronic Media

So complicated has become the feedback loop between science fiction literature and film that it makes no sense to attempt to divorce the two at the level of general inquiry. One of the first and one of the most influential collections of essays to offer a rigorous study of science fiction film was *Shadows of the Magic Lamp: Fantasy and Science Fiction in Film*, eds. George E. Slusser and Eric S. Rabkin (Carbondale: Southern Illinois University Press, 1985). Three works that productively explore the relationships between science fiction literature and film and electronic media are Vivian Sobchack's superb *Screening Space: The American Science Fiction Film* (New York: Ungar, 1988), my own *The Aesthetics of Ambivalence: Rethinking Science Fiction Film in the Age of Electronic (Re)Production* (Westport, Connecticut: Greenwood Press, 1992), and Scott Bukatman's brilliant *Terminal Identity: The Virtual Subject in Postmodern Science Fiction* (Durham: Duke University Press, 1993). Bukatman's book might be thought of as the first true study of science fiction thinking as it has become inextricably a part of and a driving force for electronic culture.

Recommended Titles

A select and painfully incomplete list. To better indicate the range and diversity of modern science fiction, few works of only technical importance to the growth of SF have been selected, my emphasis being on works that continue to hold interest for contemporary readers.

Aldiss, Brian (1925–   ). *Helliconia Spring*. New York: Atheneum, 1982. Helliconia is a planet whose sun orbits another star in such a way that Helliconian seasons range from relatively short spring and summer through an eon-long winter, or Great Year. Orbiting observers from Earth document the vast societal changes during a Great Year, allowing Aldiss to showcase his mastery of world building and planetary romance. Sequels are *Helliconia Summer* (1983) and *Helliconia Winter* (1985).

———. *Starship*. Criterion, 1959. With "Universe," Heinlein may have pioneered the story of a starship so vast and a journey so long that its inhabitants might regress to the point where they no longer know their "world" is a spaceship, but Aldiss's *Starship* is the classic development of this theme. An unforgettable novel.

Asimov, Isaac. (1920–1993). *The Foundation Trilogy*. Garden City: Doubleday, 1963. Combining *Foundation* (1951), *Foundation and Empire* (1952), and *Second Foundation* (1953), this central work of SF colonized and corporatized the imaginary future, giving SF one of its strongest legacies. The decline and fall and eventual resurrection of a galactic empire takes place against the psychohistory theories and manipulations of Hari Seldon. The trilogy, given a special Hugo award in 1966 for "all-time best SF series," has been extended with diminishing results by *Foundation's Edge* (1982), *Foundation and Earth* (1986), and *Prelude to Foundation* (1988).

————. *I, Robot*. New York: Gnome, 1950. Karel Čapek may have coined the term "robot" in *R. U. R.* (1923), but Asimov's "Three Laws of Robotics" and his positronic robot stories, here and in *The Caves of Steel* (1954), *The Naked Sun* (1957), *The Rest of the Robots* (1964), *The Robots of Dawn* (1983), and *Robots and Empire* (1985), have created an imaginary robot anthropology so powerful that other robot stories must position themselves in or against it.

Atwood, Margaret (1939–). *The Handmaid's Tale*. Boston: Houghton Mifflin, 1986. Handmaids are fertile women—effectively slaves—used for breeding in a sexist dystopian near-future world, the Republic of Gilead, run by right-wing fundamentalists. Since the framing devices that present Offred's taped account of her life as a handmaid reveal that Gilead no longer exists, Atwood's description of a dystopian world does not fit our expectations for the dystopian novel: this is primarily a personal tragedy rather than a sociopolitical polemic.

Ballard, J. G. (1930–). *The Atrocity Exhibition*. San Francisco: REsearch Publications, 1990. Originally published by Cape in London in 1970, Ballard's brilliant project is best realized in this edition that contains his lengthy annotations to the original text. This protohypertextual series of mediascape snapshots or "condensed novels" follows the apocalyptic adventures of Ballard's protagonist in a hyperpostmodern world. Ballard seems fascinated by the paratactic juxtapositions and collisions at the heart of media culture.

————. *Crash*. New York: Vintage, 1985. This edition of Ballard's 1973 novel includes his influential "Introduction to the French Edition" of *Crash* (1974). *Science Fiction Studies* devoted part of a special issue to responses to essays by Jean Baudrillard in which he explained why Ballard's brutal novel about the terrible seductiveness of injury and death through car crashes was, in fact, SF. If SF is the literature that investigates the interfaces between humanity and technology, this is surely one of its greatest—and most horrible—works.

Bear, Greg (1951–). *Blood Music*. New York: Arbor, 1985. This is one of the most striking looks at the small end of SF's longstanding preoccupation with the theme of large and small. Here, nanotechnology leads to the creation of intelligent microorganisms that "take over" the living world, a process that is finally transcendental rather than threatening.

Benford, Gregory (1941–). *Great Sky River*. New York: Bantam, 1987. Humanity/machine conflict is given a scientifically rigorous turn in this story of conflict between human colonists and a machine culture. Sequels are *Tides of Light* (1989) and *Furious Gulf* (1994).

————. *Timescape*. New York: Simon & Schuster, 1980. Scientists from a terminally polluted 1998 use tachyons to communicate with scientists in 1962, hoping to preclude some of the disastrous aspects of their time. Like Fred Hoyle before him, Benford masterfully details scientists at work, with particular attention to what he calls "the way it feels to do science, the oddly incommunicable sensation of discovering something true and strange and new," but he is an infinitely better writer than Hoyle.

Bester, Alfred. (1913–1987). *The Demolished Man*. Chicago: Shasta, 1953. Narrative and typographical gymnastics abound in this detective story in which a telepathic policeman pursues a wealthy and ingenious murderer. Both characters are intriguing, and their battle of wits is a masterful exploration of psychology. This book won, in 1953, the first Hugo Award for best novel.

————. *Starlight: The Great Short Fiction of Alfred Bester*. Garden City: Doubleday, 1976. Stories written from the 1941 to 1974, including Bester's robot classic, "Fondly Fahrenheit," and his time-travel classic, "The Men Who Murdered Mohammed."

————. *The Stars My Destination*. New York: Signet, 1957. One of the most unforgetable and most influential works of modern SF. Gully Foyle, a seemingly dim-witted spaceship crewman determined only to seek revenge on those who would not rescue him after his ship was destroyed, is driven by rage to transcend all personal limitations and becomes, almost despite himself, a kind of godlike model for human potential. Few discussions of SF's "sense of wonder" fail to invoke this novel as a paradigm, and it has exerted tremendous influence on SF readers and writers alike.

Bishop, Michael (1945–   ). *Blooded on Arachne*. Sauk City, Wisconsin: Arkham, 1982. Collection of stories from SF's most intriguing "Southern Strange" writer. Bishop is an unreconstructed humanist and his concerns often turn eschatological, if not theological.

————. *No Enemy But Time*. New York: Pocket Books, 1982. A black American time traveler returns to the Pleistocene age, joins a band of ape-like hominids, fathers a daughter, and returns with her to his own time. A complex and poignant novel that reveals Bishop's penchant for tackling tough questions.

Blish, James (1921–1975). *Cities in Flight*. New York: Avon, 1970. A collection of Blish's four "Okie" novels about migrant flying cities powered by antigravity "spindizzies," this book contains *Earthman, Come Home* (1955), *They Shall Have Stars* (1956), *The Triumph of Time* (1958), and *A Life for the Stars* (1962). These books reflect both Blish's historical interest in the American Depression and his fascination with a much larger sense of historical cycles, as explored by Oswald Spengler.

Blumlein, Michael (1948–   ). *The Movement of Mountains*. New York: St. Martin's, 1987. A bulimic M.D. protagonist is only one of the unique features in this excellent story of the emergence of sentience in Domers, artificially created mine workers designed for conditions on the planet Eridis. An M.D. himself, Blumlein uses his training to make fat fascinating.

Bradbury, Ray (1920–   ). *Fahrenheit 451*. New York: Ballantine, 1953. A world in which all books must be burned exerts a special kind of pull on readers, and Bradbury's somewhat simplistic dystopia uses SF conventions to criticize all information technologies other than books, advocating a return not just to literary culture but to detechnologized culture.

———. *The Martian Chronicles*. Garden City: Doubleday, 1950. Displaying few of the characteristics associated with Campbell era SF, Bradbury's linked stories about the colonization of Mars capture the poignancy of the vanished Martians and of the rootless colonizers from Earth. Lyric, poetic, moody, these stories were among the first to shift the focus of SF from "hard" to "soft" issues and led to Bradbury's becoming, along with Heinlein, one of the first American SF writers to achieve widespread popular and critical acclaim outside of genre SF.

Brunner, John (1934–1995). *The Shockwave Rider*. New York: Harper, 1975. Perhaps the first major SF response to Toffler's *Future Shock*, this novel about a worm (virus) in the worldwide communications net anticipated some of the major concerns of cyberpunk.

———. *Stand on Zanzibar*. Garden City: Doubleday, 1968. Brunner's dystopian view of the twenty-first century extended and intensified twentieth-century problems to present an overcrowded and violent future where technology creates more problems than it solves. Commentators note that Brunner's somewhat fragmented, protohypertextual style owes much to the Dos Passos of the *U.S.A.* trilogy. *The Sheep Look Up* (1972) turned Brunner's dystopian vision more directly toward pollution.

Bunch, David R. (192?–   ). *Bunch!* Cambridge, Massachusetts: Broken Mirror Press, 1993. Short story collection from one of SF's most eccentric stylists. Gary K. Wolfe suggests that trying to read these 32 intense stories all together "leaves one with the vague sensation of being pelted with razor-studded marshmallows."

———. *Moderan*. New York: Avon, 1971. Bunch's linked stories about the machine/cyborg inhabited world of Moderan bring to mind the darkly violent machine wars staged by Mark Pauline. Bunch is often mentioned as one of modern SF's understudied authors.

Burdekin, Katherine (1896–1963). *Proud Man*. London: Gollancz, 1934. Originally written under the pseudonym "Murray Constantine," this novel has been republished under Burdekin's name by the Feminist Press in 1993. A hermaphroditic visitor from the far future, "Person," returns to 1930s England and contemplates the lives and sexual assumptions of a priest, a woman novelist, and a murderer. "Burdekin deserves recognition as the leading feminist utopian writer of her era," writes Gary K. Wolfe, "as well as one of the most thoughtful and provocative SF writers of the 1930s—and possibly one of the more influential as well."

————. *Swastika Night.* London: Gollancz, 1937. Republished in 1985 by the Feminist Press, Burdekin's chilling antifascist novel considers a 26th century world ruled by Nazis who have added to their mad concern with racial purity a similarly mad belief in a kind of male sexual purity, with terrible consequences for women.

Butler, Octavia E. (1947–). *Dawn: Xenogenesis.* New York: Warner, 1987. A young black woman is among a small number of survivors of an apocalyptic war on Earth. These humans have been saved by aliens, the Oankali, who must crossbreed with the remaining humans if either race is to survive. Butler, one of contemporary SF's most celebrated and most challenging writers, exquisitely examines a "no-win" situation in which issues of control, gender, and racial "purity" become incredibly complicated. *Adulthood Rites* (1988) and *Imago* (1989) continue the Xenogenesis series. Butler's earlier sweeping "Patternist" series, *Patternmaster* (1976), *Mind of My Mind* (1977), *Survivor* (1978), *Wild Seed* (1980), and *Clay's Ark* (1984), addresses many of these same issues in equally complex, equally intriguing terms.

————. *Kindred.* Garden City: Doubleday, 1979. Suddenly thrown back in time to pre–Civil War Maryland, where she is a slave, Dana, a contemporary black woman from California, must protect the white rapist plantation owner's son who is her distant ancestor. This is a stunningly fine interrogation of complex power relationships.

————. *Parable of the Sower.* New York: Four Walls Eight Windows, 1993. To survive an entropically disintegrating near-future California, Butler's protagonist, Lauren, develops Earthseed, a pragmatic philosophy or secular religion built around the rigorous acceptance of change.

Cadigan, Pat (1953–). *Synners.* 1989. For several years Cadigan was not just the preeminent, but the *only* woman strongly associated with the cyberpunk movement. *Synners* shows how well she has made the cyberpunk semblance her own, with its take on virtual reality and the dangers of a world dependent on human/computer interfaces.

Campbell, John W., Jr. (1910–1971). *The Best of John W. Campbell.* Ed. Lester Del Rey. Garden City: Doubleday, 1976. Including the best known of Campbell's stories and those written under the name of "Don A. Stuart," this collection suggests the concerns and values that made Campbell SF's most influential, if not defining, editor during the 1940s and 1950s. See discussion of "Twilight" in the text.

Čapek, Karel (1890–1938). *War with the Newts.* London: Allen & Unwin, 1937. Intended as a satire of Hitlerian fascism, this story of a newly discovered sea-dwelling race called "newts" follows their history as they are first enslaved by humans and then gradually supplant them, finally flooding the continents to rid the world of its previously dominant species. The pattern of revolt and usurpation followed by the newts is similar to that followed by the android "robots" in Čapek's play *R. U. R.* (1921).

Card, Orson Scott (1951–   ). *Ender's Game*. New York: TOR, 1985. A young boy is trained to excel at a kind of virtual reality war game, only to discover that the game was real and that he has completely annihilated an alien race—the insectlike Buggers—that had previously attacked humanity. Card manages to combine Heinlein-like enthusiasm for the boy's game-training with revulsion at the ethical issues trampled by the military trainers. Sequels are *Speaker for the Dead* (1986), which, like *Ender's Game*, won both Hugo and Nebula Awards; and *Xenocide* (1991).

Carr, Terry (1937–1987), ed. *Best Science Fiction of the Year*. New York: TOR, 1986. Whether published by Ballantine/Del Rey or by TOR, from 1972 through 1987 this selection by Carr consistently singled out the finest short fiction and most promising new writers in the field. Accordingly, any volume in this series gives a perceptive view of the SF of the preceding year. Carr's highly respected mantle has now passed to Gardner Dozois.

Carter, Angela (1940–1992). *Heroes and Villains*. New York: Pocket Books, 1969. This at times surrealistic postapocalyptic novel starts from, then inverts, gender expectations as a bored and rebellious professor's daughter proves tougher than the barbarian who kidnaps and rapes her. Carter's fine writing defies labels but deserves and rewards great attention.

———. *The Passion of New Eve*. New York: Harcourt, Brace Jovanovich, 1977. Offering something to threaten any reader, this tour de force story of sex change and sexual inversion so thoroughly confuses gender expectations as to become a postfeminist masterpiece.

Charnas, Suzy McKee (1939–   ). *Walk to the End of the World*. New York: Ballantine, 1974. The first of three powerful feminist novels, the sequels being *Motherlines* (1978) and *The Furies* (1994), *Walk* sets a world in which the men of the Holdfast hold savagely to their misogynistic view of "fems" and enslave and brutalize all women. As Charnas attacks the patriarchal world presented in her novels, she also critiques many of the patriarchal excesses of much SF and adventure fiction.

Cherryh. C. J. (1942–   ). *Downbelow Station*. New York: DAW, 1981. An important novel in Cherryh's Union-Alliance future history, Downbelow Station swells with unusually well-developed characters and complicated action, centering on a huge space station orbiting Pell's World. Pell Station is a neutral site in the conflict between the colonial Earth Company and the rebellious colonies which form the Union. David Pringle calls Cherryh "the present-day mistress of intelligent space opera." Other novels set in this future history include *Merchanter's Luck* (1982), *Voyager in the Night* (1984), and *Cyteen* (1988).

Clarke, Arthur C. (1917–   ). *Childhood's End*. New York: Ballantine, 1953. Alien overlords arrive and, while benevolent, seem to control all social and political aspects of life on Earth. However, the seeming masters prove to be galactic midwives, preparing humanity for a transcendent evolution into a pure concept of mind, a metamorphosis of which their own species is incapable.

———. *Rendezvous with Rama*. New York: Gollancz, 1973. Rama, an apparently deserted 30-mile-long cylindrical alien spaceship, unfolds its marvelous secrets to human explorers. More exploration procedural than novel, Clarke's book won both Hugo and Nebula awards in 1974. Sequels, written with Gentry Lee, include *Rama II* (1989) and *The Garden of Rama* (1994).

Clement, Hal (Harry Clement Stubbs) (1922–   ). *Mission of Gravity*. New York: Doubleday, 1954. Frequently cited as *the* classic example of hard SF, this story of collaboration between an Earthman and a 15-inch-long native of the high-gravity (700 G) discus-shaped planet Mesklin also provides an interesting characterization of an alien entrepeneur-explorer and an unusually symbiotic model for inter-species cooperation.

Crowley, John (1942–   ). *Engine Summer*. Garden City, N.Y.: Doubleday, 1979. A lyrical, dreamy, and beautiful postapocalyptic novel that is a moving celebration of the oral tradition of storytelling.

Delany, Samuel R. (1942–   ). *Dhalgren*. New York: Bantam, 1975. The true test for Delany fans, this is the most complex and controversial novel from SF's most distinguished theorist. William Dhalgren's sexual and philosophical adventures in the nearly abandoned and decadent city of Bellona are presented with Joycean panache.

———. *Nova*. Garden City: Doubleday, 1968. The joyously liberating background of this sophisticated space opera presents Delany's unique vision of the future and his equally unique approach to SF. Like his earlier *Babel-17*, this book combines a kind of "lost-boy" wish fulfillment with sophisticated literary allusions and intellectual investigations.

Dick, Philip K. (1928–1982). *Do Androids Dream of Electric Sheep?* Garden City, N.Y.: Doubleday, 1968. Reissued under the title *Blade Runner* after the 1982 Riddley Scott film, this book challenges distinctions between human and android, between religious faith and electronic stimulation, between empathy and commodification. One of Dick's most haunting explorations of what it means to be human.

———. *The Man in the High Castle*. New York: Norton, 1962. One of the best known and most respected of alternate or alternative world stories, this novel explores a world in which Japan and Germany won World War II and now engage in a kind of cold war with each other in the conquered United States. More a study of cultural than of political exploitation, this fine novel also self-reflexively questions the reality of its own story, and, as is true of almost all of Dick's fiction, questions the nature of reality itself.

————. *Ubik*. Garden City, N.Y.: Doubleday, 1969. The realities of dreaming dead "half-lifers" intrude upon the realities of ostensibly live characters in this disorienting and ultimately self-reflexive interrogation of competing worldviews. See the discussion in the text.

Disch, Thomas M. (1940–). *334*. Boston: Gregg Press, 1976 (first published in 1972). One of SF's most original and most respected writers, Disch is also one of its harshest critics. With considerable justification, *The Encyclopedia of Science Fiction* describes Disch as "perhaps the most respected, least trusted, most envied and least read of all modern first-rank SF writers." 334 East 11th Street is the address of a Manhattan apartment building whose inhabitants must cope with a harsh near-future world of 2025.

————. *The Genocides*. New York: Berkley, 1965. Earth is unceremoniously appropriated by aliens who routinely try to rid it of humans—much as humans destroy garden pests—the better to raise giant alien plants. Trying only to survive, the few remaining humans live wretchedly in the roots of the giant plants. This novel is distinguished by the predictable moves it refuses to make, leaving it one of SF's bleakest works.

Dorsey, Candas Jane (1952–). *Machine Sex, and Other Stories*. London: The Women's Press, 1990. With "A naked woman working at a computer. Which attracts you most?" Dorsey may have posed one of most intriguing questions ever asked of SF readers.

Dozois, Gardner (1947–), ed. *The Year's Best Science Fiction: Twelfth Annual Collection*. New York: St. Martin's, 1995. Started in 1984, the Dozois *Year's Best* anthology joined the ranks of previous highly respected and highly influential "year's best" collections edited by Judith Merril and Terry Carr. Both as editor of Isaac Asimov's *Science Fiction Magazine* and as editor of this series, Dozois is very well positioned to influence the nature of current SF, and he has proved a perceptive judge of new directions and of new talent in SF. There is no better or more authoritative single representation of contemporary SF, and past volumes offer a clear index to the best writing of the last decade.

Ellison, Harlan (1934–), ed. *Dangerous Visions*. New York: Doubleday, 1967. In this pioneering anthology and its fine sequel, *Again, Dangerous Visions* (1972), Ellison helped energize and codify the American New Wave, providing writers with an outlet for controversially innovative stories and with a manifesto announcing that something new and exciting was happening.

————. *The Essential Ellison: A 35-Year Retrospective.* Ed. Terry Dowling. Omaha: Nemo Press, 1987. A wonderful introduction to one of the most prominent personalities in SF and one of the masters of the short story. Ellison resists being labeled a "science fiction writer," for good reason, but, under any label, his distinctive voice and stylish prose have contributed much powerful literature to the field.

Emshwiller, Carol (1921–). *The Start of the End of It All and Other Stories.* San Francisco: Mercury House, 1990. Emshwiller's writing is characteristically odd, subversive, edgy, enigmatic, and wonderful. The "title story" ("The Start of the End of the World") in this collection presents an alien invasion that first seems to the female narrator to offer a better alternative to patriarchal culture but then begins to seem a bit too much like a new patriarchy, causing her to join a new female revolt against liberators who didn't make the grade.

Fowler, Karen Joy (1950–). *Sarah Canary.* New York: Henry Holt and Company, 1991. John Clute is no doubt right when he judges *Sarah Canary* to be one of the two finest first-contact novels yet written, but this exceptional novel was enthusiastically read and reviewed by many who never dreamed it had anything to do with SF. It is a book without a main protagonist, and part of its genius lies in making the mute and chimerical title character a *tabula rasa* onto which the varied cast of "secondary" characters, all representing disempowered "Others" in the Washington of 1873, project their concerns. A finely written and infinitely rewarding novel.

Gibson, William (1948–). *Burning Chrome.* New York: Arbor, 1986. Apart from Sterling's *Mirrorshades* anthology, this collection of early Gibson stories—several collaborations—offers perhaps the best introduction to the central concerns and images of cyberpunk. And its one noncyberpunk story, "The Gernsback Continuum," offers a brilliant critique of golden age SF.

————. *Neuromancer.* New York: Ace, 1984. The novel that sold us on cyberspace and that provided what became the standard cyberpunk semblance. Sequels are *Count Zero* (1985) and *Mona Lisa Overdrive* (1988). See the discussion in the text.

Griffith, Nicola (1960–) *Ammonite.* New York: Del Rey, 1992. Several hundred years after a virus has killed all men and many women on the colonized Grenchstom's Planet (GP or "Jeep"), and the surviving women have developed strange new abilities—including that of reproducing without men—company anthropologist Marghe Taishan tries to unravel and survive the mysteries of the planet's warring matriarchies, as well as the conspiracies of her own employer. Winner of the 1993 Tiptree Award for its interrogation of gender issues, this intriguing novel features wide-ranging social speculation, explores new models for personal relationships, and charts new paths for individual growth. Less sociologically sweeping but equally rewarding is Griffith's *Slow River* (1995).

Gunn, James E. (1923–), ed. *The Road to Science Fiction*. New York: New American Library, 1977. Volume 1 in this excellent series contains short fiction from "Gilgamesh to Wells," volume 2 runs from "Wells to Heinlein," volume 3 runs from "Heinlein to Here," and volume 4 runs from "Here to the Future." Gunn's introduction and notes to each volume provide a very useful historical context and offer many insights into SF's recurring themes and concerns. Until recently out of print, the series is being republished in updated and revised form by White Wolf.

Haldeman, Joe (1943–). *The Forever War*. New York: St. Martin's, 1975. Haldeman has a gag business card that claims his specialty to be "Heinlein retreads." However, while its similarities to Heinlein's *Starship Troopers* are clear, *The Forever War* is a powerful post-Vietnam deconstruction of Heinlein's military enthusiasm.

Harrison, Harry (1925–). *Bill the Galactic Hero*. Garden City: Doubleday, 1965. This parody of galactic war training procedurals effectively lampoons the surface of Heinlein's *Starship Troopers* but leaves untouched the assumptions underlying that work.

———. *West of Eden*. 1984. This work and its sequels, *Winter in Eden* (1986) and *Return to Eden* (1988), consider an alternate line of development in which the dinosaurs not only did not die but also became technologically advanced. The series pits primitive human groups against each other and against the advanced dinosaurs.

Hartwell, David G., and Kathryn Cramer, eds. *The Ascent of Wonder: The Evolution of Hard SF*. New York: TOR/Tom Doherty Associates, 1994. While it's not exactly a case of dueling anthologies, this wide-ranging collection of hard SF stories, some might argue, represents the core of SF missing from the Le Guin and Attebery *Norton Book of Science Fiction*. The dichotomy, of course, is false, as both anthologies deserve careful attention.

Heinlein, Robert A. (1907–1988). *Starship Troopers*. New York: Putnam, 1959. Not so much a glorification of war as it is a glorification of militarized society, this remains Heinlein's most controversial work. Its presentation of space cadet training and military unit esprit remains seductive, even for those who strongly oppose Heinlein's assumptions. See the discussion in the text.

———. *Stranger in a Strange Land*. New York: Putnam, 1961. The story of a human child, raised by Martians, who returns to Earth with paranormal powers and clear parallels to Christ. That this novel became one of SF's all-time best-sellers and achieved quasi-cult status on college campuses in the 1960s suggests Heinlein's skill and unpredictability. Beneath its humorous and superficially counterculture affability, however, this novel also carries the controversial implications of Heinlein's worldview.

————. *Time for the Stars*. New York: Ballantine, 1956. Heinlein's series of juvenile novels introduced thousands of future fans to SF, and this story of telepathically linked identical twins separated when one remains on Earth and the other leaves on a starship is one of his best.

Herbert, Frank (1920–1986). *Dune*. Philadelphia and New York: Chilton, 1965. Combining Machiavellian intrigue with messianic promise, mind-expanding drugs with degenerate villains, a well-thought-through ecology of a desert world (Arrakis) with an anthropology of a desert people (the Fremen), and giant sandworms with mystical visions, Herbert's novel seemed to have something for every kind of reader and was phenomenally popular. Five sequels of diminishing interest followed, making this one of the most massive series in modern SF and making *Dune* an indispensable model of SF world making and social philosophizing.

Hoyle, Fred (1915–). *The Black Cloud*. London: Heinemann, 1957. A cloud of interstellar material threatens Earth before scientists discover the "cloud" to be a sentient life-form. When Hoyle, a prominent and sometimes unconventional Cambridge astronomer, brought his expertise to SF, he gave readers, in Gregory Benford's words, the first convincing portrayal of "the lively logic of scientists at work."

Jones, Gwyneth (1952–). *White Queen*. New York: TOR, 1993. This most ambiguous and ambivalent first-contact novel masterfully investigates a wide range of "otherness"—that of alien culture, that of gender construction, that of contagious disease. Sequel is *North Wind* (1996).

Kessel, John (1950–). *Good News from Outer Space*. New York: TOR, 1989. If Nathanael West had tried his hand at SF, surely something like this novel would have resulted. Kessel captures the sense of millennial madness celebrated in *The Weekly World News* with this tale of UFO cults and messianic evangelists.

Kress, Nancy (1948–). *Beggars in Spain*. New York: William Morrow, 1993. Expanded from the Nebula-winning novella of the same title, this novel explores the conflict created between normal humans and the genetically improved "sleepless" who have 24 hours a day in which to develop their talents. Kress deftly explores "otherness" and the ethical issues raised by the genetic design of superchildren in this striking book. The sequel is *Beggars and Choosers* (1994).

Lafferty, R. A. (1914–). *Nine Hundred Grandmothers*. New York: Ace, 1970. This wonderful collection of short stories features Lafferty's unique, absurdist blending of varying mythologies, Charles Fortean anomalies, SF themes, and whatever else amused Lafferty. The title story nicely mocks the positivistic smugness of much early SF, as a human anthropologist learns from the possibly immortal Proavtoi that some things simply cannot be learned, some questions never answered.

Le Guin, Ursula K. (1929–   ). *Always Coming Home*. New York: Harper, 1985. With its presentation of the culture of the Kesh, this daringly constructed novel set the standard for imaginary anthropology. Its nonlinear and protohypertextual form may mark an important structural moment in the evolution of SF narrative.

————. *The Dispossessed*. New York: Harper & Row, 1974. Inhabitants of Anarres, a moon of Urras, have renounced possessions when they left Urras to found an anarchist and egalitarian utopia based on the teachings of Odon, which have also produced a language suited for a society that does not recognize possession. Shevek, a brilliant physicist, leaves Anarres to return to Urras, but his Odonian idealism makes life on the capitalistic Urras impossible for him. Thought by many to be one of the finest discussion of moral and political issues in modern SF.

Le Guin, Ursula, and Brian Attebery, eds. *The Norton Book of Science Fiction*. New York: Norton, 1993. Although this collection of 67 short stories "written in English by North American writers and published in North America between 1960 and 1990" has been criticized by some for not accurately representing SF during that period, it magnificently represents one too frequently underrepresented strain of soft science, nonpatriarchal, nonmilitaristic, ecofeminist SF. It offers perhaps a better index to the present and future of SF than to its past, but, more important, it offers a wonderful range of challenging and occasionally enigmatic stories.

Leiber, Fritz (1910–1992). *The Leiber Chronicles: Fifty Years of Fritz Leiber*. Ed. Martin H. Greenberg. Arlington Heights, Illinois: Dark Harvest, 1990. Forty-four stories ranging from 1939 to 1983 from one of the most celebrated and revered modern masters of sword-and-sorcery fantasy and SF.

Lem, Stanislaw (1921–   ). *His Master's Voice*. New York: Harvest, 1983. When is a message from outer space a message and when can human "decoding" of such a message be anything more than a dangerously flawed interpretation? Lem makes this possible-first-contact story a laboratory in which he can present the infinite problems involved in radical translation. Compare with Don DeLillo's *Ratner's Star*. See the discussion in the text.

————. *Solaris*. New York: Walker, 1970, trans. Joanna Kilmartin and Steve Cox. The interface between Earth scientists and a sentient planet-covering ocean takes unexpectedly haunting forms in this magnificent study of communication, interpretation, perception, and metaphysics. Any serious attempt to understand the power and possibility of SF should include careful attention to this superb work.

McCaffrey, Anne (1926–   ). *Dragonflight*. New York: Ballantine, 1968. The first of the Pern series, including *Dragonquest* (1971), *The White Dragon* (1978), *Moreta, Dragonlady of Pern* (1982), *Dragonsdawn* (1988), and *The Dolphins of Pern* (1994). Scientifically rationalized fire-breathing, teleporting, and occasionally time-travelling drag-ons who telepathically communicate with their riders take center stage in these popular novels and in the corollary Dragonsong series that more directly targeted adolescent female readers.

McDonald, Ian (1960–   ). *Desolation Road*. New York: Bantam/Spectra, 1988. Reviewers cite McDonald's "lexical energy" and call him "a logomaniac's delight." *Desolation Road* follows the founding, growth, and unmaking of a settlement on Mars, as if, suggests *The Encyclopedia of Science Fiction*, *100 Years of Solitude* were crossed with *The Martian Chronicles*.

McHugh, Maureen F. *China Mountain Zhang*. New York: TOR, 1992. The initial cyberpunk writers hoped to refocus SF away from its preoc-cupation with Anglo-American culture. Here, McHugh does just that with a novel whose protagonist is a gay American-born Chi-nese in a twenty-first-century world dominated by the Chinese. Zhang moves in the course of the novel from being a relatively unskilled technician to being a master of computer/human inter-face design.

McIntyre, Vonda (1948–   ). *Dreamsnake*. New York: Houghton Mifflin, 1978. Expanded from her Nebula Award-winning story "Of Mist, and Grass, and Sand," this novel is set in a postapocalyptic future that seems a world made much more for fantasy than for SF. McIntyre's female protagonist uses specially evolved snakes whose bites heal rather than kill; at the same time she must con-tend with prejudice against the snakes and opposition to her inde-pendence and power as a woman.

Merril, Judith (1923–   ). *SF: The Year's Greatest Science Fiction and Fantasy*. New York: Dell, 1956. From 1956 through 1969 Merril's antholo-gies, with her astute commentaries, were the most respected index to developments in SF. Her anthologies in the 1960s, Terry Carr's in the 1970s and early 1980s, and Gardner Dozois's from the mid-1980s to the present have been highly authoritative and influential.

Miller, Walter M. (1922–   ). *A Canticle for Leibowitz*. New York: Lippin-cott, 1959. Its action spanning some 1,200 years following a nuclear war, this fine novel examines the cyclical conflict between science and religion, with a strong leaning toward the latter. Catholic monks of the order of St. Leibowitz try to preserve past knowl-edge, but their efforts ironically lead to a new cycle of technologi-cal destruction. Wonderful characterization, irony, and pathos soften Miller's Christian polemic, making this one of the most justly celebrated works of modern SF. Along with Stewart's *Earth Abides*, *A Canticle for Leibowitz* was one of the first works of modern SF to be taught in college classrooms.

Moorcock, Michael (1939–   ). *The Cornelius Chronicles*. London: Avon, 1977. Jerry Cornelius is Moorcock's role- and identity-shifting superman-everyman hero-antihero, a protagonist so serviceable that he's been lent out to other authors. In *The Final Programme*

(1968), *A Cure for Cancer* (1971), *The English Assassin* (1972), and *The Condition of Muzak* (1977), all gathered in this volume, Cornelius moves through time and parallel universes with a distinct 1960s flair, his adventures ironic and parodic but moving inexorably toward tragic limits. Both in his writing and in his editing of *New Worlds*, Moorcock played a huge role in shaping the British New Wave and its American successors.

Moore, Alan, and Dave Gibbons (1953– ; 1949–). *Watchmen*. New York: Warner, 1987. Called with good reason "the *Ulysses* of Graphic Novels," this intricately structured work is a strong reminder that SF in the 1980s and 1990s has been very successful in comics and graphic novels, many of which adapt classic SF stories and films, most of which feature strong SF and fantasy elements. *Watchmen* deconstructs the superhero myth at the heart of so many comics.

Morrow, James (1947–). *This Is the Way the World Ends*. New York: Holt, 1986. Few would have thought of staging a kind of war crimes trial following a nuclear apocalypse, and fewer still would have imagined the charges brought by the souls of the unborn dead, the corollary victims of the nuclear war. Morrow did both, with a unique blend of satire and sentimentality in this finely eschatological novel.

———. *Towing Jehova*. New York: Harcourt Brace, 1994. Let's say that God is dead (finally done in by "a bad case of the twentieth century"), and that his body is two miles long, weighs seven million tons, is floating in the ocean, and needs to be towed to the Arctic. Of course, such a literal dead God presents every bit as many eschatalogical questions as a living God taken on faith, and Morrow takes on these questions in this amazing novel.

Murphy, Pat (1955–). *Points of Departure*. New York: Bantam/Spectra, 1990. Nineteen fine stories, including the powerful and award-winning "Rachel in Love," in which a female chimpanzee with enhanced intelligence and raised as a scientist's "daughter" escapes her patriarchal-scientific environment.

Niven, Larry (1938–). *Ringworld*. New York: Ballantine, 1970. If you love technology, engineering, engineers, and right-wing philosophy, this is the book for you. Ringworld is an alien-constructed artifact a million miles wide and 600 million miles around, the perfect emblem of what *The Encyclopedia of Science Fiction* calls a Big Dumb Object. *Ringworld* and its sequel *Ringworld Engineers* (1979) belong to Niven's Tales of Known Space sequence, a sequence at the very heart of contemporary hard SF.

Niven, Larry, and Jerry Pournelle. *The Mote in God's Eye*. New York: Simon & Schuster, 1974. First contact with a well-rendered alien civilization that is not what it appears to be and challenges even the militaristic and hierarchical society so favored by Pournelle and Niven.

Norton, Andre (Alice Mary Norton) (1912–). *Star Man's Son: 2250 A. D.* New York: Harcourt, 1952. A boy's initiation story, set in a post-

————, ed. *Modern Science Fiction*. Garden City: Anchor/Doubleday, 1974. Perceptive commentary by Spinrad made this strong anthology a kind of post-New Wave revision of SF history.

Stableford, Brian (1948–). *The Empire of Fear*. 1988. The vampire myth has been a persistent subject of SF treatment, and in this thoughtful alternate history Stableford imagines a Europe controlled by scientifically explained "vampires." Related treatments of other horror myths are *The Werewolves of London* (1990) and *The Angel of Pain* (1991).

Stapledon, Olaf (1886–1950). *Star Maker*. London: Methuen, 1937. With this novel and *Last and First Men* (1930), Stapledon retired the trophy for all-time greatest sense of wonder sweep, as it offers a history of the universe and its life-forms through billions of years. Brian Aldiss calls it "The one great grey holy book of science fiction."

————. *Sirius: A Fantasy of Love and Discord*. London: Secker & Warburg, 1944. This story of a genetically enhanced sheepdog raised to a level of high human intelligence who falls in love with a human girl, the daughter of the scientist who created him, has obvious and painful parallels to Mary Shelley's *Frankenstein*.

Sterling, Bruce (1954–), ed. *Mirrorshades: The Cyberpunk Anthology*. New York: Arbor House, 1986. With his polemical preface to this collection of stories from William Gibson, Tom Maddox, Pat Cadigan, Rudy Rucker, Marc Laidlaw, James Patrick Kelly, Greg Bear, Lewis Shiner, John Shirley, and Paul Di Filippo, Sterling effectively codified at least the myth of cyberpunk and became the movement's unofficial spokesman. While several of the writers in this collection never were cyberpunks, and few, if any, would still claim that label, their movement has had a galvanizing and lasting effect on contemporary SF.

————. *Schismatrix*. New York: Arbor House, 1985. Envisioning a far future where posthuman culture has split into Mechanist and Shaper factions, the former favoring mechanical prostheses and implants, the latter genetic engineering, this novel swells with cultural speculation on the scale of Stapledon's and Asimov's, but with considerably quicker pace. *Crystal Express* (1989) collects more stories in the Mechanist/Shaper series.

Stewart, George R. (1895–1980). *Earth Abides*. New York: Random House, 1949. One of the first American works of SF to be accepted as fine literature by the academic establishment, Stewart's postapocalyptic novel quietly focuses on inexorable processes of decay and loss as the few survivors of a plague gradually slip back into a life much like that of their Native American predecessors. More an ecology of the fading of civilization than a study of human attempts to reestablish that civilization, this is one of the great works of modern SF.

Strugatsky, Arkady (1925–1991) and Boris (1931–   ). *Roadside Picnic and Tale of the Troika*. New York: Macmillan, 1977. *Roadside Picnic* brilliantly contemplates life in the wake of an alien visitation. No one saw the aliens, but it's as if they had a picnic and left six distinct zones on earth littered with mysterious rubbish that violates many of our so-called "laws" of science. The focus here is not on the aliens, but on the sad reaction of humanity—a reaction that may be a sobering insight into attitudes toward our own technology. See the discussion in the text.

Sturgeon, Theodore (1918–1985). *More Than Human*. New York: Farrar, 1953. A group of six "freaks"—diverse, outcast American children—blend their talents to form a new psi-powered psychic entity, a gestalt that suggests the potential for greater things that Sturgeon consistently saw in situations of alienation.

———. *A Touch of Sturgeon*. Ed. David Pringle. 1987. The least doctrinaire of the writers who made Campbell's "golden age," Sturgeon was the first genre SF writer to make sexuality one of his concerns. Eight of the best of his 175 or so short stories are gathered here.

———. *Venus Plus X*. 1960. This groundbreaking novel presents a sexual utopia in which a society of hermaphrodites reveals to a stereotypical patriarchal American visitor a vision of social harmony, largely achieved through the disruption of gender assumptions.

Tepper, Sheri S. (1929–   ). *The Gate to Women's Country*. New York: Doubleday/Foundation, 1988. Postapocalyptic future in which gender separation is pronounced, with women in the cities and men outside in militaristic camps. Here and in other SF novels such as *Grass* (1989), *Raising the Stones* (1990), and *Sideshow* (1992), Tepper, who is also known for her fantasy writing, combines effective storytelling, sophisticated world building, and insistent feminism.

Tiptree, James, Jr. (Alice Sheldon) (1915–1987). *Her Smoke Rose Up Forever: The Great Years of James Tiptree, Jr.* 1990. With hard-edged stories such as "The Women Men Don't See" (1973) and novellas such as *Houston, Houston, Do You Read?* (1977), Tiptree established herself as perhaps *the* outstanding writer of 1970s SF, and this collection gathers most of her best-known stories. Other collections of her fiction include *Ten Thousand Light Years from Home* (1973), *Warm Worlds and Otherwise* (1975), *Star Songs of an Old Primate* (1978), and *Out of the Everywhere and Other Extraordinary Visions* (1981).

Van Vogt, Alfred Elton (1912–   ). *Slan*. New York: Simon & Schuster, 1951. "Fans are slans" captures some of the appeal of this novel in which an alienated and disenfranchised mutant telepath—a superhuman slan—tries to prevent human eradication of the slans and to work toward replacing human "normals" with slans. Outrageous coincidences drive the frenzied plot, but the teenage power fantasy at the heart of this novel and the breathtaking adventures of Jommy Cross, its slan protagonist, have intrigued several generations of SF readers.

———. *The World of Null-A*. New York: Simon & Schuster, 1948. Gilbert Gosseyn (Go sane) practices and promotes non-Aristotelian thinking (null-A) to foil invaders and to make Earth and Venus safe for the "better thinking" so often a subject of modern SF. This crudely written and confusingly plotted polemic for Alfred Korzybski's program of general semantics has somehow established itself as a favorite of many SF readers.

Varley, John (1947–). *The Persistence of Vision*. New York: Dial Press/ J. Wade, 1978. Varley was exploring cyberspace years before Gibson named it and was writing feminist SF before it became fashionable. This collection of stories showcases his talent.

Vinge, Joan D. (1948–). *The Snow Queen*. New York: Dial, 1980. Hans Christian Andersen and heroic fantasy combine with Graves's *The White Goddess* to provide the backdrop and texture for this story of the exploitation of a barbarian world by technologically advanced "offworlders."

Vinge, Vernor (1944–). *True Names*. New York: Bluejay, 1984. First published in 1981, this novella presented a prescient view of virtual reality in which computer hackers wage competition by proxy. Vinge's version of cyberspace predates Gibson's and seems a much more accurate evocation of life in the net.

Vonarburg, Elisabeth (1947–). *The Silent City*. Trans. Jane Brierley. New York: Bantam, 1992. Available in French since 1981 (*Le Silence de la Cité*), Vonarburg's postholocaust feminist novel pits the technologized but increasingly unfertile world of the City against Outsiders. Caught between Outsider patriarchy and City exploitation of Outsiders, Vonarburg's protagonist, given special ability by reproductive technology, strives to free her children from gendered dichotomies.

Waldrop, Howard (1946–). *Night of the Cooters: More Neat Stories*. Kansas City: Ursus Imprints/Mark V. Ziesing, 1991. How would a west Texas sheriff who seems a lot like Slim Pickens have responded to the invading Martian tripods of Wells's *War of the Worlds*? Waldrop hilariously answers that and many other questions no one else would have thought of asking in this delightful collection of nine of his brilliantly warped stories.

Watson, Ian (1943–). *The Embedding*. London: Gollancz, 1973. Whorfian and Chomskian assumptions about the shaping power of language run through this fine novel that examines the relationship between language and reality in children taught an artificial language, in the language used by Amazonian Indians, and in the attitude toward language that brings aliens to Earth.

———. *The Flies of Memory*. New York: Carroll & Graf, 1991. Aliens arrive in a giant pyramid spaceship and announce: "We have come to your planet to remember it." But remembering seems to involve matter transfer, as the places "remembered" disappear and reappear elsewhere, namely on Mars.

Wilhelm, Kate (1928–   ). *The Infinity Box*. New York: Harper, 1975. Brian Stableford says that "Wilhelm has no peer as a writer of realistic near-future SF stories examining the human implications of possible biological discoveries." This collection of stories more than justifies that claim. More recent collections of her stories include *Listen, Listen* (1981) and *And the Angels Sing* (1992), and five of her novellas are gathered in *Children of the Wind* (1989).

————. *Where Late the Sweet Birds Sang*. New York: Harper, 1976. Cloning allows a "family" to survive the ecological disaster that destroys the United States, but Wilhelm's novel questions whether the cost of this survival has been too high.

Williams, Walter John (1953–   ). *Hardwired*. New York: TOR, 1986. Williams rode the wave of cyberpunk for all it was worth, and this novel of earthbound rebels against orbiting multinational corporate powers offers fast action in a dense cyberpunk semblance.

Williamson, Jack (1908–   ). *The Humanoids*. New York: Simon & Schuster, 1949. Based on Williamson's well-known stories of overprotective robots, "With Folded Hands" and " . . . and Searching Mind," this novel explores some of the ethical implications of rebelling against humanoids who take their prime directive—"To Serve and Obey, and GUARD MEN FROM HARM"—to stultifying extremes.

Willis, Connie (1945–   ). *Doomsday Book*. New York: Bantam Spectra, 1992. One of the most consistently delightful and challenging writers in contemporary SF, Willis, whose unsentimental vision manages at once to be hard-edged and empathetic, has been called a "post-feminist." Here, she uses time travel to transport her female historian protagonist to an alternate fourteenth-century England, where her experience interrogates the blending of Christian and patriarchal worldviews. Her previous uses of time travel to present alternate histories in the award-winning stories in *Firewatch* (1985) and the novel *Lincoln's Dreams* (1987) have established Willis as one of the most respected and most promising voices in contemporary SF.

Wolfe, Bernard (1915–1985). *Limbo*. New York: Random House, 1952. Hard to find and harder still for the squeamish to read, this complexly written story of a post–nuclear war world in which men cut off their own limbs ("Immob") to prevent war is consistently mentioned as one of the most underappreciated works of American SF.

Wolfe, Gene (1931–   ). *The Book of the New Sun*. New York: Simon & Schuster, 1980–1983. A mammoth work published in four volumes, *The Shadow of the Torturer* (1980), *The Claw of the Conciliator* (1981), *The Sword of the Lictor* (1982), and *The Citadel of the Autarch* (1983), with a coda, *The Urth of the New Sun* (1987), *The Book of the New Sun* has been accepted by critics as one huge masterpiece rather than as a series. Set in a far future in which civilization on Earth has regressed into a medieval-like analogue to the worlds so prominent in sword-and-sorcery fantasy, Wolfe's novel is indisputably SF rather than fantasy and indisputably one of the great achievements in modern SF.

―――. *The Fifth Head of Cerberus*. New York: Scribner's, 1972. Three novellas that only gradually reveal their strong interconnections make up this brilliant evocation of two sister planets, Saint Anne and Saint Croix, in the decadent and destructive wake of colonization by Earth. Wolfe's complex vision and narrative skill make this a stunning work.

―――. *Nightside of the Long Sun*. New York: TOR, 1993. Wolfe's "Long Sun" series now extends through *Lake of the Long Sun* (1993) and *Calde of the Long Sun* (1994), with a fourth volume to come. Schoolmaster-priest Patera Silk is pushed toward becoming the ruler of the city of Viron in this series whose overtones become ever more theological, as the higher powers shaping events on the planet Whorl are revealed.

Womack, Jack (1956–   ). *Ambient*. New York: Weidenfeld and Nicolson, 1987. With this novel Womack opened what is planned to be a five-part "ensemble" of novels set in a cyberpunkish near-future New York, dominated by multinational corporations that prosper amid general economic collapse.

Wylie, Philip, and Edwin Balmer (1902–1971; 1883–1959). *When Worlds Collide*. Stokes, 1933. A huge rocketship "ark" is constructed to save a specially selected few people from an Earth doomed to be destroyed in a collision with a wandering planet. *After Worlds Collide* (1934) follows the survivors to a new planet where they discover cities built by a vanished civilization.

Wyndham, John (1903–1969). *The Day of the Triffids*. Garden City: Doubleday, 1951. Master of what Brian Aldiss has termed the "cozy catastrophe" novel, Wyndham combines two manmade disasters in his exciting postapocalyptic adventure: a series of satellite superweapon explosions that leave blind all who watched them and possibly alien, genetically engineered mobile plants with deadly stingers who prey upon blinded humans. Civilization "as we know it" crumbles, but Wyndham's sighted survivors quickly regroup and begin the slow but steady task of reestablishing British society and reclaiming territory from the pesky triffids.

Zamyatin, Yevgeny (1884–1937). *We*. New York: Dutton, 1952; current ed. New York: Penguin, 1993. Zamyatin's dystopia, first published in 1924, makes Orwell's world of *1984* seem like a vacation, albeit an unpleasant one. In the thirtieth century, D503, an engineer and builder of the first great spaceship, moves from his mathematically insured faith in the One State to the diseased condition of having a soul—and then back to unquestioning faith in a state where freedom of any sort is precluded. This greatest of twentieth-century dystopias has greatly influenced most subsequent efforts, particularly Orwell's.

Zelazny, Roger (1937–1995). *The Doors of His Face, The Lamps of His Mouth and Other Stories*. Garden City: Doubleday, 1971. Both the title story and "A Rose for Ecclesiastes" are among this frequently electrifying author's best known. These stories are among the best of the American New Wave.

———. *Lord of Light*. Garden City: Doubleday, 1967. What seem to be Hindu gods are the products of technology used to insure its human wielders' power on a colony planet. When humans revolt against these "gods," technology and myth become blurred in this superbly imaginative and stylishly complex novel.

Zoline, Pamela (1941–   ). *The Heat Death of the Universe and Other Stories*. Kingston, New York: McPherson & Co., 1988. The title story alone makes this collection worth reading, but the other four stories also feature Zoline's determination to bring together women's daily experience with SF tropes. See the discussion in the text.`

INDEX

THE AUTHOR

Brooks Landon is Professor of English at the University of Iowa. He is the author of *Thomas Berger* and *The Aesthetics of Ambivalence: Rethinking Science Fiction Film in the Age of Electronic (Re)Production*, as well as numerous articles on science fiction, science fiction film, and twentieth-century American fiction. His *Horizon of Invisibility Homestead* web pages can be found at **http://www.uiowa.edu/~english/landon.html**.